Front Row Seat:

Brass Bands and British Culture in Uncertain Times

Peter Hardy

Published: 2023

Published by: Front Row Cornet

ISBN: 9781399960854

Contact: frontrowcornet@gmail.com

Printed and bound by CPI Group (UK) Ltd, Croydon, CR0 4YY

Acknowledgements

Thanks are due to the following:

Barbara for extreme tolerance and forbearance during the writing of this book.

Simon, John, Dennis and Pete for reading, commenting and encouraging.

Sarah for an early proof-read and helpful comments.

John Cawood and Stephen Allinson for pilfered anecdotes.

Johnny Purkiss for the books I have destroyed through overuse.

Moira for proof-reading

Anyone who read early excerpts.

Stella for getting me back into banding.

John Whittle and Mark Wears for the band at my mum's funeral

Rochdale Metropolitan Youth, Kingsway Youth, Golcar, Huddersfield & Ripponden, Uppermill, Dobcross and especially Meltham & Meltham Mills bands.

Paula, Hannah, Warren and Lisa, for helping to make me the cornet player I am today...

...

Contents

The Areas

Whit Friday

British Culture in Uncertain Times

About this book

I first began playing in brass bands as a child. I left as a teenager, self-conscious about being involved in something so evidently uncool.

30 years later, I casually mentioned to my son's school teacher that I used to play the cornet and soon found myself press-ganged into her local band. I expected to hang around for a few weeks before making my excuses and quietly leaving. Instead, I became a permanent member. After a few years I left for a better band. I was hooked.

Given my youthful ambivalence, I was intrigued to understand what was drawing me back and began to keep a diary. This eventually became the story of a year in the life of Upperthong, a fictional Pennine village band.

I soon realised that it was not just what happened in the band room that was important to me, but a wider sense of what might be termed band culture. The more I considered the history and culture of brass bands, the more it became impossible to avoid the general influence of British history and culture.

—

There are two factors which I hope distinguish this book from other books about brass bands. The first is the attempt to communicate a personal sense of what it is like to be part of a band. The second is to locate bands within a larger frame of British culture: to consider the place of brass bands in a 200 year sweep of British history from the early nineteenth century to the present day. These two threads are woven together in brief chapters balancing the storyline with discussion. This is intended to make it accessible and appealing to the general reader. The brevity of the chapters invites the curious to dip in at random.

Since the book explores notions of British culture it is hoped that it will have a broader appeal than just the brass band movement. Amateur musicians from other disciplines, whether choirs, orchestras or even rock bands, may find something of their own experience here. Likewise, those involved in more general community activities and groups may also identify familiar themes. In the words of William Blake, this book attempts "to see a world within a grain of sand." By understanding the culture of a Pennine village band we can get a sense of what might drive British culture in general.

Some readers may consider that within this exploration of British culture lie two problems. The first is that the approach to culture draws on archaic roots and is at best regarded as outdated, or worse rejected, by contemporary academics and government agencies alike. The second is that the terms English and British at times become difficult to distinguish. The separation of notions of Welsh and Scottish identities would not have provided a similar problem for people beyond England's borders.

—

It is now nearly twenty years since what is arguably the last major book on brass bands, Roy Newsome's *The Modern Brass Band*. Most of the classic brass band texts were written in the later twentieth century, in times of post-war certainties. It is also over twenty-five years since the release of *Brassed Off*. Those were very different times from our own.

This book began life in the shadow of two shocks to our understanding of a coherent Britain and its place in the world: the Scottish independence referendum and Brexit. Before the dust had settled, the Covid19 pandemic added a further disturbance to both national life and local community. It almost goes without saying that we now live in a digital age.

Having offered an understanding of British culture, the book concludes by attempting an analysis of its current condition, how it might be shaped in the future and the contribution that brass bands are making in uncertain times.

1. Christmas

Blow

It all begins with the lip: puckered; pinched at the edges where it is held firmly; relaxed in the centre where an aperture is formed. The lips are rolled slightly inwards. The jaw is dropped a little to create a gap between the teeth, then pushed forward so the top and bottom are better aligned. The mouthpiece is already in the cornet; the cornet is raised to the lip. Breathe. Blow. As if it were that simple...

Given the capacity of brass instruments, it is easy to be seduced by the notion that their sounds are extruded with extreme stress. Perhaps there is another way of looking at it. Sound is ultimately vibrating air, and so it may be considered that all tones, all music, exists in potential in the environment. Before these notes may be heard they must be imagined; they must be visualised then brought into being. This is surely the essence of magic. The true musician is like Tinkerbell flitting delicately with a golden wand. A deft touch to the air, the articulated breath, is what gives us music. But I am not Tinkerbell; I am Captain Hook's crocodile.

The lip can be a point of obsession for brass players, especially those with smaller mouthpieces such as the cornet. For brass players, that word "lip" usually indicates the muscles forming the aperture we blow through, more properly referred to as the embouchure. Embouchure is a French term meaning the opening of a passage, tube or pipe. It is no surprise to learn that in France they refer to the instrument's mouthpiece as the embouchure - just to confuse the British, obviously.

Most players have to adapt the ideal embouchure to their physique, their overbite or the straightness of their teeth. Maybe the perfect embouchure is centred, resting on the top lip to allow modulation by the jaw. However, in practice most players may rest more heavily on one lip than another or play with the mouthpiece to one side. Some have stories of having to rebuild the embouchure to address bad habits formed early on.

Amateur musicians sometimes grumble about their lip going, meaning the muscles of the embouchure have become too tired to hold their shape. When the lip goes the player is unable to hit and hold notes; this usually happens during a demanding rehearsal or performance. It is noticed in the upper registers first: the note becomes strangled, then flattens; and finally fails. Later the higher notes can't be hit at all. On longer, quieter passages an unbearable tension can be felt building at the corners of the mouth; phrases that could be comfortably played at the start of the session aren't completed.

Having seen the archetypal jazz trumpeter it is easy to conclude that playing is about wrestling the instrument with ballooning cheeks. The ideal is somewhat different, the aim being to ease the mouthpiece pressure and make the airflow as economical as possible. In the lore of banding is the example of the teacher who suspends the instrument from the ceiling, compelling the student to play hands free with the lips alone.

For developing players there is a temptation to markedly increase the mouthpiece pressure when attempting higher notes; this leads rapidly to soreness and fatigue. The bruised sensations from playing like this can linger for days, however some pressure is unavoidable. I recall photos of Miles Davis with the imprint of the mouthpiece embedded in his face.

Rehearsal

Two bright red dots, then black. The lane is flooded with light and a doubled figure dashes for the barn, cutting to the far side. Dark again, starless. Light returns; this time it stays. Out of the car, we take the cases from the boot, and, heads down, grope our way towards the band room. We are miles from anywhere here up on the moor and there is no shelter from the weather as it drives in.

Scuttling past the great double doors we nip down the side into the old outhouse, spiral round the flag-stoned corridor, budge open the sticking door and emerge from behind the curtain into, well, not exactly Narnia. I can never orient the internal geometry to the external geography, or understand how the two combine. This is a place out of joint, out of time, out of the world. Those with an esoteric bent might consider it a type of sacred, ritual space, but we'll have no truck with that nonsense.

It is warm in here, a welcome contrast to the cold night; the heating has been on since six. At one end the percussion is piled around an empty fireplace, at the other the kitchen counter. Mick is already brewing up; we ask for two teas but are refused. Emphasising the point, he leans towards us, elbows on the chipped formica counter, chin resting on locked fingers. Mick seems a strange choice for this slot, his vocation to obstruct, not to serve; we must trick the guardian of the urn into dispensing tea. Tonight he is ecstatic, formidable, with his new stone wall defence. James has decreed that from

11

now on there will be no drinks on the stand during rehearsal. Mick's challenge is a size ten postman's boot nudging the yapping terrier off the doorstep but wiry Tina springs straight back, nipping at his ankles. "Bollocks to that," she says, "he's not stopping me having my brew. Who does he think he is? Get that tea made, two sugars."

My current obsession is that the warm fluid is an aid to playing, boosting circulation in the pinched lip on chilly evenings. Athletes stretch their legs before running to loosen up. There is a school of thought that says brass players may benefit from a little athletic preparation too - after all, we use the muscles of the face when blowing. On the other hand, maybe it is not the face that warms up but the bellows, the muscles supporting the lungs; this is where the real work happens.

Many players won't perform without having warmed up first. Some I know have a twenty minute blow before they leave home; on the other hand there are top class players who play straight out of the case, no problem. Several books explore the subject: Duke Ellington's trumpet star, Cat Anderson, advocated spending a quarter of an hour blowing the quietest note possible, Whisper G, barely a breath; the Stamp and Caruso methods suggest buzzing on the mouthpiece and playing pedal tones, sounds well below the accepted range of the instrument.

Get to band early and you can have a chat with whoever is hanging around, such as Chairman Jack, though that is a little risky as he might collar you for subs. I have a good rapport with Geoff, "a total band nerd" according to Super Sue, but tonight he blanks me completely. He is too polite to dismiss me; it should be blindingly obvious that he is warming up. One or two of the others will just get their instrument out of the case and have a headlong blast into anything that takes their fancy, but not Geoff.

The great thing about Geoff is you can have a detailed discussion about the minutiae of brass technique: the different theories and approaches, the pros and cons. When I raise the topic with anyone else they just look at me like I'm a complete nutter. Geoff has also identified some gaping holes in my musical education and is providing me with a trickle of CDs copied from his collection of brass band LPs. He hopes that this careful tutelage will broaden my awareness of our brass heritage.

The period before the rehearsal starts is a window into the soul of the band; so much can be inferred from how a player uses this time. Geoff has his ear for detail and the music students play increasingly complex runs and arpeggios. Those less confident are limping through passages that trail off at the point of technical difficulty. Consider also the guilty, they haven't played since last Monday but know they should have sorted out that tricky passage in the second movement - they're just going to have a quick look at it now. Finally, one or two individuals may have been sitting there for a quarter of an hour and still not touched their instruments - too busy gassing away to their neighbours. I mention no names. Cassy! Nicola!

I catch the sniggering behind me on the back row, Chris rolls out the latest joke for his impressionable sidekick, Luke. Beyond them, the mutterings of our very own Statler and Waldorf - their down time is spent in withering dissections of the conductor's shortcomings. They say they've seen it all and in Jim's case he literally has - literally literally. Jim joined on third cornet in very short trousers in 1947 when the band restarted after the war.

If I've got to rehearsals early, I go round the pictures on the band room wall and play Where's Jim? He's in most of them though he's harder to spot when he had hair. One day I was talking through this archive with him, and we stopped at a band portrait from '87, (1887). I asked him, "Where are you in this one, Jim?"

"Y' cheeky bugger!"

Lurking across the floor, our two tenor trombones stand running in their slides. Andy scans the room and whispers asides like a latter-day Thomas Catesby. Sometimes I have sidled over eager for a whiff of conspiracy, but the topics of conversation are at odds with his stance.

We become a swelling, undulating sea of sound, crescendi collide with glissandi, an occasional fanfare soars overhead. A foghorn bellow says Big Michaela is in her seat. The room is filling up, but I am beginning to get a little concerned by the empty chairs around me on the front row. The clock says we start in five minutes.

That void in the centre of the horseshoe is filled. A manilla folder thumps the lectern, which rocks with the impact. The buff burden slides, finally falling to the floor. James barrels around, wrestling his coat onto the nearest chair. Grunts of greeting grace the closest seats; he bends to the carpet and rootles around in the cardboard wallet like a truffling pig. Heavy scores slap the desk. A quick two step shuffle. He raises his arms, stretching his jacket to bursting and untucking his shirt. Clearing his throat, "Red books."

Every band I have ever played with has started rehearsals with hymns. Some conductors will refer to this as warming up (hymn tunes are undemanding as they are slow and low). A range of tempi, keys and times get the band on its toes and sight reading. Hymns may introduce some technical element that will be important later on; dynamic control is a favourite, quieter, quieter, never the other way round for some reason. Another method is sub-division: breaking the beats into ever smaller chunks to develop precise rhythmic coordination within the band. Hymns also expose the fatal flaw of any poor band, intonation: the ability of the musicians to play together in tune.

The conductor's use of the red book shows something of their general musicality. Some might start the rehearsal with the same tune every week, *Aurelia* for example, perhaps the only hymn they willingly play. Others make random selections or open suggestions to the band; you can't play in a band and not love a good hymn tune. One or two conductors look for the lyrical sense, the ebb and flow of verse and chorus, and mark these out for the singing of an imaginary congregation. Most aim for a seamless sea of sound, pushing the band's breath into the start of the new phrase. Either way the hymn tune establishes disciplines of tone, co-ordination and dynamic.

Tonight, James offers the choice to the band; Chris pipes up, "number five". James stares over, head cocked slightly to the right, left eyebrow raised. No band ever plays number five - EVER!

Cornets

She says, "Oh, you play the cornet do you? That's interesting."

I correct her, "Used to, past tense."

Undeterred, she counters, "No such thing, what are you doing on Monday night?"

I reinforce the point, "When I say used to, I mean thirty years ago."

She persists, "A small detail, we're desperate for cornet players. Y'll be reet."

I play my trump card, "You are also overlooking the fact that I no longer have a cornet."

She reveals the strength of her hand, "But we do... Monday night in the chapel basement."

Upperthong practice in an old stone barn, Wellhouse in a chapel basement, the term chapel doesn't do it justice. In its time it was a Baptist temple complex spread over the best part of an acre - what is now called the chapel was merely the Sunday school. Above our heads, the hall floor is pounded by a Zumba class; we huddle in the burrow below. Extensive efflorescence breaches the plastered walls; two puny heaters battle back against the implacable damp. I am taken into the inner sanctum, the store, piled with instrument cases and a large wardrobe full of uniforms. "We won't worry about them now. We'll get you sorted with a cornet first, then you can get bugling." Some say that a cornet is just a bugle with ideas above its station.

The bugle is a single tubed brass instrument with a mouthpiece and bell. It will be tuned to a specific pitch. For most band instruments, in relation to orchestral (C) pitch, this is Bb; the soprano cornet, tenor horn and one of the basses are tuned at the higher Eb.

An open bugle will produce a fundamental note, nominally C, above which will be higher notes created by changes in the rate of airflow and embouchure. These higher notes are known as harmonics and begin to cluster more closely together as the pitch [in physics, the frequency] of the sound rises. But, notes are never just a single frequency; harmonic ghosts haunt all beautiful tones, breathing into life a warm, round sound. By contrast harsh and piercing electronic tones, such as fire alarms, contain only one pure frequency. After C, the first harmonic will be G, then 1st octave C, E, 1st octave G and so on. There is a slight problem: the fully chromatic musical range has 12 semitones. To create this it is necessary to have a range of tube lengths available - consider the pipes of the organ.

Before the nineteenth century, changes in pitch in brass instruments beyond the harmonic series were achieved by swapping shanks, different lengths of tubing, into the horn body. In practice this allowed the instrument to be tuned to different keys but didn't extend the number of available notes. Trombones may be considered to have a movable shank [the slide] to allow an infinite possibility of pitches. The first move to chromaticism, for an instrument to play all the tones and semitones of the octave, was addressed with keys in the manner of the clarinet; keys change the resonant properties of the tube. Whilst there were virtuosi of the keyed bugle it was held to be an unsatisfactory system. In his PhD study, *The Nineteenth Century Brass Band in Northern England,* Roy Newsome suggests that it didn't translate well to the larger bores and tubes of the instruments at the deep end of the band.

In his essay, *A Brief History of Piston-valved Cornets,* Niles Eldredge notes that experiments with valves began in the early decades of the nineteenth century: Stölzel and Blühmel patented a valve in 1818 which was used in the two valve cornopean; in 1829 came the first French patent for the three valve cornet we know today. These valves move up and down in cylinders when pressed, like the pistons of a car engine; descendants of this technology are present in the instruments I will inspect tonight.

Excavating battered cases from the dust of the store, I register the style and condition of the rough sarcophagi: peeling pasteboard caskets with rusted catches; splintered plywood boxes bound by leather belts and bungee cords; small trunks, their velvet interiors carved with pockets for manuscripts, mutes and mouthpieces. Examining the cornets: a selection are battered and tarnished almost beyond recognition; a few seem presentable enough to warrant lifting them out of their cases. Testing the valves, the first responds reasonably well but the pistons of the next rise and fall slowly like the wheezing of an iron lung. The last instrument is completely seized up. No joy.

The piston valve is a precise and complicated mechanism. In most contemporary brass instruments three additional tubes have been added to the bugle body; valves allow these to be joined individually or severally. Valves turn tubes into labyrinths with connecting passages embodied in the piston. Eight valve combinations create eight fundamental tones which together with their harmonics, encompass all the notes of the instrument's range.

Piston valves are believed to have triumphed because they can be more easily manufactured under industrial conditions than a keyed instrument. They also operate effectively across the whole range of tube bores found in brass bands. However, valves may have ultimately prospered due to the talented entrepreneurs who championed the system. The most notable of these was Adolphe Sax, now most famous for another musical innovation, the saxophone.

During the 1840s Sax developed a whole family of brass instruments; the tenor horn and baritone are the instruments that still bear the strongest family resemblance. Sax may be credited with the invention but the Distin family are considered the prime movers in promoting and developing the instruments. It is surprising that the Sax name has slipped into obscurity in brass band circles, at one stage a number of ensembles acknowledged his influence. My favourite? The Mossley Temperance Saxhorn Band.

Despairing, I reach for the final case. Despite their generous intention I am not convinced the band is going to be able to offer me a playable instrument. And, suddenly, there it is, the Holy Grail. It is still a respectable, not too tarnished, silver with that unmistakable round stamp on the bell. If

17

ever there was a portent, this is it. Memories of the school band flood back. Most of us were playing instruments that could only be deemed instruments because they corresponded to a general physical description. There was an exception: an act of forgotten benefaction had endowed the top chair with a Sovereign cornet. It came in a case lined with a rich blue velvet; as a physical object it had the lustrous presence of the crown jewels. You needed sunglasses to look at it. Time has dulled the instrument in my hand but it is suddenly animated with the spirit of that precious horn. The valves work, the triggers work, but do I work? I put the cold metal to my lips and squeeze a plaintive wail from its tubing. It will be a while before I am playing the cadenza from *Napoli*.

Back in the band room I am keenly aware that my playing is truly painful on the ear. My recruiter, Sheila, smiles benignly and indicates that quality is not critical at this point. Noel, sitting on my right, keeps muttering "Jesus Christ!" like a fervent evangelical every time I put the cornet to my lips. He is not a practising Christian.

Wellhouse were still a presence in the area fourth section contest but with so many vacancies numbers were beginning to take precedence over talent, a point I exemplified to a T. Experience spread across the generations: a smattering of the long retired dignified the upper echelons; little legs swung from big chairs in the junior parts. Some of the children were clearly being mentored by older family members, parents or grandparents.

Our band was in a period of consolidation, so I was told. The conductor had plans and he was already working on filling those empty seats. Numbers were not the limit of his ambition, and the only dissonance was not that being wrung from my cornet. It became difficult to avoid the conclusion that no matter what was actually happening in the band room, he thought he was conducting Brighouse.

Folders

Through the curtains again. I look around, the chorus sit in a line on the far side of the kitchen bar. We have never been introduced in the six months I have been here but I am slowly learning names. As a group they are peripheral yet significant. I think of them as the chorus as they form an extramural buffer for Chairman Jack: echoing his thoughts in discussions; offering support to his plans and proposals. Recently, Tina discovered they are his bulwark; they form the majority of the committee. It is not unusual to have non-players as officers of the band, most people join to play not administrate, but this grey wall has always struck me as incongruous.

Jack leans against the bar with his briefcase open. "It looks like you owe a tenner," he gazes at Tina expectantly.

"A tenner? Bloody hell, I only paid you the other week. Do you make it up as you go along, or what?" Tina is not happy.

"No, it's what it says here in the book, look in the column for November," says Jack, ever the literalist. "You could pay by direct debit if you like, then I'd never need to bother you."

She sighs, "I'll have to pay you next Monday."

He peers at the ledger, "It'll be twenty then, it's the start of December."

Tina takes a breath, thinks better of it and slides over to Mick for the tea.

"I set up a direct debit." I say.

"I know, I wish everyone were like you. "

A pause. "Oh, I was checking the lists for the job a week on Sat'day, I haven't got y' down."

I'm surprised, You should have, I'll be there."

Jack bites his bottom lip then asks, "You don't know anyone who could play on the front row d' y'? We've at least one chair that's still empty."

I apologise, my band contacts book is pretty blank, the few contacts I have may not make the grade for a second section band. We have our standards, how closely I meet them is another matter.

I started playing in bands just over five years ago, after a very long break, and have been slowly working my way up the sections since then. The band may have a dilemma, I am not the best player in the world, but keep the seat warm enough to get us through most jobs. Numbers are increasingly a problem for all bands, so sometimes it is prudent to stick with what you have rather than insist on the best. I didn't know it then, but the end of the evening was going to provide a textbook example of this.

Doreen has just finished tuning the timps in the newly reconfigured percussion corner. "You couldn't give us a hand with these could you?" She hands me half a pile of dog-eared red folders. Negotiating my way through stands and seats I deliver wallets to chairs.

Cassy and Nicola are already in position, "Oh, Christmas folders!" they chorus.

"Didn't we get Polar Express last year or was that at college?" asks Nicola. "Here it is. I know what we should get... Frozen!"

Cassy is enthusiastic, "Yeahuheah, that'd be dead good."

"*Let it go, let it go. Turn away and slam the door*" They belt out the chorus, rocking from side to side before collapsing in giggles.

I look at them blankly. "You know?" says Nicola, talking slowly as if to an imbecile, "from the film..."

Confused, I echo, "Film?"

More clues are required. "Derr... Frozen, cartoon, princess, singing..." They give up in hysterics.

Squeezing into the angle between horns and baritones I offer a pad to Kevin, in the band about three months and just getting used to bass trombone. The seat was empty and he'd always fancied it, anyway, the other two trombones were already taken. I thought he was doing OK, at the very least he seemed to be going away and practising his part. Eavesdropping on whispered asides after rehearsals, I was not convinced everyone was so forgiving. If I was happy to see the positive developments James was clearly more focussed on Kev's faults, there had been a number of attacks sweeping in over the last few weeks.

"What's in here?" he asks, as I hand him the folder.

"Christmas stuff, the usual, probably not much you haven't seen before, *Santaclaustrophobia, Christmas Swingalong.*"

He pauses, "Don't know 'em."

I am all too familiar with them. "Really, what stuff did you used to play at Christmas?"

"Nothing, the band I was playing in didn't really do Christmas."

Raised eyebrows register my surprise; Christmas is usually the most intense part of the year for brass bands.

"I was working away for ten years," he explains. "I've just moved back, it wasn't like round here."

"You should pick it up easily enough," I say, "most of it is pretty straightforward," which is true enough. However, as a cornet player you always have others to rely on, unless everyone fluffs that is. Sitting on the front row there will be plenty of times I don't play in quiet passages and leave the part to the two top chairs, Katie and Super Sue. Things are a little different if you are the only one on a part, as is the case for the bass trombone and soprano cornet.

The room is filling up. James is early and in deep conversation with Jack, who is looking slightly uncomfortable. I struggle to imagine what band topic could warrant such intensity.

Tonight's rehearsal revs up the Christmas programme. Instead of hymns we kick off with the slower, quieter carol arrangements, but they aren't quiet enough for James' liking. He is clearly not in a good mood; a few ragged entries are picked up and we restart some pieces several times - a general aura of irritability descends.

Moving up tempo, there are some lines for bass trom that are not handled well. Kev is given the opportunity to perfect them but he generally doesn't, he needs a little more time to get his slide around them. What begins as a slow jog of challenges accelerates until the interventions fly thick and fast like a flurry of jabs in the closing round of a title fight. It doesn't escape anyone's attention that he is the only one singled out for this treatment.

Kev sits there taking the blows; we listen to his playing slowly disintegrate. First, there is the trickle of doubt about the entry, where exactly does this fall? When the entry comes there is that blurring of articulation, the wobble at the start of the note, a minor glissando as he lips the note into pitch. Tension creeps in at the edges of the lip and the notes start to crack, but these can't be salvaged by support as his breathing is shallow, not deep and full. Struggling to find the slide position, the notion of subdivision, the metronomic reckoning of the very substance of the beat, becomes a distant memory. In short it could be said that Kev is well and truly on the ropes.

Rehearsal finishes and Katie, leaning forward, suggests to James that he may have been a little out of order. James, in a better mood at this point, brushing it off, says he has no problems with Kev, Katie has read too much into it. This is possibly somewhat disingenuous as on the other side of the room Kev looks like thunder. Ex-services, he vacillates between explosive force and parade ground self-discipline, but there is no reckoning.

—

Buckling her seatbelt, Tina turns to me, "What a twat, eh? Did you see the way he was laying into Kev? Who does he think he is? He'd better not try that with me or I'll tell him where to get off." She pauses, reflects.

"Do you think he's trying to get rid of him? Some conductors are like that. When I played with Holme Silver I turned up one night, I was only sixteen at the time, like, and there was this bloke sat in my seat. I says what's going on? And Laycock, the conductor, he says, "Whitwam's playing second baritone now and you're not needed."" She inhales deeply, "I was so humiliated I didn't know what to do. I just turned and left, nobody said anything, they all just watched it happen. Nobody said owt, just sat there like lemons." She is briefly immersed in the agony of the memory.

"And do you know what? Two years later they need a new baritone player, so Laycock... The bastard! He has the nerve to ring me up and ask me if I want my seat back! But, at that point I'm playing for Hinchliffe Mill in the third section. I tell him I'd love to, but it would be too much of a step down to play in the fourth section again. "I thought, you can stick that where the sun don't shine."

Performance

Uniform in one hand, case in the other, I round the corner at the back of the Con Club. Big Michaela is emptying the van. Thrusting the mute box at me, she instructs, "Take this upstairs." After a deep breath, I ask, "Whatever happened to please? Anyway, I need to drop this lot off," waving jacket and instrument, "don't worry, I'll be back."

I don't mind being asked to help, I expect to help, but I resent being ordered to help. Big Michaela's style lacks subtlety, tact, diplomacy and their many synonyms. Describing an encounter with a famous Yorkshire showjumper a friend observed there is a fine line between plain speaking and plain ignorance. Sometimes I wonder which side of that line Michaela is on.

Big Michaela has always been Big Michaela, right from the moment she joined the youth band, aged nine. There was another Michaela who was two years older, but even so and even then she wasn't as big as Big Michaela. At that point we should change our punctuation as she was surely merely big Michaela to distinguish her from her smaller namesake. And so it remained, until her middle teens when she left the band to pursue her other interest, rugby; it requires little in the way of imagination to visualise her diving into a tackle in the Challenge Cup final.

Rugby was where Michaela properly grew into her name, the three letters gaining rank and status like stripes on a sergeant's arm. That syllable acquired an inflection it is hard to convey in print, inflating like a truck tyre. There is a subtle emphasis in that simple word, you would never enunciate the big in Big Michaela as if you were merely talking about a large object like a big bowl or a big box. Big Michaela has the sort of name that fills the room before she crosses the threshold.

Unfortunately for Michaela, but luckily for the band, rugby took its toll on ankles and knees and she returned to the fold in her twenties. It is no surprise that she plays B flat bass, the biggest instrument in the band, a bass in a case takes some shifting and there are more reasons than one why I play the cornet.

Basses are not the only bulky items in the band room. Once upon a time, a band may have been supported by a percussionist with a modest kit or a big bass drum. Since the 1970s bands have been augmented by a symphonic percussion section: timpani, tuned percussion, not forgetting the minor paraphernalia. It resides in the band room because of the sheer size of it all, as do some of the larger instruments.

On concert nights, Michaela commandeers the long-wheelbase transit from the family business to make sure we can get everything moved. Her Dad usually lends a hand and one or two of the chorus help, too. Intermittent grumbles complain this duty falls on too few shoulders; resentments and grievances bubble under the surface. Tonight, it is cold and not only has the van to be unloaded, but everything has to be moved up two flights of narrow stairs. Choice expletives are already wafting out of the club's back door.

Michaela is in full spate, "It's alright for you lot, swanning in when you feel like it. We've been on the go since five, not that we get any thanks for it."

Her Dad chips in, "Aye, it's alus the same few doing the donkey work, it'd be nice if someone else did it for a change."

Appreciative of their efforts as we are, it is still possible to wonder if their martyrdom precludes any sense of the contribution of others. Stripping naked and hauling the band tackle over the moor with a stout rope might still not impress. Their important contribution to the band is entirely voluntary and freely given, but they somehow seem immune to the sympathetic resonances of reciprocation.

Sometimes it is not enough to do, sometimes it is important to be seen to be doing. Against my better judgement I agree to help Chris wrestle the big timp up the back stairs. I feel it is prudent to take the top and let him shoulder the bulk at the bottom. This tricky task is complicated by the drum's protective jacket. Loosely lagged like the boiler of an old immersion heater, the copper body defies our grip. Dragging it the final yards into the main hall, the clicking of music stand assembly suggests we have entered a knitting convention.

Sue directs her yonderly nephew, Luke; they're sketching out the band stand with shiny metal pylons. Rolling the timp into place, Chris calls over, "She's got you under the thumb there, Lukey boy." Luke grins bashfully as he wrestles with the tangle of the latest stand.

Doreen looks up from the drum kit she is assembling, "Not like that y' daft so and so, y'll brek it." Taking the stand from his hand she points to the wingnut that secures the neck. "You've got to slacken this off first, otherwise the twisting will shear the metal. If you look in there," she nods towards an old wooden ammunition box, "there's always a couple of headless stands. They're not cheap." Luke tries to free the nut with no success. Doreen turns to Chris, "Go on, you do it."

Chris turns puce, "Bloody hell, who's done this up, King Kong?"

Pairs of committee members wheel stacks of chairs; the club steward explains how they need to be stored at the end of the night. Glancing back to Chris and Sue, black jackets, white shirts and sombre ties make them look like a funeral directors' convention.

The band layout is taking shape. Right at the back, the drum kit is assembled, the big percussion in place - there will be two percussionists to support the kit player tonight. In front of all that scaffolding are four chairs, two for the higher pitched E flat basses and two for the deeper B flats. They sit behind three tenor horns and the flugel. Of the wings to either side, the inner seats on the right are the two euphoniums and two baritones in front of the three trombones. Opposing their imposing bulk are the four solo cornets and their six piece back row, from the front: soprano, rep, two seconds and two thirds. For those familiar with the choral tradition: the solo cornets generally take the soprano, main melody, line at the top of the band; the lower cornets and tenor horns are the altos, with the tenor part handed to the euphoniums and baritones. As to the bass part, this may be rather obvious.

Taking in the scale of the concert room, the Con Club is far grander than its name suggests. It seems more like a medieval hall; above us a church high roof is braced with sturdy timber trusses. Anticipating Merrie England fixtures, I find instead a newly fitted bar, formica topped tables and those red cushioned chairs with gold steel frames that can be found in every hotel from Accrington to Zanzibar. The steward is dealing beer mats onto the tables. "What's the fire limit for this place?" I ask.

"We can get 200 in here for a big event." I'm impressed. He says, "You've got a lot of chairs out there".

I explain, "25 for the band with three percussion."

Weighing up the logistics, "I imagine that's a nightmare to get together. It's bad enough organising the cricket team."

Nodding slowly, "Herding cats," I say, "herding cats."

On stage, Tina hangs black banners from the silver stands. Banners tidy up our appearance, add visual coherence and conceal sheaves of battered manuscripts. They also identify us to the audience and confirm the seriousness of our intent. Other musical ensembles use banners too, but for me they fit into that troubling category: band regalia.

Acknowledging our origins, the banners use the emblem from Bates's Mill. Back in the 1860s old Bates had been canny, recognising the musical enthusiasm in the workforce and realising a band could offer valuable publicity for his products. Supporting wholesome, improving and cultured pursuits might also lessen the allure of baser temptations such as the demon drink. A moral workforce would be a healthy workforce, and a healthy workforce would be less likely to honour Saint Monday and clock in on time for a full week's work.

Despite the strength of the case, Bates was reluctant to spend any money on setting up a band. Instead, he struck a deal whereby he offered a low interest loan for the purchase of instruments and uniforms and the free use of the mill premises for rehearsals and storage. This worked out well for both sides; the band soon recouped its investment in prize money, paid off the debt and built up some healthy reserves. Honouring their patron, the band adopted the mill emblem as their own.

Unfortunately, there is also a dark side to this tale; the band's emblem has always courted controversy. With its inverted pentacle and severed goat's head it has often been said that the band's early success came from being in league with the devil himself.

Busy behind the banners, pads placed on chairs, we sort the programme; sheets rustle into order. Rocking back and forth, we whisper and mutter the names of the pieces: Talmudic scholars reciting our Torah.

Cantor James intones the sacred sequence, "March, solo, carol then medley…"

A questioning chorus replies, "Solo, medley, carol?".

The instruction is repeated, "No: solo; carol; medley."

Our calm, contented chorus responds, "Right. Solo, carol, medley."

A lone, ad libitum voice floats over from behind the horns, "What was that, solo, medley, carol?"

A final exasperated unison concludes, "No… Solo. Carol. Medley."

A pause is followed by a protracted, keening "sorry", like a round amen.

I juggle two pads simultaneously to support the dep in the next chair. Gormless Luke excavates the detritus in the pad box in a frantic search for his folder, carpeting the surrounding floor with old programmes and running orders. "Luke. Luke!" commands Sue. Luke looks towards her, "I've sorted it for you. It's on your chair."

Scanning the ring of tolerant faces, he blushes as the information lodges. "Ohhhhhh."

Sue nods very firmly and very slowly, "On, the, chaiiirrr."

Grinning bashfully, he shambles off behind us.

Programme sorted, all that remains is to tidy up the boxes, cases and covers. These are placed in a neat pile in the corner of the hall before we drift off to the changing room downstairs.

—-

Warming up in the snooker room, those with larger instruments test stiff lips on cold, clutched mouthpieces: it is the buzzing of a busy hive. Smaller instruments are plugged with practice mutes: a whining cloud of angry gnats.

Navigating the narrow gangways has become difficult, the larger cases are stacked in all available spaces. The silver-grey cover of the snooker table disappears under a litter of cloth as we change from blazers and ties to jackets and dickie bows. Gold brocade glints in the gloom.

Seated at the edge of the room, I apply oil to the cornet's valves. Glancing up, the shadows cast by the snooker light shade make it difficult to distinguish individuals. A few collaborate with the back fastenings of bow ties or straighten out collars, "Who do you think you are, Eric Cantona?"

My mentor joins me, "How's it going, have you been listening to any of those recordings?" Geoff's most recent tutorials have featured different versions of our next test piece.

"Yes," I reply, "I tend to go for the GUS one, but it seems to be played a bit faster than some of the others. I don't know if they've been speeded up because I'd swear it's at the wrong pitch, too."

"Not so," says Geoff, and explains that by the early twentieth century brass bands had arrived at a position where the movement's tuning pitch was out of step with the rest of the musical world. It was only in the mid-1960s that brass manufacturers rationalised their production and decided to bring band instruments into the prevailing orthodoxy. This means the 1960s recording was appropriately pitched for its time. Coincidentally, this insight aligns with some of my own musical research and I am able to disrupt Geoff's flow by affecting an erudite air. I tell him I understand that in 1939 there had been an international moratorium on musical pitch. He will surely savour the irony that the world achieved perfect harmony just before the outbreak of the Second World War.

Geoff isn't easily put off his stride and continues his lecture. The 1963 change in pitch meant that bands had to replace their instrument stock to meet the new requirements. Not all bands could afford to replace their instruments to conform to the new standard. Many economised by adding length to the various tubes [or slides as they are known - they are movable and removable by sliding them]. I remember coming across these instruments as a child, and I still have one, they were characterised by the brass collars fitted to all the slides.

Apparently, the instruments of the original bands were set at a pitch similar to that used today. In the middle of the 19th Century the pitch shifted upwards to comply with orchestral standards, what is now known as the "Old Philharmonic" pitch. This change may have been introduced to add brilliance to the string sound. Unfortunately, the higher pitch put a strain on operatic voices and the convention drifted downwards as the century drew to a close. It only took the brass band movement 70 years to catch up and adopt the "low pitch" standard. Players must have felt their cheeks pushed in by the G forces of such rapid change.

Today's lesson draws to a natural conclusion as Geoff nudges my elbow, "Can you see what I see?" With his index finger he describes a line across the room, "Someone doesn't look very happy..." At one extreme stands James, his suit making him the most easily identifiable figure in view. He lies at the end of an axis constructed by Kev's glare. Incandescent pinpricks burn in the darkest corner of the room. James's right arm swings metronomic, his left leafs through a score. If he is aware of Kev it is not obvious. These observations are interrupted as my attention is commanded by another presence.

Andy is making his way round the room drumming into everyone how we will walk on stage. It looks better to arrive in an organised fashion rather than just drift on. In his wake we commence the sub-assembly into our sections. I wait for James to give a pep talk, but it doesn't arrive. He gathers up his scores and checks their order. Deep in the gloom, amongst the milling figures, I sense the surly presence of Kev drifting towards him as surely as a shark in dark water. He stops some way away as James opens the door.

Andy might be getting us into order but I feel we are lacking a focus. I realise the reason we need an extra dep for tonight is because we are missing our principal cornet, since this is the job that fires up the Christmas season her presence is important. Turning to Chris, I ask, "Where's Katie?" Wearily, he shifts his gaze to the ceiling, out of the corner of my eye I catch a knowing look from somewhere in the horns. Before I can ask any more questions we are on the move, nudging into line as we climb the stairs.

We hear the request to "put your hands together for Upperthong Band," and march on stage to the thunderous applause of thirteen people.

Uniform

In keeping with the spirit of the decade, my youth band wore a purple polyester shirt tucked into the bottom half of a school uniform. This was complemented by a navy blue, nylon tie featuring a sublimated version of the town crest. I still keep the tie rolled up in a corner of my sock drawer, I outgrew the shirt some years ago. It was only when I joined Wellhouse that I was confronted with the full sartorial implications of the band tradition.

In the popular imagination, bands are inextricably linked with caps and dress jackets. Headgear has slipped out of fashion but the jackets remain, either off the peg in the familiar shop sizes or bespoke. The latter is a good idea at the time but fitting new players into old clothes can quickly become an almost surreal experience. Uniforms are expensive and for cash strapped bands their replacement will always be drifting down the agenda. Somewhere, there is a band room cupboard packed with musty, threadbare jackets that will just about do for another year.

Uniforms are just one aspect of banding that has encouraged and sustained entrepreneurial activity. According to Gavin Holman's paper *How Many Brass Bands?*, there are now around twelve hundred active bands in the UK. In the last decade of the nineteenth century there were at least seven thousand. During the golden age they were a very popular form of entertainment and a source of civic pride. Most bands were generating the funds necessary to equip themselves with both instruments and uniforms, that's a lot of jackets. As late as the 1980s there was a shop in Huddersfield specialising exclusively in band uniforms.

Contemporary youth bands are likely to choose hooded tops, and a number of adult bands have chosen polo shirts or a DIY approach to presentation. With reduced income a dose of pragmatism can be useful, but my experience suggests any competitive band will want a proper uniform, although this view may not be shared by all band members. I confess to harbouring ambivalent feelings and am not the only person in my household who considers the uniform with a sceptical eye.

The stage jacket has become a touchy subject at home, when Bee first found it in the wardrobe it was received with a mix of incredulity and derision. Whilst her choir clothes were dignified with the term uniform I had a band costume, like it was something for a fancy-dress party, like I was assuming a comic role. It is one thing to harbour doubts, it is another for them to be exercised by someone else.

Bee told her friends of the new discovery; sitting at the kitchen table they'd affect a disinterested tone and ask about the band. Gradual facial distortions betrayed the foundations of their smirks. Questions about the jackets collapsed incomplete in a chorus of helpless cackling. They may have found it funny, but I didn't. Band uniform is a serious issue, it is very important. It is no, laughing, matter... Is that understood?

—-

Christmas is now in full swing with two jobs in one day. First up is the Upperthong parish church service. The band has a long-standing relationship with the church; we play three regular concerts here each year, a fixture of the village calendar since well before the Second World War. For reasons I am not entirely clear about, we aren't putting on a proper Saturday evening carol concert this Christmas; the village will have to make do with a traditional service instead.

This morning we expect the congregation to take their place in the pews but churches haven't always had seating. Up until the late Middle Ages church services retained the flavour of a Dionysian cult with a singing and dancing congregation. It wasn't until the fifteenth century that the authorities began to successfully purge this ecstatic form of celebration. By the seventeenth century the transition from peasant dance to high church theatre was complete, and the decorative qualities of both the liturgical setting and the clerical costumes took centre stage.

Gowns and robes define the choir and clergy as do the uniforms of many professions and occupations. In hospitals, clothes are often colour coded to denote medical specialisms. Police uniforms confer legal power and authority. The military adopted uniforms when standing armies were developed, these became increasingly colourful until the advent of the repeating rifle - at which point wearing a scarlet tunic on the battlefield could seriously damage your health. Band uniforms often refer back to these military precedents, but we haven't adopted khaki and camouflage as our audiences tend not to be armed and hostile.

There are band uniform traditions that predate the military influence and the elder statesmen of the Cyfarthfa ironworks band had rather natty velvet suits. Some contemporary bands have decided to move on from the stage jacket style. I have seen coloured shirts, shirt and waistcoat combinations and, on Whit Friday, reprehensible forms of fancy dress.

Before a note is blown, the band uniform suggests our spectacular role. It reinforces our status as performers and helps command attention - as if the sound was not sufficient. If the uniform serves an external function, it also serves an internal one: the uniform emphasises our sense of belonging to a group. As a child learning the cornet, membership of the band was something to aspire to; it was a special moment to at last be identified with the uniform.

Uniforms aren't exclusively institutional clothing and informal uniforms seem to be increasingly popular; no opportunity for creating and wearing them seems to be missed. I wonder if this, perhaps counter-intuitively, may suggest anxieties about social identity and belonging, things that up until quite recently may have been taken for granted. Popular culture seems to take every opportunity to mark out membership of groups, no matter how ephemeral or transient.

One recent tributary of this tradition is the styling of rock band merchandise, now adapted to a broad range of situations: think of the stag do tour t-shirt. Celebratory t-shirts may also be found on pub crawls, but subtle or simpler markers are often used: fright wigs; colour codes; whatever. The band also engages with this tradition, our marketing guru has commissioned a range of goat themed, apres contest, leisure wear which is proving rather popular with the band and its followers.

School uniform is another common code of formal dress. Britain has a long-standing fetish for this not widely shared by our continental neighbours, an enduring legacy of the public schools. The current incarnations of the state-funded school system accommodate a range of approaches. The more sensible end may use polo shirts and sweatshirts or formal shirts, clip on ties and V neck pullovers. Other schools favour the pretension, expense and down-right impracticality of blazers.

School uniforms have the benefit of suppressing flamboyant display and excessive individuality whilst emphasising a collegiate identity. Another strength may be that they suggest the process of education is inherently special and so deserves particular care and attention. If uniforms set the scene for learning they may also help focus the attention when making music.

Wearing the uniform reminds us of our musical responsibilities, and that the band is greater than the sum of its parts. On the other hand, the uniform may also offer the licence to behave in ways that may be denied in daily life; it gives the opportunity to be special. The uniform provides the permission to perform.

—

Brass buttons bedazzle, glinting fractals reflect from sinuous silvery surfaces, the band outshines the Christmas tree. Embroidered jackets stake our claim for centre stage, the dais of the chancel, decanting the choir from their stalls. They still stand on ceremony, and process down the aisle to our overture in their freshly pressed surplices. The vicar, out of step with the occasion, wears her vestments as a hedge wears a sheet on a windy day.

If we were somewhat dispirited by playing to the void at the Con Club, we are amply compensated this morning. Membership of the church guarantees a place at the highly desirable local primary school and this may be contributing to our full house. The excellent attendance is not just a token gesture. This congregation has arrived ready to sing, and we can hear them as we play - which is rather gratifying.

Katie, our principal cornet, is absent. Again. Christmas is exposing the weak points in her commitment to the cause and as a result the front row is left with a skeleton crew of two. Unfortunately, both Sue and I see that empty chair as a threat rather than an opportunity. We are flying against a well-worn tradition of the brass band world; bands are generally hierarchical and competitive; the key seats have sometimes been the battleground of bitter ambition.

Upperthong's most recent examples were the two euphonium players resident when I joined. Tina christened them Bill and Ben, they were inseparable, squabbling siblings. According to Andy they were "fighting like rats in a sack". Chris's critique focussed on their hairstyles - "two bald men fighting over a comb". Acrimonious disputes occasionally erupted in rehearsals, to everyone's frustration. I am pleased to report that our current Euph's are both on the same page and playing in tune.

Karen is encouraged to leave the rep chair in the shadows of the back row and step up to bask in the spotlight on the front. She demurs, preferring the comfort of familiar territory. Rep is an abbreviation of repiano, sometimes spelt ripieno in older scores. Ripieno is an Italian term referring to an accompanying body in orchestral music. In the brass band, the rep bridges the gap between the back and front rows, sometimes playing supportive um pahs with the lower cornets, at others carrying the melody with the front row. It also takes its own solos or may duet with the principal.

The rep is one of the most important cornet parts. Traditionally the four strongest cornet players in the band will be the top two on the front row, the rep and sop, short for soprano. Since we are only playing carols today, Karen's move would only have affected the appearance of the band and not its sound as she is playing the same part as the solo cornets. Our melody line is also supported by the flugel.

Whilst the rep is a cornet role, the flugel is a unique instrument with the same B flat pitch as a cornet. In written parts the flugel is often paired with the rep, though it may get its own solos. The timbre of the instrument is much deeper and richer than a cornet because of its large bell, somewhere between that of a cornet and a tenor horn. Flugels have found favour in jazz since the late nineteen sixties as they offer a mellow contrast to the more strident B flat trumpet and in some continental European brass groups they are the dominant melody instrument.

For cornet players with ambition, the flugel can be the most sought-after seat in the band after the top chair. It is also highly desirable for the slacker musician having more rests in the scored parts, it also tends not to be asked to play at too high an altitude and gets a few tasteful solos.

We lost our last flugel player shortly before James joined, she went from a sense of duty when her partner, Bill (not Ben), flounced off. There was some jockeying for the position between Sue and myself but we were blindsided when James brought in Geoff, a free agent after a long stint with Slaithwaite, one of the better local bands.

It transpires there were sound biological reasons for Karen's desire to stay on the back row. A couple of times during the service she disappeared into the vestry to cope with waves of morning sickness. In the end she didn't need to move as we were surprised by a late arrival; after the service James introduced Jenny to the band, she is being lined up as soprano for the areas. The sop seat is another of our persistent vacancies. After glancing a couple of times at the empty seat in the far corner of the band, I wonder if the bass trombone might also be about to fall into this category.

—

Disrobing in the vestry, I ask around, "Where's Katie?" At her mum's for Sunday dinner, apparently. "Really?" I think that shows a remarkable lack of commitment. The principal cornet is the figurehead of the band, as I imagine the leader of the orchestra to be. I admit, I am unfamiliar with the mores of orchestras, maybe the leader is like the conductor and is untroubled by the mortal concerns of administration. However, the principal cornet of a village band should be more like the boss of a labouring gang, leading by example, setting the work ethic. They should be the first one putting the stands out and the one putting the last case back in the band room - maybe that's an exaggeration.

Alan offers an opinion, "Neil cut her a lot of slack. He had a real soft spot for her, she could do no wrong in his eyes. When she was thirteen, she was principal cornet in the Sellars youth band."

Jim remembers, "She was on the front row at Hepworth when she were fourteen, but she's definitely drifted for a while now. I don't know if it's personality, motivation, whatever. You have to question why she wasn't here for this morning's stint."

"It does rather beg the question why she is still in the band if she can't be bothered to turn out for jobs," Alan concludes.

Jim taps the side of his nose, "Bear in mind that our principal gets fifty pounds a month retainer."

"So, if she is getting some sort of honorarium, why isn't she turning out?" I muse.

Cassy, passing by, chips in "...because she's a lazy cow and anyway she's probably hung-over from last night."

"Miaaooww," counters Sue from across the room.

"Well, what's your version?" asks Cassy. "Come on, you've got to face it, we all had to get up this morning and get here - why can't she? Plus, I've had to sort the kids out as well. And, she missed the Con Club job for some half-baked excuse." She pauses. "Deep breath!"

"Where did all that come from?" asks Sue, as Cassy wanders off to put her horn in its case, "though she does have a point." I catch James's eye; distracted from his chat with Jenny, that little interaction has not gone unnoticed.

James isn't the only one to speak with Jenny, she gets passing thanks from most of the band and some compliments on her playing. This is how it should be, and from my experience I expect Jenny will have one eye on how the band treats her this morning. If she is thinking about a permanent move she will want to know the band is at a performance level that will challenge her, but also that it will be a friendly and sociable environment. Let's hope those boxes have been ticked.

That might have been the end of the job but it was not the end of the day. We finished the afternoon in Beaumont Park [winter coats with the band logo], in a proper park bandstand, no less. There was a good turnout, and we played well into the dark. The local primary school choir took to the stage in the interval. We feared their departure would clear the park of their families, but we held a healthy crowd until five.

As someone who looks askance at the contemporary incarnation of Christmas, I now love these carolling jobs. After all, with declining church attendances how many opportunities are there for communal singing? If brass bands can give people something important like that, well, it must be worth a mince pie or two at the very least.

Military

The band was John, Paul, Ringo and George, although there was always speculation about number five. Paige, Plant and Jones said the band was over when the drummer died. But, if your band has been going for 150 years how many people playing tonight were in the original line up? We had our picture taken after the parish church job, twenty of us standing there in the nave in full dress. Our band is solid, permanent and will endure.

Imagine the physics lab, a block of brass on the table. Place a sliver under the microscope: solid. Magnify and it quivers with the vibration of the molecules. Enlarge again and the atoms become insubstantial, void not particle; before your eyes the metal disappears.

If you expect players to stay a decade then that is three out, three in every year. No band I have played with over the past five years has turned out the same group twice. We are always in motion, always changing; we are a sense of historical continuity, an enduring purpose. Over time the band is not its members, nor that musty rehearsal room with a shelf full of instruments and a wardrobe bursting with mothballed jackets. The band is not those cabinets of manilla envelopes bearing the name of an engineering works with a three digit phone number. The band does not exist.

If you attend enough local concerts, you will notice the same old players cropping up in strange new seats. Bands don't exist in isolation, they exist in dynamic community, in culture. They are an ecology: sharing players; sharing instruments; sharing music.

That sheet on the stand is barely legible; this is its fourth home. Follow its journey through the hazy outlines of the faded stamps: Pennine; Todmorden Old; Lockwood; and yours. With a straight face the librarian has stamped his contraband to show its latest residence. As you go to call the copyright police you realise the faded inscription in the upper right hand corner says the piece was arranged by your own conductor.

The copyright police would find slim pickings in most band rooms, and especially ours; we spend hundreds of pounds on new music every year. Our main library has over a thousand scores; we have four libraries. Jim gives me a guided tour as he lays out our latest acquisition, already stamped. His archive is a private place, a monastic scriptorium whose floor floats free above the kitchen ceiling.

Jim swaps the old sheet from the ring binder; the new page keeps the titles in order. "Right, so the way we do it is, in the ring binder everything's in proper alph'betical order but on the right-hand side we have the catalogue number, see? Then on the filing cabinet drawers we have the file numbers. So, this is going in the second drawer down of this cabinet, 1,000- ." He looks at me, "Why d' we do it? Cus if y' put everything in letter order y'll end up having to keep shufflin' folders from one drawer t' t' next," which I have to agree makes sense.

Indicating another set of cabinets with identical numbers, "That's the old library, it's all gone out of fashion and nobody wants to listen t' that stuff now. Nobb'dy else wants it 'n' wi' can hardly throw it out." I peruse its catalogue of unfamiliar titles and drag out a couple of scores. These only serve to confirm Jim's appraisal.

Spurred by impulse, I dig for *Coriolanus*; I remember the youth band trying this out one night. What sticks in my memory is not the sound but the number of notes and bars that were crammed onto that single yellowed sheet of foolscap card; a contemporary print would be at least four pages long. But I can't find it, it's not in its place. "'appen, must have lent it out to someone, I don't expect we're likely to see it again now."

Ranks and rows of marches regiment the middle shelf. Above it, bulge broad, buff folders, "What's all these, Jim?"

He stops and peers over, "Now that, now that is the *really* old stuff. That's the old Victorian music." Pointing to a short section, "these are all handwritten scores. There's some in there that were written by Edwin Swift for contests he took us for." He adds wryly, "before my time you understand?" Out of respect, I spare him my sarcasm. "Then this lot over here is when they started printing the test pieces for Belle Vue. We must have won the British Open with one of them," he muses, peering at the faded paper.

"Have you played any of them?" I ask.

"We got one out for the last concert we did at the town hall. It was utter crap so we put it straight back away again. I doubt we'll ever play it but it's still band history."

Downstairs, at the bar, James chats with Jack, sandwiched between them, Katie. A few words drift in my direction, "commitment... inspiration... leadership... area champions." Incrementally, Katie's posture lifts with each locution. Unarticulated thoughts swim behind her eyes, slowly she shifts her gaze from one man to the other.

Paul pauses from the process of removing and replacing each slide and valve on his baritone; the greenish tinge of the metal offers an insight into his maintenance routine. With an open hand and quizzical expression he gestures to the empty seat by his side. "No Tina tonight," I say.

"How come?"

I give him the bad news, "Thursdays, she's on 2-10 for the next month."

Paul weighs it up, "James won't like that. I'm off next Thursday, too." I express disappointment and enquire as to what could possibly come between a man and his band. "Regiment Christmas reunion."

The military connection is strongly entwined with brass band history. One of the foundation myths considered by Roy Newsome in *The Nineteenth Century Brass Band* is that some of the earliest bands were military, or at least private bands on the military model. Clegg's Reed Band, dating from the late 1700s, are considered an important case in point.

Later, in 1815 at the end of the Napoleonic wars, mass demobilisation created a cadre of musicians who were able to transmit their skills and knowledge to the wider community. A problem with this theory is the likely quality of the musicians.

Until late in the century British military bands had a poor reputation. The music college at Kneller Hall was only established in the 1860s, in response to a particularly egregious celebration of the Queen's birthday during the Crimean War. At which point, the military hierarchy had been humiliated by the disparity between their military music and that of their opponents and allies.

Roy Newsome also seems unpersuaded that brass bands in general emerged directly from the traditions of church music groups. Looking elsewhere, the founding date of Stalybridge Old demonstrates that organised amateur music groups were flourishing in the new industrial towns by the second decade of the nineteenth century. Since the types and availability of brass instruments were constantly evolving throughout the 1800s, Stalybridge Old would not have been recognisable as a brass band at the time of its inception. The current instrumental formation was not possible until the 1850s.

Slaithwaite, where I now live, provides a good example of how, over time, a number of bands may have formed and dissolved - some existing contemporaneously, others sequentially. A portion of these bands had a decidedly ersatz reputation, referred to locally, colloquially and homophonically Germanically, as "waffen fuffen". I suspect they were the pub rock combos of their day, but higher impulses eventually prevailed.

Ultimately, Slaithwaite was a cultured musical milieu, by the end of the nineteenth century having at least a couple of choirs and a symphony orchestra to complement the village brass band. It might be stretching a point to try and prove that bands have naturally evolved from older ensembles in the manner of Darwin's Galapagos finches. However, knowing musicians to be a culturally promiscuous lot, it is possible to imagine how traditions might develop, overlap and merge.

The instrumentation of the early groups was most likely to be a mix of brass, reed and percussion. Initially the brass was weighted to the bugle (and trombone) and, from the second decade of the century, its progeny the keyed bugle and ophicleide (and trombone).

A fuller family of brass instruments didn't enter circulation until the 1830s. This is when historians identify the establishment of what many

41

regard as the first entirely brass band, the Cyfarthfa Ironworks band of Merthyr Tydfil.

Early brass bands often benefited from the assistance of benefactors such as philanthropic industrialists. In the final analysis, most ended up being self-financing through commission and subscription. Embryonic band forms may have been strictly civilian, but the military connection became significant in the middle of the century.

By the late 1850s, there was fear of a return to war with France and new militias were formed. In his general history of the movement, *Brass Bands,* Arthur Taylor suggests that in many cases a significant proportion of the capitation grant was directed into building bands. After all, the bands were necessary for adding a dash of style to drills and parades, an essential recruitment tool.

Occasionally, local bands were hired by the militias to avoid the greater costs of creating their own. These arrangements may have allowed bands access to practice spaces such as drill halls as well as free or subsidised uniforms. This may be a reason why band uniforms from the middle of the nineteenth century onwards often had a parade ground style.

Militias, volunteer forces and rifle brigades - most notably commemorated in the march ORB (Oldham Rifle Brigade) - continued to be supported until around 1910. A number of bands adopted military identities to garner martial largesse; there were concerns that this was more to the benefit of the bands than the military. Ultimately, a parliamentary committee was established to investigate the matter. With history in mind I sarcastically suggest to Paul that James will be encouraging him to attend his reunion. "You think?" he smirks.

Cassy elbows in, "What are you two sniggering about?"

"Nothing to bother you," replies Paul.

"So strictly boys only, then? Whatever happened to equal opportunities? I think this is a matter for the committee."

Paul gives her a stern look, "You'd better watch your step or we'll have to send you to the Ladies Committee."

Cassy gives him a puzzled reply, "Ladies Committee, what's that?"

Paul explains that until the late 1980s the band had been supported by a ladies committee who had fundraised with cake stalls, raffles and the like. They had also taken responsibility for cleaning the band room.

"Oh, that's it, is it? So, you expect us to be grovelling around on our hands and knees scrubbing whilst you lot have a blow and disappear off to the pub?" she folds her arms and sits back, upright, indignant.

"Sounds alright to me," says Paul, "What do you think?"

He turns to me. "I think I need another cup of tea..."

Upperthong is composed roughly two to one male and female, my experience of bands has always had this gender mix and it is the norm for most bands I know. The rejuvenation of brass bands in the wake of the Second World War properly opened the door to women players. All the pictures I recall of bands from before that time are exclusively male and there are a number of academic studies that focus on the role of brass bands as a masculine recreation. However, it should be noted that women were trickling into bands in the 1930s - at that time there were also one or two all-female dance bands.

Earlier, in the Victorian era (as Gavin Holman demonstrates with articles posted on his IBEW website), there were well established traditions of women in brass. Women were especially prominent in America, with many well-known female soloists, especially cornet players.

Ron Massey's brief history of *Marsden Senior School Boys' Band* features a warm pen portrait of the professional music career of Sylvia Hampson. In 1942 she became the first girl to join that band. Six years later she turned professional with one of the all-female ensembles referred to earlier.

As far as Upperthong is concerned, the gallery on the band room wall demonstrates that by the early 1950s the band was no longer an exclusively male preserve. This was no doubt helped by schools actively supporting girls to learn brass instruments. Whilst the efforts of the Ladies' Committee were of great value, its presence implies a very unequal approach to matters of gender in the band world until relatively recently.

Drifting to the kitchen bar Andy says, "That looked fun."

I consider the appropriate response and decide it was, "a bit of good old sexist banter. I thought I'd leave whilst I was still in one piece."

This prompts an Andy anecdote, "I remember when I started playing as a kid at our colliery band."

I think, "That sounds hard line..."

He reassures me, "Nah, it was a good laugh. I remember this one bloke saying how welcoming the band was. He goes, completely straight faced, "aye lad, we're not fussed, we'll have anyone in, it doesn't matter as long as you can blow, that's all that counts". He says, "we'll accept all sorts here - we even had a woman in once...”” Andy continues, “We might have got into the Twentieth Century in that way but we have a way to go in some others.”

“What do you mean?”

He poses a question, “Well,” allowing me to prepare for some serious thought, “if you were going to use one word to describe this band, what would it be?“

I think I understand where he is heading, “You mean, white?” I ask.

“On the other hand,” he adds, “you could say at least we attempt to embrace sexual diversity.”

I’m puzzled, “What do you mean?”

This incurs mild exasperation, “Do you wander round with your eyes shut, or what?”

This doesn’t improve my understanding, “I’m not sure what you’re getting at...”

“I’ll let you work things out for yourself...” He pauses, his face lights up, “Speaking of enlightened attitudes... I remember this one night. After practice we were in t’ welfare and to move with the times, it was back in the eighties, I thought I’d get a bit experimental, like. So, I goes to the bar and says, “I’ll have a white wine, please”. The barman looks me straight in the eye. “Is thar a poof lad?”” *(att. J. Cawood)*

Even though I am standing at the kitchen counter I don’t get that second cup of tea because as I turn to challenge Mick James raps loudly and impatiently on the lectern.

—

As the cornet case clasps click closed, I notice Katie and James sharing a brief joke. I admit a grudging respect for his man management. Katie was a different player tonight, the best performance she has given for several months; she is worthy of her seat. James then turns and offers a thumbs up to our new bass trombone player, introduced at the start of the evening and by the end proving that he will also raise the standard of the band. This leads me to suspect some Machiavellian machinations have been going on out of sight, and come to that, in plain sight...

Just as I make to leave my seat, chairman Jack shuffles forward to deliver his notices and finalise the plans for Saturday night. Instead of seizing the opportunity to round the evening off in style, James decides to step in and demonstrate that his diplomacy still has a serious skill deficit.

At the start of the evening James showed he could read Katie's character and build her confidence; he now demonstrates that Big Michaela presents as something of a closed book. This is more than a surprise. Whilst there are undoubtedly some subtle and sophisticated characters in the band, it is safe to say that Big Michaela is not one of them.

As the announcements move to the discussion of logistics, James is direct. "Michaela, on Saturday you need to have the van here for about six and we need to be at the club by quarter to seven." Turning to Chris and Dan, "You two need to be here, too, to help Michaela load up." They are all taken aback, but Michaela goes straight into the attack.

"What do you mean I need to have the van here? When has this been discussed?"

James recoils slightly, "Well, we move the stuff in your van, don't we?"

Michaela disagrees, "Let's get this straight. I usually bring the van, but after I have been asked. As I recall no-one has asked me if it's available on Saturday night. And this Saturday it isn't because Dad's off to York with it." She crosses her arms and glares at James whilst a red tide rises.

Michaela may be on fire but she has nothing on the incandescent glow that emanates from Chris, "What do you mean, we need to be here at six. Since when have we been here to take orders, eh?"

It dawns on Jack that matters may be sliding wildly out of control, "I think there has been a little misunderstanding here. I think James was just asking..." Unfortunately, he only manages to add fuel to the fire.

"Asking, my arse," butts back Michaela. "There's a big difference between asking and telling and everyone in this room knows it when they see it." She begins to perform the theme from her favourite aria, "Me and Dad put ourselves out for this band hauling stuff around, but we do it as a favour not because we're told to. Anyway, like I've just said, this is the wrong weekend to do this because I can't have the van."

Whether this is true or not I can't say, but if it isn't it is a masterful block that creates something of a non sequitur. A Gary Kasparov might choose to use such a moment to lean back and reflect on the overall game plan. James on the other hand apparently refuses to recognise the concept of the immovable object even though Michaela is evidently the human embodiment of this concept in both temperament and physique. I don't wish to be disrespectful but in a head to head contest I can only see one winner and it won't be him.

James wades in, flapping his arms like an exasperated penguin. "Well, can't he change his arrangements? You knew this was coming up, so surely you were going to bring the van?" Michaela eyes him up and decides to let him stew. She bides her time like a wrestler circling an opponent, considering her next move, which might possibly be a full nelson.

Chairman Jack flounders and flails as James and Michaela stare each other out. Jack has some sterling qualities that have served the band well, but conflict resolution is not one. I can see his natural instinct may be to head for the door, but he summons his remaining courage and averts the apocalypse.

"I'm sorry, Michaela, very sorry. I feel this is all my fault. I should have asked you, and I'm sorry I overlooked it." Looking grey and very weary, "James, Michaela is right. I think we need to leave it there. We know we need a van and we have a few days left." He sighs, takes a deep breath, "One way or another we will get something sorted for Saturday night, Michaela."

Jack looks at the floor. "I think we need to leave it there..." Reviving, he observes, "Anyway we seem to be eating into valuable drinking time. Is everyone going to the pub?" We are, but the question remains, how are we going to get everything to the cricket club?

But that is not the final disaster of the evening, "Whoa, hold on, hold on, there's one more thing." We all pause. "The committee have been looking into booking a coach for Whit Friday, we just need to confirm everyone's available as far as they know. We want to get a feel for whether it's a goer or not." The date is announced, and there is a fumbling of phones, or diaries for the Neanderthals and Luddites amongst us. There seems to be a general assent.

As we resume our exit, Katie speaks up. "Oh, shit. I've just booked a holiday for that week."

Unthinkable, Whit Friday and no principal cornet, what will we do?

Funeral

"We do quite a lot of funerals, two or three a month; we call ourselves *Brass Handles*. There's quite a regular slot up at the crem, too. We did one the other week and they asked for a march. We played *Blaze Away*..." *(att. S. Allinson)*

A funeral might not appear to be the most compelling engagement until it is understood that for hymn tunes, without a doubt, brass is best. Playing in a smaller ensemble brings out the best in brass players. Us lesser lights from the lower sections may believe that in the full band we can get away with bum notes, missed entries and other venial sins. However, when the ranks are thinned everyone knows that their individual performances are in plain sight which means making that special effort to shine. The commitment to quality makes funerals a good job.

I am returning a favour. Tony, one of their cornets, is laid up with a cold. Tony sets the benchmark for reciprocity; there have been many times when he has filled an empty seat for Upperthong and so I am only too happy to help.

Today's service is worthwhile with some mournful favourites from the red book, *120 Hymns for Brass Band* published by Wright and Round. I have never come across a band that doesn't use it. I have my own cornet copy at home; hymn tunes are an essential practice aid. *Hail, Smiling Morn* was a particular favourite of the deceased, she requested it be played as the mourners departed. It's a hymn (or more accurately, a glee) with a banding significance, particularly in this area, and is played first thing on Whit Friday morning in all the Saddleworth villages. *Hail, Smiling Morn,* carries a great burden of tradition; William Rimmer even arranged it as a march.

As we play at recession, the congregation shuffle past the vicar and relatives en route to dinner at a local pub. The band are also invited. I am tempted but have to get back to work.

This morning is a sombre occasion, but there are traditions where the aftermath of a funeral has been marked by some levity. In *Brass Bands and New Orleans Jazz,* William Schafer states that in their tradition bands belonged to lodges and funeral societies, like the Oddfellows in the UK. Stalwart names abounded: Eureka; Preservation; Excelsior... Bands were required to lead the cortege to the cemetery gates, processing with dirges and slow marches.

Reassembling later, after the interment, the return was typically dynamic, featuring upbeat classics like "*When the Saints*" and "*St Louis Blues*". The music might also have poked fun at the bereaved, if they had a temperament that would allow it, with tunes such as "*Lady be Good*" for a widow. I am fascinated by that tradition and its energy but born in dour climes I fear such levels of exuberance and spontaneity will be forever beyond my reach.

The New Orleans tradition began at the end of the nineteenth century as the military style of American brass bands was taking the form popularised by Sousa. It formed at the confluence of two tributaries, the urban and the rural. Urban bands had trained musicians teaching instrumental technique, reading and theory; on the other hand, rural bands usually learned by ear. The two strands collided when rural musicians moved to the towns and teamed up with their formally trained peers. This mingling of the written and improvised gave birth to the music that became known as jazz.

Initially, these American bands may have been similar to their British counterparts, but their stylistic evolution developed both the music and the ensemble structure. In the 1920s, a jazz band would use several types of brass and reed instruments and, say, a dozen musicians. By the 1950s the expectation was that the cutting-edge groups would be quintets or quartets. A decade later, they started to embrace electric and electronic instruments such as bass guitar and keyboards. Meanwhile, back on this side of the Atlantic the more that things changed the more they stayed the same.

Having been brought up around what I assumed to be the spiritual home of brass bands - that topographical palimpsest on which many of the important popular movements of the nineteenth and twentieth centuries are inscribed - it has been easy to overlook the fact that there are differing brass traditions that have developed their own identities. Other comparisons with musical developments across the Atlantic, such as are set out in the Hazen's book *The Music Men*, help shed more light on the evolution of the British tradition.

From early in the nineteenth century there were at least as many, if not more, village type bands in the USA than the UK and they were often using similar instrumentation. These ensembles could be found in the tiniest hamlets and they performed many of the same functions as their British counterparts: leading parades; providing the background music for promenades, and of course; concerts.

By the latter half of the century, it was clear that American bands were not going to pursue the exclusively brass route taken in Britain. This was due to factors such as: the influences of instrument manufacturers; the post civil war traditions of the American military, and; exemplars such as the Sousa band.

The marching bands that evolved from these roots are still popular at schools and universities and may involve huge numbers of musicians, flamboyant costumes and extravagant parade routines. I believe they occasionally perform classics from the British quick step repertoire whilst on manoeuvres, marches such as *Ravenswood* and *Roll Away Bet*.

In contrast to America, the British brass band found its mature form of 25 seats in the second half of the nineteenth century and has retained it ever since. The legend (according to Meltham Mills) has it that sometime in 1871, the adjudicator John Gladney was summoned to face the wrath of the band. He had delivered a withering criticism of one of their recent contest performances and was challenged to justify his opinion; his presentation convinced the band to hire him as their conductor. Gladney's preferred instrumentation was so successful that it was soon adopted by other bands and subsequently enshrined in contest rules.

There was no comparable defining moment on the other side of the Atlantic because band contests did not command the same prestige. A singular, and perhaps unexpected, piece of technology created this divergence of the American and British musical traditions: the railway.

The rapid expansion of the UK rail network had a profound effect on the establishment and popularity of the band contest. Entrepreneurs, notably Enderby Jackson, forged agreements with the rail companies, chartering trains to take Sunday trippers from their home towns to distant contests. Some larger contests attracted crowds in excess of 15,000. Affordable travel and the size of the prizes made it entirely feasible for bands from the fringes of, for example, Bradford and Huddersfield to enter contests in Manchester or Hull on a regular basis.

The demands and discipline of the contests began to define the brass band, indeed some brass bands were formed specifically because of the lure of prize money. Impossible distances and the wide dispersal of settlements in the continental USA meant that a similar pattern was unlikely to become established there. Contesting could never have the same cultural impact as it did in Britain; it couldn't exert the same formative discipline upon the ensemble structure. This created circumstances that allowed bands to continue to evolve, though bands as the British know them may have prospered under the auspices of the Salvation Army.

UK contests had a secondary effect that reinforced the band format. Over time a virtuous cycle was created: bands needed a repertoire and to play the repertoire a specific band formation was required. Music publishers with an exclusive focus on brass bands commissioned pieces favouring the scoring of the successful ensembles.

Another important innovation in this field was the introduction of a journal system, the most famous of these were published by Wright and Rounds, Boosey and R. Smith and co. Journal subscriptions provided bands with a regular flow of new music, allowing them to build and expand their libraries. Some enduring classics of the band repertoire were published in this way. Any well-established band will have a copy of Vaughan Williams' *English Folk Song Suite* engraved with a journal title; those original copies have now yellowed with age.

Conversely, the wide variation in band formats before the explosion in music publishing was exacerbated by the fact that without support from music publishers conductors usually had to transcribe and arrange for their own musicians. This created a situation at some early contests of bands ostensibly playing the same piece of music whilst offering radically different arrangements and interpretations.

British brass bands have endured in their current format for 150 years and the Americans generously recognise the ensembles' qualities. There are now a good number of what the Americans call British-style brass bands, but their national association has only been in existence since the 1980s. Similarly, in some European countries there is a very strong growth in brass bands. The European Brass Band Championships can no longer be regarded as a euphemism for a British band contest in a foreign country.

The European Championships began long after Upperthong's finest hour, the peak of our current contesting ambitions is the Yorkshire area contest. Late February or early March, St George's Hall, Bradford, the date resonates more clearly than Christmas. Mediocre (it sounds so much better than awful) results over recent years have placed the band in jeopardy, another poor showing and we will become a third section band. This would be unconscionable.

Anyone with a passing acquaintance with band contests will be familiar with the aspiration to quality. This emphasis on finesse and the creation of high art has always been integral to competitions and so competitions have always been fundamental to any band's strategy of self-improvement. Not all observers have considered contests from this perspective.

In the Victorian era, when rival bands brought crowds of supporters to competitions, it was not unusual to find a rowdy and partisan atmosphere. In his essay *Brass Band Contests: Art or Sport?*, Clifford Brown suggests this puts the bands more in line with sportsmen such as boxers and footballers than the refined inhabitants of the opera house. Using the measure of Victorian critic Matthew Arnold, the bands may have been musical ambassadors of the mob. However, this is a minor distraction from the higher purpose of the brass band.

During the so-called golden age, bands were the only way that many working class people would encounter examples of European art music; selections from opera remain a mainstay of the classic band repertoire. Bands have always been complex entities: educators; entertainers; competitors, and; carriers of civic pride. A notable anecdote of band history reports how the Irwell Springs band of Rossendale emptied its local village to take a train load of supporters to one prestigious contest. Whilst Upperthong can't expect many villagers to follow us to Bradford in February, the area competition is still as intrinsic to the band's purpose as those competitions of the nineteenth century.

As we drive away from the church our thoughts turn from the funeral to preparations for the areas. Stephen voices the concern that his band has lost too many members recently and for the second year running will have to withdraw. The bass player, whose name escapes me, is looking forward to another year in the championship contest with Marsden. I am not too bullish about Upperthong's chances of retaining our place in the second section. This is a topic of conversation that is soon exhausted and we lapse into private silence.

Stephen shatters our reveries with news of the morning's missed opportunity. "I haven't told you, but that turned out to be quite a posh do. I could kick myself. If I'd known they were public school I'd have charged another hundred quid."

Culture

"Where was Dan tonight?" asks Chris, "It's not like him to be missing."

Jim fills him in. "We did a job in Honley this afternoon. He was sitting down waiting for me to give him a lift home, I turns round and he's snoring like a hippopotamus."

Chris nods, "Did you see him on Sunday morning in the service?"

"Oh, yes, I remember that, alright," says Jim, chuckling.

Chris continues, "Afterwards, I says to him, did you catch any flies there, Dan?" He mimics Dan sleeping, head back, mouth open. "He goes, "you what, you what?"" I says, you were sock on there, mate. He goes, "I weren't, I were wide awake, what 'r yer on about?"" He jerks around in an agitated fashion.

We enjoy the joke but this is underpinned by a heavy dose of sympathy for Dan's circumstances. For the past few months he has been on contract to an agency covering the night shift at a local internet warehouse. It has been put to him that during the festive rush he may choose to work seven nights a week or not at all. Luckily for us, Andrew was able to step in and save the day; in honour of his contribution, I stand the round.

Setting the beer before him I confess, "I love playing round the streets at night."

Andrew grumbles, "it's all right for you with a cornet." His grievance hangs between us.

"Yeah, I can see that a bass is a lot to lug around," I concede.

"That's not the half of it," he informs me, "it's the valves..." I am a little confused as surely a valve is a valve whether you are on the street or in the band room "...they freeze up. It's OK for you with a cornet, the valves are always warm. With a bass the tubing's always cold. On a night like this they're always freezing, the valves actually seize up on you." I admit that had never occurred to me.

This is not Andrew's only educational purpose, as well as being a fine bass he is a southern anomaly reminding us of the wider reach of the brass band movement. We are parochial and insular, like musical hobbits; he is our Gandalf, a messenger from a cultural world beyond our shire. Andrew is from Southampton; he was cultivated by the Hampshire Music Service.

Hampshire were a notable contributor to the post-war development of brass music. In the 1970s and 80s the county youth band competed in the championship section under the baton of John Knight. Knight was one of the first peripatetic teachers taken on by the county and a contributor to Gammond and Horricks' anthology *Music on Record 1: Brass Bands.* Knight championed brass as ideal instruments for the young because common key signatures and techniques of lip and valve allowed relatively easy switches between instruments and parts. He also believed that brass provided the fastest route to creating a pleasing ensemble sound, a claim that must resonate for those familiar with the violin.

Some would argue that the advent of electronic instruments provides better musical options for young people. Before becoming too enthusiastic about these, it may be worth considering the words of jazz pianist Keith Jarrett. Jarrett rose to prominence playing keyboards in Miles Davis' electric fusion bands at the end of the 1960s, "I can't even tolerate my own playing on electric keyboards. It's not about the musical ideas - the sound itself is toxic." I don't entirely agree because I love the keyboard sounds on Miles Davis' jazz-rock albums and the playing of Herbie Hancock and Joe Zawinul. What I think Jarrett may have been trying to say is that there is a difference between pressing buttons and making music.

What is most instructive about Knight's writing is that he builds the sense of the larger scheme that was needed to propagate youth bands. He was a founder of the Schools' Band Association which worked closely with the music publisher Max Hinrichsen to publish an appropriate repertoire. They were complemented by a national association of teachers advocating for the development of musical tuition. These were initiatives that allowed ideas and resources to be developed nationally and for skills and knowledge to be shared by teachers and musicians from local authority music departments across the land.

Enthusiastic educators combining in associations created an enlarged musical world for young people. This activity was not centrally planned or driven by government policy, however they relied on properly resourced music departments at a local level. Other fruits from this associational culture included national festivals of youth music (what was happening for brass was mirrored by other musical forms). Musical associations were also able to commission new repertoire from composers including some, such as Malcolm Arnold, of international standing. Repertoire development also extended to encouraging young composers.

Andrew creates a lively sense of the character of Knight as a conductor, suggesting someone who could be loved and feared in equal measure. On the podium he always commanded full attention, Andrew fixes a manic stare to demonstrate extreme vigilance. Knight lived into his 90s and hundreds of former students were in attendance at his funeral.

There is an important lesson that might be learned from Knight's professional life. It is that the boom in youth bands in the middle to later decades of the twentieth century depended not just upon giving young people the opportunity to learn brass instruments, but the creation of a wider culture to promote and propagate brass music. Culture is a word that haunts the pages of this book.

—

In *Keywords*, the critic Raymond Williams noted that culture has more meanings than almost any other word in the English language, it covers territory from art to biology, agriculture to sociology. The roots of the word are in the French *cultura* and *couture* which in the Middle Ages were concerned with agricultural or horticultural ideas of nurture: cultivation.

By the 1500s these meanings were being applied to forms of personal development that we might include within the term education. It was possible to speak of someone being cultivated in the sense that they were knowledgeable, sensitive, refined and discriminating. But meaning is not static and with the arrival of the internet culture is one of many words that are required to bend with the times.

A common understanding, and perhaps culture's most frequent contemporary use, is to describe styles of social organisation which may stem from tradition or systems of belief. We may speak of an office culture, a culture of bullying or the need for a culture change; it may be applied to small groups of people but also nations or religions. We may speak of English culture or Islamic culture, or suggest that "they do things different over there". In this sense it has become the property of disciplines such as sociology, anthropology and even business management.

Culture has strong associations to artistic expression: music; literature; art; theatre... Thus, culture offers a means of understanding: how a society celebrates itself; how it considers the world around it; the world it has emerged from and; the world it aspires to create. This is the sphere that still just about clings on to the term "the arts".

The arts are increasingly viewed as cultural products, commodities or entertainment within a market society. In this guise it is common to hear references to painting and sculpture as artefacts for sale in the fine art market or theatre and music as the cultural industries. References to music education are often framed within arguments for developing talent to retain competitiveness in the international pop music business.

The organisational and the artistic strands of culture fuse and become a way of defining the texture and quality of a society. When we speak of the culture of Ancient Greece, we refer both to the political and intellectual traditions it developed and the buildings and art it produced.

The buildings, the architecture, enabled the social interactions in the agora and theatre. The visual artworks portrayed the people who inhabited these places. The famous playwrights, storytellers and philosophers wrote about what it meant to be Greek: the values and the virtuous life. Also bear in mind that the current obsession with gyms, and indeed our ideals of physical beauty, have been handed to us by the Greeks.

In *Culture*, Terry Eagleton makes the distinction between civilisation and culture. He argues that civilisations may have common physical characteristics, for example their buildings might look the same, but culture is the set of attitudes and beliefs that determine the way they are used. Culture is the force that animates a civilisation.

We understand Greek culture as the expression of a refined society, but culture doesn't always have to be infused by such lofty ideals. In their own ersatz way, the punks of the late 1970s and early 1980s might be considered as a cultural, or to be more sociologically correct a subcultural, phenomenon. They had a rudimentary musical and sartorial style, but also forms of self-organisation and a "literary" genre: the fanzine. There was a code of ethics in play too, this was militantly anti-commercial as might be expected from impecunious youth.

The punks can take their place in the evolution of expressions, understandings and experience of culture that has been a current of British life for the past two hundred years. Similarly, it is unarguable that John Knight was at the centre of a burgeoning culture. His life's work suggests that he straddled the two horses of culture: as a form of artistic expression, and as a way of doing things. These elements are all pervasive in the experience of playing in a brass band, more than that they are both inseparable from what I grew up to understand as a British way of life.

—

The modern ideal of cultivation as a project of art and education first flourished in the nineteenth century. Its earliest expression came in response to a philosophical movement called Utilitarianism whose leading light, Jeremy Bentham, argued that the application of reason could achieve the greatest happiness for the greatest number.

An important component of Utilitarian practice was the new "science" of economics, and it is no surprise to see that Utilitarianism was closely associated with the rising, mill-owning, middle class. Bentham was a supporter of the 1832 Reform Act which extended voting rights to the nouveau riche; the Utilitarians opposed the enfranchisement of the general (male) population.

The Utilitarian ideals of efficiency became closely associated with the factory system. By the 1830s it was possible for Thomas Carlyle, in his polemic *Signs of the Times,* to decry these effects as creating the mechanical age. It was his view that mechanisation did not just turn the bodies of factory workers into machines, but their minds also.

The most memorable observation of this moment came over twenty years later from the pen of Carlyle's friend, Charles Dickens, whose novel *Hard Times* is still taken as a benchmark for criticism of Victorian factory conditions. Dickens provided eloquent illustrations of the problems of the period, but as Carlyle was writing *Signs of the Times*, the Romantic poet Samuel Taylor Coleridge had already begun to propose rarefied solutions. *The Constitution of Church and State* is the first British book to use the word culture in a concerted manner.

For Coleridge, the purpose of cultivation was "the harmonious development of those qualities and faculties that characterise our humanity" and was the measure of society. Whereas a cultivated persona may have been a desirable trait in high society, Coleridge felt that it was something that needed to be a feature of society as a whole. To this end he proposed the creation of a caste of enlightened educators, the Clerisy. They would be "the learned of all denominations; the sages and professors of... all the so-called liberal arts and sciences." Coleridge framed his Clerisy as the servants of a national church, whilst this idea was informed by his own religious sensibility, the ideals of human cultivation went beyond a Christian doctrine.

The experience of industrialisation had suggested to its critics that left unchecked it would crush the human spirit. Coleridge argued that human virtues were fragile and in need of both protection and nurture through institutions of education and cultivation. Victorian virtues received a clearer definition in the middle decades of the nineteenth century. They began to achieve a more coherent symbolic expression through the disciplines of the arts, and in particular the visual arts. The great Victorian champion of the arts as the repository of culture and virtue was John Ruskin.

It is unfortunate that Ruskin is now most celebrated for the debacle of his marriage, depicted in the film *Effie Gray*, as he was the foremost critic of art and society in the century's middle decades. In *Culture and Society*, Raymond Williams shows that Ruskin argued that art and society were inseparable; the arts are an expression of society and in turn the arts shape society.

Ruskin's criticism of art and society arose from his consideration of the nature of beauty. He proposed two types of beauty, the beauty of form and appearance, which he termed *typical beauty*, and "the joyful and right exertion of perfect life in man", or *vital beauty*. Great works of art were those that expressed the "universal grand design" through typical beauty, and society was at its best when it allowed man to express his natural joy in the perfect life.

Ruskin also took up the argument of an earlier critic, the prominent Catholic architect, AWN Pugin (the designer of the Palace of Westminster), that the goodness or virtue of art was dependent on those qualities being present in the artist: a corrupt artist would be unable to produce perfect work. By extension Ruskin pronounced, as Williams quotes: "The art of any country *is the exponent of its social and political virtues. The art or general productive and formative energy, of any country, is an exact exponent of its ethical life. You can have noble art only from noble persons, associated under laws fitted to their time and circumstances."

What was happening within these debates and movements around culture was the creation of a new secular language of public and social virtue. This was a battle to re-establish the centre ground of public morality from the utilitarian pursuit of money to a refined, humane sensibility. If Ruskin was preaching, others were practising.

From the middle of the nineteenth century, a movement of Mutual Improvement Societies began to develop momentum. In *The Intellectual Life of the British Working Classes,* Jonathon Rose notes that the societies had large memberships and often created their own libraries stocked with philosophy and great works of literature. It is significant that a number of early Labour MPs credited their radicalisation with a critical reading of classic literature. They were more likely to be influenced by conservative authors, such as Walter Scott, rather than say the works of Karl Marx.

Rose suggests that at times up to 20% of the working class were involved in what might be considered intellectual pursuits. In contrast, in her history of *The Mechanics Institutes of Lancashire and Yorkshire,* Mabel Tylecote notes that the formal educational reach of these particular organisations was quite limited. She argues that they nevertheless had lasting effects on attitudes to education and literacy.

It cannot be entirely coincidental that this is the backdrop against which brass bands sought to define themselves as producers of music of enduring artistic quality. If brass bands are viewed as the musical wing of the British industrial working class then the higher artistic aspirations of the brass band movement fit squarely within the framework of Ruskin's thinking. By embracing these aspirations, the common people were staking a claim to the right to cultivation, to the personal development that was available to other classes within British society. They were now becoming equal participants in the shaping of British culture in all the important senses of that word.

The gathering confidence of the working class was a major theme in the last classic Victorian work on cultivation, Matthew Arnold's *Culture and Anarchy*. Unfortunately, as far as Arnold was concerned the working classes provided the potential for the anarchy in the title.

In Arnold's analysis, Victorian society was composed of three strata: the Barbarians, the leisured upper classes with a vested interest in maintaining the status quo; the Philistines, the materialist mill owners obsessed with the accumulation of wealth and the machinery that created it; finally, the Populace who in 1866 alarmed Arnold by storming Hyde Park in certainly their tens and possibly hundreds of thousands in what modern news media would call a pro-democracy rally.

Arnold regarded the populace as rather rough and unformed, and thus posing the greatest danger to the national balance. He did not follow Ruskin in considering the plight of the working class as a clarion call for social justice. However, it would be unfair to cast Arnold as wholly unsympathetic, he was more aware than most of his contemporaries of social reality due to his day job as an inspector of schools.

Arnold followed Coleridge in seeing the solution to the problem as a reinvigoration of a sense of national culture, and in seeing the means to this end as being best pursued by cultivation. He saw this cultivating project as the duty of the state and is therefore a significant figure in the development of a national education system. I can't help thinking that if Andrew had paid more attention when he was on stage with the Hampshire County Youth Band, he may have noticed the ghost of Matthew Arnold nodding approvingly in the wings.

—

By the 1950s the industrial working class, or in Matthew Arnold's terms the populace, had arrived in the national consciousness as a fully formed, three-dimensional entity. A number of important writers such as Shelagh Delaney, John Braine, Alan Sillitoe and Stan Barstow, were producing plays and novels rooted in the world of terraced houses and factories. Ordinary people now had the skills, confidence and opportunity to write about their own lives in the way that the middle classes had previously been able to write about theirs (think of Jane Austen). There are a number of factors that are surely relevant to the creation of this moment.

At the start of the twentieth century, the baton of nearly three hundred years of pro-democracy campaigning had been handed to the Suffragettes. They finally pushed Britain over the finishing line to become what we would now regard as a fully democratic, modern state. This led to improvements in the general conditions of life for the majority of the population. Most notably, the 1945 general election opened the door to the introduction of the National Health Service. According to Danny Dorling and his colleagues, in *Poverty, Wealth and Place in Britain,* prosperity became more evenly distributed than at any other time in modern British history, a situation that was to continue until the end of the 1970s.

The labour government that swept into power in 1945 may have been equally swiftly removed, because of its failure to end rationing and post-war austerity, but it had consolidated social improvements of international stature. One of its achievements was an expansion of education provision that would surely have met with the approval of Matthew Arnold.

Brass bands also had a place in this picture as from the end of the Second World War they were established performers in the major concert halls (at least in the north of England). From early in the century, the movement had been slowly developing its own art repertoire through test piece commissions: the standard bearer was Percy Fletcher's *Labour and Love* composed in 1913. Cyril Jenkins also made lasting contributions, publishing *Coriolanus* and *Life Divine* at the dawn of the following decade. By the 1930s bands had truly arrived as a fully formed art ensemble when Elgar composed his *Severn Suite.* Whilst they were a significant cultural force rooted in popular experience, they were barely considered by Richard Hoggart in his reflections on ordinary life in the 1950s, *The Uses of Literacy.*

Hoggart celebrates and admires his community's traditions: from the minutiae of family life; to individual hobbies and private interests; to the clubs and associations, sporting, drinking and otherwise. However, he was also concerned that this was a moment of potential crisis, "the ideas for which their predecessors worked for are in danger of being lost, that material improvements can be used so as to incline the body of working-people to accept a mean form of materialism as a social philosophy." The subversive force that he identified as undermining working-class culture was the world of mass media: the cinema; cheap periodicals; soon to be tabloid newspapers; and pulp fiction. All these were more readily available and more readily consumed than ever before.

It was perhaps no coincidence that the publication of *The Uses of Literacy* coincided with the start of Harold Macmillan's tenure in Downing Street. In *A World Still to Win,* Jeremy Seabrook and Trevor Blackwell argue that the Conservative party's response to Labour's post-war cultured austerity was to promote and improve forms of material comfort. By the end of the 1950s, this strategy was proving popular and successful; Harold Macmillan felt confident enough to proclaim, "you've never had it so good."

Hoggart was observing a sea change in the values that had shaped the working class: he was bearing witness to the birth of the consumer society. The values that the flourishing print publications were introducing were ones of material advancement through the acquisition of consumer goods. The attitudes and postures that readers were advised to adopt were ones that might be purchased, rather than the examples set by more local role models. The arrival of the consumer society moved the centre of cultural renewal from within the communities Hoggart describes and into the offices and print rooms of the publishing world and media entrepreneurs. Other forces also affected this shift.

Changes in the types and availability of media were complemented by shifts in work patterns and occupations. British industry was now being forged in, what Macmillan's Labour successor (Harold Wilson) summarised as, "the white heat of technology." The post-war world was creating a new class of white-collar technical employment, these posts were filled by the brightest alumni of the traditional working class.

The progressive expansion of the school system was also shifting the idea of where the responsibility for cultivation should be housed; it was no longer accepted that self-improvement must necessarily take place within the community. An expectation was developing that the school system might now take responsibility for cultivation. The extent to which it is capable of doing this has always been a moot point.

By the 1960s the more adventurous and better educated cohorts of the working class were finding opportunities for advancement, moving into the technical jobs created by the post-war industrial renaissance. New private housing estates appealed to the emerging white-collar workers; they left their old communities to enter a brave new world. But this was not the only exodus.

Whole communities were decanted from slum neighbourhoods of cities such as Liverpool and the East End of London into new towns such as Skelmersdale and Harlow. They gained better housing and a cleaner, more spacious urban environment but lost the community connections that had defined their inner-city experience.

These emigrants became a new formation in society, occupying a middle ground between the tight-knit, communitarian traditions of the industrial working class and the up-tight aspiration of the inter-war suburban middle class. They were more likely to define their political interests in narrowly economic terms and regard their economic fortunes as being determined by their own efforts and aspirations. Many still felt able to rely on the dependable industrial models of employment but at the same time were more willing to move to better their position than previous generations.

In *The Private Future*, architectural critic Martin Pawley noted that by the late 60s the average mortgage only lasted for seven years. This represented the breathing space for those ascending the housing ladder, as succinct an example as any of the diminishing importance of community networks. The first house price bubble, the so-called "Barber Boom", came in the early 1970s.

These developments caused, at first, unseen fissures in the previously bi-polar political landscape; the new demographic lacked a political identity and more importantly a political home. They wouldn't have to wait long for a political leader who instinctively sympathised with their world view.

In the decades after Hoggart, the dominance of print declined to be overtaken by visual media. Over the past half century or so it has crept from a glass-fronted, laminated, wooden box in the corner of the living room to become Gollum's ever present "precious" in our pockets. In our private and also our very public moments we caress small, slim screens, our faces bathed in a beguiling glow. Our heads have been turned down and inwards; our notions of culture are increasingly individual curations.

If we have been seduced by electronic sirens, we have also chosen to be led by politicians who have urged us to leave the world of public duty and enter one of private gratification. Their standard bearer was a grocer's daughter from Grantham. To use the language of Thomas Carlyle, she represented the return of the "genius of Mechanism". To use the language of Coleridge, she represented the rise of "a contemptible democratical oligarchy of glib economists." An important think tank providing her with policy ideas was the Adam Smith Institute, the name calls to mind one of the inspirations for Jeremy Bentham's Utilitarianism.

The significant directions of Margaret Thatcher's cultural revolution were to denigrate the principles of collective organisation and the ideals of mutual benefit. Her first step was to roll back the achievements of the populace by attacking the trade union movement and reducing its capacity to: organise protests; influence public policy; and provide effective funding for her political opponents in the Labour Party.

A second strand of Thatcherism was an attack on the notion of cultivation as demonstrated by a utilitarian approach to education policy. This cast Thatcher, in Arnold's terms, as a latter-day Philistine.

As far as brass bands were concerned, the most damaging effect of these changes was the de facto abolition of most music tuition. This stifled the supply of talent which had led to the brass band movement reaching a state of robust health by the early nineteen eighties. The website *4 Bars Rest* has demonstrated that the number of bands entering the area contests is now only 75% of what it was in 1988.

A third front of Thatcherism was to downplay the influence of the state and replace it with the disciplines and mechanisms of the free market. The "mean form of materialism" that had so troubled Richard Hoggart was to be the nation's salvation.

There were some notable examples of how this policy direction undermined both core "big C" and "small c" conservative institutions: the promotion of out of town retail sites undermined the livelihoods of small shopkeepers; Sunday trading laws dealt a blow to attendances at high church and small chapel alike; liberalising licensing conditions for supermarkets and the discounting of alcohol off sales eroded the takings of local pubs and Con Clubs. A by-product of this was that venues that had provided bands with regular performance opportunities began to close.

In summary, the project of the Thatcher years could be seen to be to dismantle ideas of the public, the civic and the bureaucratically democratic and promote private and particularly economic initiative. The former could be seen in the shrinking of the civil service, the hacking back of local democracy (eg the abolition of the Greater London Council), the sale of social housing and the withering of public transport.

On the economic front, where others may have chosen to resist or mitigate, Thatcher's response was not to stand in the way of developing or underlying trends: cars should drive where they liked; shops should sell what they wanted when they wanted; banks should lend what they liked in deregulated financial markets, and; workers should adapt to the demands of their employers.

Despite the conclusions that may be drawn from her attitude to British institutions and traditions, Margaret Thatcher was certainly susceptible to the grosser symbols of patriotism - but she clearly struggled to understand a larger sense of society. In a much-quoted 1987 interview with Douglas Keay for *Woman's Own* magazine she stressed that there was no such thing, instead she emphasised the importance of individual economic responsibility and the virtues of neighbourliness. What was most troubling was that here was a Conservative Prime Minister with no sense of national culture. Culture was in crisis.

—

The post-Thatcher crisis of culture received two major statements during the New Labour years. Those hoping for some form of renewal or revival were left either cringing or weeping as Tony Blair celebrated "Cool Britannia". Almost a decade later Gordon Brown had a go at defining "British Values", ostensibly a response to the 2005 London bombings. The idea fell flat but it is significant that it was resurrected by David Cameron's Education Secretary, Michael Gove.

Gove framed his initiative as a response to a multi-cultural moment when Britain was experiencing unprecedented immigration from both within the EU and also the wider world. However, from a broader perspective it is hard not to see it as a cry from the heart of a government that was becoming increasingly disconnected from its own cultural roots. This is especially so if we accept that a central theme of Brexit was an attempt to reclaim a drifting sense of Britishness and that one of the key figures in that campaign was Gove himself.

If the utterances of Blair and Brown and Cameron and Gove seemed superficial and one dimensional, the government wasn't altogether devoid of serious thought on matters of culture. There is a certain irony that the most coherent example of this was to be found in the book setting out the agenda for David Cameron's *Big Society*. Cameron's attention might have wandered as soon as he'd dreamt up the idea but Jesse Norman wrote his manifesto with the zeal of someone seizing the opportunity to set out their most firmly held convictions.

Towards the end of *The Big Society*, Norman identified something: that can be a central, unifying force within society; that has been neglected for too long but is accessible to all regardless of age, social class or disability; that promotes "individual self-discipline" and "mutual respect" and gives "insight into other cultures"; that can be "intensely competitive or highly co-operative"; which "demands reflection on its own history and development" and indeed has a "long and distinguished history"; which never "loses its essential connection with the human emotions, or with emotional truth." He championed a cause that "is one of the hallmarks of a civilised society". It is a cause John Knight would have recognised.

Cricket

At middle school, I prided myself on my athletic prowess. Sports day was approached in the spirit of a conscientious objector and games lessons eluded for years on end.

Cornet tuition gave me a legitimate parole from sporting torture. Perched on a piping hot, cast-iron radiator, I peered down through cabbage-misted condensation. Classmates shuddering with the first spasms of hypothermia skittered out of the changing rooms onto the cold concrete path. Lifting my eyes, I watched sheets of grey rain drive down from Blackstone Edge, anticipating the moment the storm would howl across the playing fields, rip through shirts and shorts and flay their skinny legs.

Occasionally, my brass teacher was absent and I had to join the ordeal. In my first year I banded together with a couple of others at the corner flag. Discovering that outsize cotton rugby shirts could be pulled down over reddening knees, we fashioned makeshift survival tents. In file, we took turns shielding each other from the cold rain stinging our backs.

That final year, I was roped into rugby. Standing on the touchline I stared at submarine feet as the gentle tide leached the last of life. The lake lapped my shins, and as the game commenced I understood that catching the ball would provoke a violent baptism: a certain and total, frigid immersion. The pack advanced, gathering momentum like a squad of screaming US Marines, forcing my face under water until, gasping, I finally confessed, "I love rugby!"

In summer's haze I sloped off into the long grass by Betty Nuppy's Lane, lying undetected like a hunting lion, safe from the cork and leather projectile that flew across the field. At high school, when physics allowed me to calculate the product of mass and acceleration, it only confirmed the wisdom of my decision.

In later years, I had to sit my son down when he insisted he wanted to join the local cricket club. I was afraid he hadn't understood the life-threatening nature of the game. I soon realised his choice was a sound one, and we began to enjoy the midweek excursions to the farthest reaches of the league. There were the postage stamp grounds, like Scholes, where all teams were ordered to exercise a skilled restraint and keep the ball within the boundary. Holme Bridge had half a ground mirrored by a twenty foot stone wall topped with a chain link fence. Broadoak sloped gently, lazily up away from the main road. Somewhere beyond Chimney Lane was a beautiful Shangri La, an isolated, rural cricket idyll. Marsden was scooped from the hillside; its grass bowl grandstand afforded a full view down the valley. Then there were the level grounds nudging professional standards: Golcar, Linthwaite, Skelmanthorpe and our home, Slaithwaite.

Touching his teens, my son's talents were recognised by the club and I was able to spend large chunks of Saturday afternoons sitting on a bench with a book or newspaper. He claimed he was the best bowler, I had to agree. However, whatever the truth of the matter, he was ordered to patrol the distant perimeter and only given token overs. He claimed he was the best batter, I wasn't convinced. Despite, or possibly because of, his protests it was also made plain he couldn't expect to do anything other than prop up the batting order. The real education here was not the skills and strategies of the adult game but one of humility and sacrifice. These lessons, I realised, would require extensive repetition before they were appreciated.

I came to understand that the band ethic was also the cricket club ethic: the team is more important than the player and the player serves the team so that all can play. Equally important is that the talents of all are appreciated and exceptional talent is encouraged. It feels appropriate that our last big engagement of Christmas should be at a village institution with a parallel tradition. As the date approaches, I find myself looking forward to playing at Upperthong Cricket Club.

—

Upperthong's cricket club has a long and distinguished past and the licensed clubhouse almost qualifies as the village's second pub. Gallery walls celebrate the great teams, the cups, the shields and the prizes. In common with our rehearsal room, faces appear and reappear in team photos at twenty year intervals: fathers are replaced by sons in a hereditary roll call. Like the band, the cricket club is also not in the division history dictates is its rightful place. Despite the obvious parallels there is a subtler layer in the experience; as I push through the doors past and present rub shoulders.

Even before we have set up the room is half full, scattered tables with disparate groups. Everyone seems to know each other, there are nods and greetings, shouts over. Rounds are bought, deferred and tallied. Groups split and recombine as stragglers arrive; seating is rearranged and tables butted together. Children tear about, adults attempt to exert some control but the leashes are clearly fraying. One or two from the band leave a half built music stand or a pile of folders to chat to familiar faces. I clearly sense the overlap between the band and the club, the band and the narrower world. This scene jogs my memories of working men's clubs.

Working men's clubs are now a dying breed but for the youth band they were an important source of income. Club jobs jammed Sunday afternoons, weekend evenings or, on occasion, school nights - they were a mixed blessing. On the one hand there could be several hundred people in the audience, the downside? Most smoked.

Unventilated concert rooms were cloaked in choking fog. The far side of the room became a myth, invisible through the swirling haze. These ordeals left eyes streaming, clothes stinking and lungs gasping for clean air. If I catch a whiff of a cigarette in the street now I have a blast of nostalgia for pubs, clubs and football terraces: football terraces in particular - nostrils pricked by the eruption of the final mounting tension.

I can appreciate that the smoking ban may have had a detrimental effect on business for the licensed trade but as a lifetime non-smoker I can't understand how anyone would want to take a step back to that era. The other feature of the working men's club was that, unlike a concert, the audience was not necessarily there to listen to the band.

Battering against a wall of chatter is never a problem for a brass band. Unless you manage to play really quietly there is no chance of being drowned out. Still, it is essential the tables get the message, we are here to play; from that point on things should fall into place. As a church has an order of service, as a contest has its process, so the club job has a form: win them over; involve the room; turn those lively conversations into an audience.

The conductor plays a vital role and needs a vaudevillian patter; there are crude rules to follow and it is not difficult to succeed. He (and I am more inclined to see this as a male role) needs to strike a pose somewhere between a fairground barker, a music hall master of ceremonies and a stand-up comedian. He needs to throw in some games and quick quizzes, a running joke with a well-known member of the audience, the summoning of small children and of course a good singalong. At Christmas this impromptu choir inevitably demands serial renditions of *Rudolph*, *Jingle Bells* and *Away in a Manger*.

Some argue the best way to fulfil his role is for the conductor to enter the same state of consciousness as the audience. Unfortunately, intoxication always presents problems for a band navigating the border between order and chaos. But to begin with, we have to deal with that wall of chatter; a brisk march shuts them up.

Reaching under my chair for something to wet my lips I find water. Jack has a stern view on banding and bacchanalia: a job is a job and should be taken very seriously - no drinking until after the show. The committed are not going to obey the letter of the law but the spirit is clearly noted, no one will disgrace themselves with erratic playing. Given my own level of ability it seems foolish to do anything that would take that standard lower.

After establishing ourselves, the relationship with the audience begins to build. James knows the ropes: he thanks them all for their appreciation and for their attendance; he praises the club and compares it favourably with similar institutions, "How lucky you are, how lucky you are… fine building… great club… proud traditions… Upperthong community… how special, how rare, especially in modern times. And now to get us in that Christmas mood a medley, feel free to sing along." Facing the band, he bends forward, whispers, raises eyebrows, points to the percussion for the drum roll intro… and we're off again.

Applause: the rapport is there. "And now to change the mood a little we shouldn't forget that Christmas is a time to spend at home, by the hearth, and remember the good times of the passing year. Now, we'd like to play for you a song that brings those sentiments to life, a song made famous by the great Cliff Richard…"

Cliff Richard, Cliff bloody Richard! I cringe, I convulse, I almost go into spasm. If there was one thing that epitomised my teenage ambivalence to brass bands, it is that genre known as band cheese. As far as I am concerned, Cliff and his ilk are mature gorgonzola. Nudging Sue, she giggles, she knows my views. I whisper, "At least it isn't *When a Child is Born…*" Straightening our faces, we prepare to play… the audience love it, some croon along, James has them in the palm of his hand. And so it goes until we round off the first half.

Trooping to the away team changing rooms we prepare for that band ritual, the changing of the jackets. I have been pulled up before, "You go to the bar in your walking out jacket, not your stage jacket". There is the eminently reasonable argument that this way you don't get a pint of bitter sloshed over it. However, in Upperthong I have been increasingly convinced it is because someone has a love of doing things properly, not slovenly, and she is usually found behind the percussion.

Jack's booze embargo has been breached, he doesn't mind, it's the principle of the thing and we are all comfortable with that. I am reminded of one of the working men's club traditions that is missing tonight - the club committee always stood the band a drink at the interval. Drink. To the uninitiated this simple word may seem to encompass a world of beverages; there it was reduced to a single meaning: pint of bitter.

That first pint arrived at the age of twelve. Gripping the glass bucket in both hands, the undrinkable brown liquid tilted through the foamy head towards my unsuspecting lips. It would be a number of years before I successfully navigated that particular rite of passage. The conductor, on the other hand, received homage and tribute from the audience, throughout the job a steady trickle of men delivered pints to his table.

One Sunday at the Legion, the conductor's table was stacked with more than a gallon of beer. At this distance it's a scenario I regard with a dreadful fascination. Did he drink it all? Did he get home? Could I drink that much and live? I will never know. It is not a situation I could ever imagine and I won't be trying it out tonight. Given that most of us are driving home this evening the current beer embargo is something of a *fait accompli* anyway.

Non-alcoholic drink in hand, I stand at the bar. Nearby, Jack and some of the older committee chat with members of the cricket club. A little further along is a tight knot with Andy, Alison and James. They are laughing, but there is something harsh in James' face, his is not a spontaneous amusement.

Katie, close by, seems uneasy, sensing it may be the done thing to join in but unable to fully commit.

Nicola is at my elbow as I grumble with Sue, "Cliff Richard... band cheese..."

Geoff sidles up and takes us to task with his customary earnestness, "You shouldn't talk about music like that."

"Like what?" asks Sue.

"Band cheese... It's not cheese, it's music," insists Geoff.

"Yeah, of course it's music, but it's still cheesy music. That's why we call it band cheese." provokes Sue.

"No, I disagree. You're wrong, you can't call it that."

"Why not?"

Geoff is fired by a passionate intensity; Sue backs off like a B movie heroine. "If you call it cheese then you are devaluing the music and the audience. It isn't for us to tell the audience what they should or shouldn't like. We try and play music that they'll enjoy and if they enjoy it then we've done our job. If we start getting sniffy about the music then that'll come across, we'll play it badly and it will become bad music. It is our responsibility to make it good music. That's why we're musicians."

Chris brushes past, looking at his watch in an exaggerated fashion, "I think you're a bit early Geoff."

"What do you mean?"

"Well, we usually get the sermon at 10:30 on a Sunday morning not 9:30 on a Saturday night." He laughs and pats Geoff on the back.

Whilst on the one hand Chris has hit the nail on the head, I can't help but have a sneaking admiration for Geoff's integrity and commitment to his art. For all the uniforms, the rehearsing twice a week, the arcane contests, the purpose of the band is to provide music for its audience.

For village bands like Upperthong most of the audience lives close to the band room and always has done. In the nineteenth century it was perhaps the only social music in the village. The band would have played for dances, church services, village fetes, parades and more. The village would have appreciated its band, would have been proud of its band. Its band was a great band, possibly the best in the country - sometimes. Not only was the band giving them good music, it may have been giving them the only music they heard apart from their own singing. In that sense, tonight, we are part of a continuous thread stretching back one hundred and fifty years.

Now, our music is under threat: it has become devalued by the cinema, the gramophone, radio and TV. Economics has evicted us from public events and replaced us with amplified sounds. But, good music badly amplified is execrable and execrable music badly amplified is now inescapable. However, we still have something of value to offer. The skein linking band and village may have become frayed and tattered over the decades, but tonight it still holds firm.

Time to return. Changing back, then lining up against the dressing room wall for an ordered re-entry. General rowdiness and the dead acoustic drives the volume, the night becomes a hard blow. Fatigue follows, forcing unconscious compensation: we blow harder. An hour of hard blowing is contraindicated for playing a sweet slow melody and our sound drifts away from Christmas. Quiet passages demand keeping a weather eye out for splitting the high note mid phrase, I hope my lip will hold. Swimming that first full length, hoping you won't drown in the deep bit in the middle of the pool.

James feels our fatigue and gives us a break. Wheeling out a few old jokes, he relishes the ribaldry the mood demands. Time for a bit of audience participation; the older children sense what is coming and make themselves scarce. "The band say they've had enough of me. They say they need a new conductor. Personally, I think it's outrageous... What's that you say? You agree with them? OK, if you think you can do better come up here and have a go. Come on... what do you mean, no? You've no choice, now, you've dropped yourself right in it." The audience laughs. "What's your name?"

"She's Betty."

"Betty? Right, Betty love, you come up here. Come on, look sharp. We haven't got all night." Betty duly arrives, "What do I do, do I just wave the stick around?"

"Does she just wave the stick around?" he flaps his arms, exaggerating, and gazes at the ceiling exasperated, "Oh, Betty. It takes years, years of practice to be a great conductor."

Chris chips in, "So that's the problem? You never practice!"

The band sniggers and the audience laughs. "We'll have a little less of that if you don't mind." James affects indignation.

Betty raises the baton: she is Simon Rattle. She taps the conductor's stand before waving her arms in the air; the band plays fast. Waving slowly to bring the band under control, Jingle Bells becomes a ponderous dirge. Speeding up, the band races and the audience love it. As the moment winds down James sees that little Ellie is standing close to the front looking longingly at Betty and the baton.

"And who do we have here? What's your name? Don't be shy."

"She's Ellie"

"Are you Ellie?" Ellie nods. "Is that your mum Ellie?" Four year old Ellie nods again. "Would you like to conduct the band Ellie?" Ellie clearly would. James leads her in front of the band but the band can't see her, someone fetches a chair for Ellie to stand on. She has the baton, wide eyed she assesses the band and then turns to look at her mum. The audience sighs, "Aaaaaah."

"What would you like the band to play, Ellie?" James leans in, "Away in a Manger?" She nods. She stands on the chair in front of the band and carefully waves the baton as, softly, we play *Away in a Manger*.

The mood settles, James mines this mawkish seam. As the applause for Ellie fades, he turns to the band and whispers, "Change of plan, Mary's Boy Child." Leafing through the folder we find the square of paper with the tune and it's seven million repeats. Even swapping verses with Sue can't protect my lip from disintegrating like the jelly in a hot pork pie. This endless sonic trudge transforms wistful reverie into neurasthenic stupor. Before James can realise the error of his ways and turn the tempo round Jack ambles to the fore.

"Good evening, Ladies and Gentlemen. Can I just say how delighted I am to be here with you all once again for another Upperthong Band Christmas concert. It's nice to see old familiar faces and some new ones, too. It's been a bit of an up and down year, the last twelve months, but we're ending on an up because six months ago we finally appointed a new permanent conductor in the wake of the retirement of Neil." He pauses and looks into the audience, "I'm very pleased to see that you've been able to join us tonight, Neil, and the band wish you all the best and have fond memories of your many years service. Thank you very much for your decades of hard work." There follows some brief applause.

"I think you'll all agree Neil's shoes were big ones to fill but we finally think we have found the right person to fill them. I'm sure you'll join me in putting your hands together for James who has done such a smashing job tonight."

He continues in this vein for a while longer. His delivery, dogged and deliberate, has something of the quality of a Lancaster Bomber approaching from the middle distance; this is not a TED Talk and my attention wanders. After a while everyone applauds and I wait for Jack to sit down, but he doesn't. Instead, he commences an elaborate and extended ritual of presenting gifts and tokens to all the members of the chorus, thanking them profusely for their service.

Jack turns to leave the stage; I survey the room. Some children are very boisterous still but the younger ones have collapsed from all the larking and the lateness of the hour. Cassy's husband cuddles a sleeping heap in the corner; a good few of the small children here tonight have parents in the band. I catch myself thinking, "How could they possibly sleep through this?" forgetting they have literally been brought up with banding from the womb. I have attended numerous rehearsals with pregnant women blowing happily away, as indeed Karen is tonight. Sudden sounds may be expected to wake babies but these infants sleep through practice and concert without disturbance. Cassy claims her baby will only go to sleep if they play her the march *Knight Templar* - some lullaby!

Jack returns, "Sorry, I nearly forgot... the raffle!" Raffles seem as integral to a band job as marches and hymn tunes, my lips have always rejoiced at such *longueurs*. Youth band sets were often interrupted by an even more sacred activity. More recently, I recall an engagement with Wellhouse one Remembrance Sunday; it was at the local Legion, we had been booked to play for the service in the club's function room. Embarrassed by how little we had to do we decided to embellish the end of the proceedings with some sombre music in the patriotic style. My attention was soon drawn to a restless figure at the edge of the stage. As we finished our first number he collared the conductor, "Can you get off now? We want to start the bingo."

Raffle over, Jack departs. We are revived, moving up tempo for a couple of tunes. Finally, we wheel out the twelve days of Christmas. Back row cornets divide up the tables, quickly coaching them on their chorus. The dry run concludes with table one belting out, "...and a partridge in a pear tree": the short straw. By the end of the evening, they will feel like they have spent the night doing star jumps in a gym.

When all is done, we launch straight into a rousing refrain of *Merry Christmas Everybody*, ably demonstrating the band's facility for twisting any tune to our purpose. Turning base metal into brass, the room roars along. James gives his thanks, the band stand and take a bow. The audience cheers; they demand an encore.

Immediately, everyone is dreaming of a white Christmas, just like the ones they used to know, collectively crooning and swaying to such infectious effect that the band is pulled along. Savouring the applause, standing, bowing, we wish them a merry Christmas, once at tempo, then a swift dash down the home straight.

A peel of clinking glasses returns to the bar as we put the music in our folders. Some of us head straight for the changing rooms; we really shouldn't have been wearing these jackets tonight. My shirt is sticking to me and I'm still surprised my glasses didn't steam up.

In the brief moment it has taken me to pack up my cornet the banners are boxed, most of the stands are folded and volunteers are being recruited to dismantle the percussion. Andy is taking charge, directing the operations of a human chain.

In Upperthong there is usually a niggling point of conflict around who does or does not help out. A close tally is kept by some members observing the skivers and the shirkers. My experience suggests anyone joining a new band would be well advised to be seen to pitch in. This is something that is always noticed and if you feel vulnerable about your position, a willing helpfulness will be a casting vote in your favour. It is the experienced players and those brought up in the band who are the ones most likely to help. For them it is instinct: reflex.

There is a humility and sense of service which is deeply ingrained in band culture. This is most noticeable in experienced deps who have no obligation to stay but generously help pack up. Conversely, those who see themselves as superior or indispensable may be the last to arrive and the first to slope off, but the best of us are surely part of the band? And tonight we are all in the band; all hands are on deck. Even Katie is putting some stands away - unheard of. I wonder what Cassy will make of that transformation.

There is still the matter of a full drum kit and a variety of tuned percussion, including xylophone and timps. The question hangs, how are we going to get this lot back to the band room? How did we get it here in the first place? Students of the miraculous will not be surprised to learn that it came in Michaela's van.

Mountains have been moved, seas have parted and now the van waits for us in the car park with its doors open. There is a secret to effecting such transformations which Michaela patiently shares with all who enquire: "All you have to do is ask nicely."

Vib

Tonight, is our second stint busking at Tesco. For a while Geoff and I are the only cornets, so he suggests we divide the verses one each. This appears to be an eminently sensible bit of teamwork; little do I suspect his hidden agenda. He seizes his moment and deftly nabs the role of conductor, setting a tempo that is somewhat slower than my ideal. Sharing the verses also has the effect of making them solos - of course, I am utterly focussed on giving a good account. However, when it comes to Geoff's turn, I can hear the vibrato creeping in. I challenge him, "Who do you think you are, Philip McCann?"

At the end of his distinguished career with Black Dyke, Philip McCann released a series of CDs titled *The World's Most Beautiful Melodies*. I understand they were a bit of a hit on Classic FM. They serve as a manifesto for his cornet style: light; soft; and purring with perfectly controlled vibrato.

Vibrato is a technique that introduces a tremulous oscillation to a note to enrich the sound; it is particularly popular with orchestral strings. Instruments such as guitars have fixed points, called frets, to secure the pitch of notes. Fretless instruments such as the violin and cello rely on the skill of the player to create the desired string length. Richard Sennett offers an eloquent insight into the cellist's vibrato technique in his book, *Respect.*

Vibrato is a rocking motion of the left hand on a string which colours a note around its precise pitch; waves of sound spread out in vibrato like ripples from a pool into which one has thrown a stone. Vibrato begins at the elbow, the impulse to rock starting from that anchor, passing through the forearm into the palm of the hand and then through the finger.

Cornet virtuosi have traditionally produced vib with an oscillation of the jaw. Some trumpet disciplines create vibrato effects by agitating their fingers on the valve caps. Vib was introduced into brass band technique to add a warm emphasis. Some conductors suggest it is a means to smooth over problems with intonation. Richard Sennett insists that before attempting vibrato, "a cellist first master the capacity to play perfectly in tune." A cellist who has not mastered perfect pitch will produce a sour vibrato, "precise pitch is our version of artistic truth."

There is a view that vibrato was advocated to emulate the strings of an orchestra; the cornet has at times been described as the violin of the brass band.

Vib may have long been a stylistic distinction of the brass band sound but not all brass music subscribes to it; it is used very sparingly in orchestral situations and jazz. The opposite end of the spectrum is exemplified by trumpet virtuoso, Haken Hardenberger. He came to prominence in the late eighties, famously working with the conductor Elgar Howarth at Grimethorpe, where he switched from trumpet to cornet. His style is muscular and punchy, as may be expected from a trumpeter, but the vibrato is kept firmly in check. Hardenberger's CD *At the Beach* is essential listening for any young cornet player.

Vibrato may be regarded as an embellishment, an optional styling, but as a child it was impressed upon me that it was the very foundation of cornet technique. To play without vib was unthinkable, regarded in the same light as poor intonation or sloppy articulation. Ironically, contemporary conductors may now have to request vibrato to round the sound of the band.

If I were to hazard a guess at the reason for the relative demise of vibrato, it might be that from the late 60s onwards many talented young brass players were able to study band instruments in higher education. Conservatoire professors with an orchestral trumpet pedigree would be instructing their students to play "straight", a radically different approach to technique than the pedagogues of village bands. As these students in turn became teachers or conductors, they would inevitably introduce alternative approaches to style.

Historically, the band world was hermetic, at one remove from the classical mainstream. Brass bands are a lived tradition and strongly self-reinforcing, stylistic development has been an almost incestuous phenomenon. Until the 1960s amateurs seeking role models and inspiration would have found them in their own band rooms, at local performances or from hearing occasional radio broadcasts. In the 1960s other options became more widely available.

One reason that the 1960s were able to experience Beatlemania was the huge growth in the ownership of record players, these were high status items. At the top end, they were styled in the manner of the centrepiece of any bourgeois salon: the sideboard. Those lower down the social scale might aspire to something more portable, like a Dansette. This was a record player in a suitcase, if your suitcase resembled a carpenter's toolbox.

The spread of this technology allowed young brass players an opportunity for more leisurely study of the soloists of the day. Brass band records were readily available from all good record shops; famous bands often had recordings issued at budget prices. Big name bands were also increasingly likely to play large halls around the country and by the 1970s abridged concerts were broadcast in prime-time slots on national television. This may be one reason why the final arbiter of cornet style is still held to be James Shepherd as his career coincided with this moment.

James Shepherd is still regarded by many as the definitive cornet player. His slow melodies recorded in the sixties and seventies are marked by a keening vibrato. This particular timbre is no longer found as the cup of the contemporary cornet mouthpiece is much deeper and the bore, the diameter, of the instrument's tubing is now broader. Together these create a bigger, mellower sound. Jim Shepherd is also the foremost exponent of another brass technique which is synonymous with bands: triple tonguing.

Triple tonguing is a way of articulating triplets (groups of three notes) exceedingly rapidly and is fiendishly difficult to master. As a seven year old I was in awe of his interpretation of the cornet solo *Pandora*, recorded with Black Dyke around 1970. A child savant, I thought to myself, "I'll never be able to play like that," and I was right. On *Youtube* there is a grainy video of Shepherd playing *Pandora* with a band in Saddleworth Civic Hall near the end of his career. The recording may be ropey but you are left in no doubt as to why he gets a standing ovation.

There are many of Shepherd's solos that are the definitive interpretation, one of the most outstanding is *Cleopatra*, also recorded with Dyke; his triple tonguing is like the purring of a hummingbird's wings. Geoff says of the great man, "He pins you to your seat with his articulation". He pauses in his reflection, "I tell you what though... the best cornet solo recording ever...Maurice Murphy and Leyland Band. It must have been done well after he left Dyke, maybe when he was with the LSO, I'll have to check. All of it, it just comes straight from here," he thumps his chest. "Even the cheesy stuff is sublime..."

Shocked, I turn to him, "Geoff, did you just use the C word?"

Tonight, Geoff is clearly using his solo carol verses as an informal slow melody contest. We confer after each one to discuss our phrasing. I give up on the vib when my verse of *Silent Night* suggests I have a bad case of the delirium tremens. Our ultimate purpose has been to make the ensemble sound sublime, but I am not sure we have succeeded. When Chris finally rolls up he tells us straight. "Bloody hell, it sounds like a funeral!"

Chris isn't the only late arrival. Sue misses the first half hour, punctual as ever. After fifteen minutes, in her feline way, she drags Nicola off for a tea break. On her return she sits with me and Chris. I explain that I have only played two bum notes the whole night, she is astonished. She tells Chris that it's great sitting next to me because she gets a full view of James's face when I err. The expressions apparently encompass rage, horror and the sort of incredulity you might experience if you opened your front door and found a house full of ostriches.

—

Standing in the supermarket car park we end with a whimper and not with a bang. The Christmas season has taken up a month of our calendar but now it is finally over. I have done at least a dozen jobs in this time. Tina shares her responsibilities with another band and, depping included, insists she has been out every day. However, in this moment we struggle to acknowledge that the stands have been folded away for the last time and we will not see each other again until rehearsals start in January.

It feels that there ought to be some form of ceremony to mark this transition and separation, because I never feel more intensely involved with the band than Christmas. Instead, I place the bag of stands and music in Geoff's car boot and wait for him to close it. He extends his hand, "Well then, merry Christmas."

I reply, "And a merry Christmas to you." He extends the greeting to Tina in similar style. "I suppose that's it, I say."

Geoff looks at us both and says, "I suppose it is." After three weeks of carolling it is hard for the three of us to accept that we have put those Sally Army books away for another year. "Take care," he says.

"I will," I reply. Tina and I turn to walk away, "It's the areas next..."

2. The Areas

Sounds

In Victorian times if you wanted music, you would probably have to perform it yourself, perhaps by singing or playing the piano. Music would also have been found: informally in pubs and front rooms; more formally in concert halls, churches and chapels and of course; in weekly band and choir practices. In the intervening years the development of technology that records, distributes and reproduces sound has radically changed our experience, understanding and appreciation of music. These developments began, ironically, at the same moment that brass bands were becoming a major musical force.

The 1860s saw the first tentative steps being taken to record music. In the 1870s Edison etched the imprint of sound onto wax cylinders with the phonograph. By the 1890s Berliner had invented the first reliable system for reproducing recorded sound: the gramophone.

The early twentieth century introduced what we now know as records for general sale to the public, and by the 1930s these had reached a wide enough circulation to make Louis Armstrong the first global pop star. Armstrong in his turn had been inspired by the discs of an earlier American cornet player, Herbert L. Clarke.

The record reached its mature form (the long-player or LP) at the end of the 1940s. It was superseded by the cassette tape and then the CD which could be played on the Walkman and Discman respectively; music became increasingly portable. With the arrival of the internet, the iphone and digital network coverage, almost any recording can be summoned anywhere, at any time with a finger stroke on a glowing screen.

Technology has altered the terms on which music is encountered. The change has been so radical that if most people are asked if they like music their first thought will be of a favourite recording and not of performance.

From the middle of the last century recordings were no longer merely the means to allow people to hear a celebrated piece of music, but the definitive experience of that music. Developments in recording technology also allowed the creation of styles of music that were previously unimagined. Multi-track recording enabled artists to build up layers of sound that it would be impossible to perform live. In the present day, sound synthesizers and digital technologies enable music to be composed and produced within the circuit boards of machines without any need for skilled human performance. This holds as much for the rarefied world of "art" music as it does for pop.

Changes in music production have been mirrored by changes in consumption. The appreciation of music is now often a solitary rather than a social experience: the speaker in the living room; the headphones on the train, or; the radio in the kitchen. However, personal choice may be conspicuously absent from many of our encounters with music.

From being a rare and elusive creature, music has now assumed the mantle of a stalker. It is inescapable, lurking at every turn: drizzling out of the radio in the corner of the barbers; tinkling down the telephone for a half hour on hold; chirruping out of the cheap speaker in the rattling lift; booming and banging in the bar and pub; or pacifying late night passengers in the bus station. This may not be the music of your choice but it is likely to be that most offensive type of music: inoffensive music. The quality of the sound reproduction enhances the disturbance: played on tinny speakers at a level that cannot command full attention yet cannot be ignored; or blasted out at a volume that deters all thought and conversation.

So called "canned" music (a term coined by Philip Sousa) is often used with specific intentions, as was observed by pop musician Brian Eno with his Music for Airports. *This has not gone unnoticed in the world of commerce, and there are now companies that compile soundtracks for specific business environments.*

Music directs customer behaviour, for example, encouraging restaurant diners to stay and relax or eat quickly and move on: music as nudge, music as social control. For the listener it may also be the sound of security: a salve for anxiety in a new situation; or something that takes the edge off the loneliness of an empty room. Such music enhances the mood or atmosphere (the ambience) but does not demand exclusive attention.

At the end of the nineteenth century ambient music received a conscious redefinition from Eric Satie, who was said to protest if people tried to actively listen to his compositions. Viewed as a radical gesture at the time, ambient music is nevertheless part of a noble artistic tradition. Much courtly music from the Middle Ages onwards would have been expected to serve this purpose, the minstrels in the gallery are a good example. Other more recent forms are: the organ playing in the church as the congregation arrives; the string quartet in the Palm Court tea rooms or; the brass band billowing over the fields at the village fete. What all these performances have in common is that they are specific to social occasions or public events; they are an intrinsic part of the moment. The musicians present are playing a social and cultural role, as indeed are the audience.

There is a qualitative difference between this type of "live" ambience and the regurgitated recordings with which we are bombarded in public spaces - in shops, cafes and call centre queues. Music encountered in this imposed form has become another type of background noise, like the sound of traffic. At this point music ceases to be music, and no-one will ever want to ever listen to Vivaldi's Four Seasons ever, ever again.

Recorded sound might dog our every footstep in the public realm but it may also be sculpted into the soundtrack of our lives. Developments around the recording and distribution of music have allowed us infinite control of what we might listen to in our private moments. This portability of music may be a defence or a liberation.

Headphones on the train create privacy in a public space, imposing a sense of order and control in an oppressive acoustic environment. However, new technology has the potential to offer us much more: climb a mountain with a phone in your pocket and watch the sunrise as Richard Strauss intended or; dance by the light of the silvery moon to the strains of a Bluetooth speaker. Bringing music along may make events more of an occasion, and a later replay will help recall and reconstruct memories. At first glance there is something slightly puzzling about the power and significance of music in these scenarios.

Music as an art form is exceptional in that apart from the lyrical content of songs it is entirely abstract. Theatre, painting and literature have attempted to produce literal representations of human experience whereas music provokes responses through the co-ordination and sculpting of sound alone.

We have imposed our own order on sound: the notes, or pitches, all correspond to specific frequencies. Some of the differences in frequency between notes (known as intervals) have obvious mathematical relationships, but mathematics slips adrift in the western chromatic scale - especially in its "well-tempered" incarnation.

Western music is something of our own creation rather than an expression of the underlying cosmic order (though students of Bach may beg to differ). Yet, it is something we all instinctively grasp. As Stevie Wonder said, "music is a world within itself with a language we all understand".

Stevie Wonder was close to the mark but could have gone further: music is not just a language, it is language. Or, more accurately, music shapes spoken language as all speech requires rhythm, tempo and pitch to be effective. From an evolutionary perspective, the vocal communication of chimpanzees, the whooping and chattering, incorporates these elements and so suggests that the music in speech preceded the words. Without the elements of music speech would be flat and monotonous like the unwitting comedy of the computerised Stephen Hawking. If music is integral to speech, it is also integral to culture in general.

Referring back to that touchstone of civilization, Ancient Greece, Anthony Storr reports that music was woven into all aspects of performed art. Poetry could not be divorced from music; the sagas of Homer were spoken with the accompaniment of a lyre. Note also that the chorus was an essential component of Greek drama. Those familiar with Christian liturgy will have some understanding of how music may have traditionally been an intrinsic part of poetry. It is not only language (in poetry and song) from which music cannot be separated. The art form with which music is perhaps most closely linked, and a fundamental form of social expression, is dance - music and movement.

Dance has been a defining feature of human ritual, celebrating the most important events in both an individual's life and the life of a society, from time immemorial. This relationship is so fundamental that cultures may be defined by both their folk dance and folk music traditions.

If music is an expression of cultural identity, then in an absolute sense music is essential to identity. However, the celebration of this identity is not an individual matter of personal choice. If music is to have meaning it must be a social and collective experience: like playing in a brass band.

Wisdom

Here's a bit of maths. There is a direct correlation between the degree of deafness experienced in the right ears of the front row and their status in the band. This is not a consequence of talent; this is a consequence of their proximity to the sop, the soprano cornet.

I have no wish to disparage a fine instrument or the many fine players associated with it; I only wish to recognize its sonority. The intensity of the soprano cornet during the bass solo of a Whit Friday contest march is a marvel to behold, but that concentrated blast of high volume, high frequency sound would be deemed an industrial hazard in another context. The Upperthong front row has been hearing clearly in both ears for the past year, tonight that may change.

Sopranos in choirs generally sing the top melody lines. In a band these lines are taken by the solo cornets, they are the band's soprano department. The sop is akin to an operatic lyric coloratura - it tends to cover high cornet parts, add altissimo flourishes and provide descants - for example, in *Arkthiyerald.*

The sop is pitched in the key of Eb, significantly higher than the Bb cornet, and at times may play an octave above. It looks very similar to its sibling but on closer inspection has less tubing and a clamped, mouthpiece receiver in the manner of the flugel. Whilst a cornet player could swap to flugel mid-rehearsal and make a reasonable job of it, the sop is an entirely different matter. James suggested I give it a go early in the summer; I struggled to produce a single note. I needed a new anatomy, an extra pair of lungs. The sop demands the power of an industrial compressor and a high-pressure hose.

Jenny has been engaging her high-pressure compressor for several weeks now. Tonight, I notice that as she eases her way to her seat she is hesitant, slightly anxious - but she's still new to the band. She is just beginning to warm up as I brace myself for my confrontation with the guardian of the urn.

I am wrong-footed, thrown off balance - Mick smiles. He nudges a steaming mug in my direction as I approach the counter. Is this a Damascene conversion to hospitality? Is it the product of a New Year's resolution? Or, have I passed my probationary period and, in his eyes, become a fully-fledged member of the band? Dazed, in shock, I only manage to squeeze out a faint "hello" and a fainter "thanks".

Back on the stand, Jenny is having similar trouble with her instrument; the notes just aren't flowing. To try and get around the problem, she starts low and creeps upwards until she hits her threshold. Like a novice climber going free-style up the local quarry, she has reached the point of vertigo. She understands how far from the ground she is and starts to feel anxious about reaching higher, looking down not up. I am a sufferer myself: I think of it as altitude sickness. Geoff notices too and understands.

Geoff does not suffer, Geoff has transcended these mortal terrors. "So many people stress about high notes but there's no such thing as high notes, there's only notes."

I say, "Wow, that's a bit Zen for a Monday night, Geoff."

He pauses and focuses his thoughts, as if listening for a distant voice. "What I mean is, you can't play the note unless you can hear it. When you can hear it *then* you can play it. Then it's not a high note, it's just another note." He generously allows this to sink in.

I nod, slightly dumbfounded.

"The Americans, the jazz guys, they have this term "slotting". There's this little window where the note is, like you're pushing it through a letterbox. You know, you've got to find that gap right between the brushes?" He closes together finger and thumb to demonstrate. "...and then you push it through." He holds his hand close and flat at eye level and gently chops, fingers forward, "That's how you've got to be with high notes. You've got to direct the air into that window, into that slot." Geoff, generously allows me to meditate on this insight as we turn our attention back to Jenny.

The grim spectre of Jenny's next note hovers in front of her. She tenses, bottles her breath and launches into the void. She gains a purchase, a tremulous squeak, but just at the point I think she is consolidating her hold, she slips. The instrument falls from her face propelled by a heavy, spluttering sigh. She slumps, deflated. Geoff strokes his chin as if coaxing the genie from the magic lamp. There is a time to speak and a time for silence. Geoff's ineffable wisdom hangs in the air between us.

Slightly unnerved and a little intimidated, I venture, "Well, she hit it…"

Geoff sighs wearily, "Nah…You don't hit notes, you *play* notes. Notes have quality, they have form, they are *music*. If you hit it, it's just a sound…"

Our moment of meditation continues to unfold until a cod Kung Fu voice interrupts. "When the golden cornet rings the notes of heaven, then shall your soul be awakened. You still have much to learn, Grasshopper."

"Hi, Chris."

Slightly agitated, he admits, "I thought I was late."

"You are," I reply.

"So what's he on about tonight then?" he asks, cocking his head towards Geoff and making ironic eye contact. Geoff does not match his mood.

"The trials and tribulations of the soprano cornet," I reply.

"What, you mean Jenny?" he asks.

"In an oblique way…"

"Well, I suppose she doesn't look like a sop player," he observes.

"So, tell me, what's a sop player supposed to look like?" asks Geoff, irritated.

"Well, I suppose, like a fat bloke who's about to explode." Whilst there are very few soprano players who could view that as a compliment, it strikes a chord. "Anyway, where is everyone?" asks Chris, scanning the empty seats.

"This is it," I half shrug and sweep my hand round the room, "it must be because of the Bank Holiday, you know how it is… I'm surprised it hasn't been cancelled." But James is at the helm and he beckons us to stand with him on deck as he plots a safe course to Cheltenham.

There are 11 of us tonight, I am the sole solo cornet. Within ten minutes of the start, we are tacking towards that phrase, somewhere out there on the high Cs, the one that has been intimidating me for the last fortnight. I hit the notes and my lip holds, but swimming in the shallows of my conscious mind I hear the voice of Geoff, drawling like Alec Guinness. "It is not enough to hit the note, one must play the note. It is not enough to hit the note, one must *play* the note..."

On the surface James is taciturn and seems to accept my efforts, this may be because he has no other option. I hope my performance is compelling and that the matter is put to rest. However, I note the expression on his face as Jenny blurts out a demanding passage: it is not a happy one. At least he has the nous not to repeat his performance with Kev from before Christmas. Nevertheless, I sense there may be trouble ahead.

—

On the way home afterwards, we wonder aloud as to why we have ended up in Upperthong when we both live five miles away in Slaithwaite. Since Slaithwaite has a very respectable village band of its own it would make more sense if we both played a short walk from our front doors. In my case it is because when I left Wellhouse in search of a more challenging band Slaithwaite had just been promoted to the second section. I was concerned I might not meet their standards and didn't want to suffer the indignity of rejection, perhaps with good reason. The village has a national reputation for a very high standard of amateur music stretching back to the nineteenth century.

A good starting point for understanding how this tradition may have developed is the book *Slawit in the Sixties* by John Sykes. The sixties in question are the 1860s. For the uninitiated Slawit is a common local abbreviation for Slaithwaite, also known as Slathwaite, but never Slay-thwaite. (For a while the local train guard was a wag who would announce "...calling at Slaythwaite, Slathwaite and Slawit". He was replaced by a robot.)

Whilst not dwelling too heavily on musical life in Slaithwaite, *Slawit in the Sixties* offers glimpses of community music in Victorian times. Sykes' first encounters with music were in the church choir, he joined at an early age and the choirmaster taught him to read music. In turn, Sykes taught two pupils for the price of a candle a week. Clearly, some tuition happened informally through mutual exchange and general musical knowledge may have been widely spread.

The choirmaster was likely to have been paid but unlikely to have earned a living from his role. There were a number of ways such an income could be supplemented, for example, the middle of the nineteenth century saw a growth in the ownership of pianos. Mastery of the instrument was a desirable accomplishment for the children of the well-to-do and they would have needed teachers. Some historians have remarked on a surge in the number of music "professors" around that time.

John Sykes briefly played the tenor horn in his local band, which may have been the Slaithwaite Victoria Band. This has no relationship to the current Slaithwaite Band which formed in the 1890s, initially rehearsing at Shred, up on the moors, a mile or two above the village. This decade was an important one in the cultural history of the village, with the establishment of the village philharmonic orchestra which still promotes a season of concerts in Huddersfield Town Hall. This obviously came long after the time of Sykes' reminiscences. What is of particular interest to those with an interest in brass band history is that during his time in the band, Sykes claims he played alongside Edwin Swift – it's plausible.

Edwin Swift rose to fame in nearby Linthwaite and in 1855, at the tender age of thirteen, was appointed that band's conductor. Along with John Gladney and Alexander Owen he was one of the three great conductors of the late Victorian age, though he would be past his thirtieth birthday before he claimed to be a full-time professional musician. It is entirely likely that Swift was doing some conducting on the side in Slaithwaite. Unfortunately, Sykes struggled with the tenor horn and soon gave up.

Sykes' band practised in the Lewisham Hotel, situated near the westbound station platform and within 200 yards of my front door. The Lewisham Hotel was close to Lewisham Rd. The reason there is a road in a Yorkshire mill town named after a London borough is because the land in both areas is/was owned by the Earl of Dartmouth. There is a corresponding Slaithwaite Rd in Lewisham joined with Lingards Rd, another name with a link to this part of the valley. The Lewisham Hotel closed in 1966 and was subsequently demolished but the site is marked by a plaque on a retaining wall.

One of the Lewisham Hotel's later inhabitants, and a subject of the memorial plaque, was Haydn Wood. During my time at Wellhouse I was taken to task for calling him *Highden* after the surprising composer - it's *Heyden*. He wrote two popular songs that are still played as slow melodies, *The Roses of Picardy* and *A Brown Bird Singing*. Slaithwaite Band have at times recorded both these and his march, *Merrydale*.

Haydn Wood is still remembered by a youth music festival in Linthwaite and the *Haydnwoodmusic* website. The current Slaithwaite band rooms is at Ing Head and was purpose built in the 1920s long after the times of both Wood and Sykes.

I assume that Sykes gave up on the horn because of a lack of tuition. He was probably left to find his way around the instrument from a few guiding principles and bits of advice. In *Brass Roots,* Roy Newsome (himself a distinguished conductor of Slaithwaite Band) suggests that the bandmaster was supposed to have responsibility for the musical development of the players. There would be obvious limits to the amount of attention that could be given to those learning their instrument.

I wonder if bands had a very high turnover of members, there would be a tremendous amount of luck involved as to whether new recruits grasped the fundamentals of technique and not a tremendous amount of support if they didn't. A friend corroborated this, he told me he started to learn trombone with one of the local bands when his children were small. The guidance he received was minimal and he almost gave up, instead he decided to pursue private lessons. He says he once read an interview with the trombonist Denis Wick lambasting the quality of tuition in the brass band movement. He checked on Wick's background and found that he rose through the ranks of the Salvation Army and so was probably speaking from bitter experience rather than elite prejudice.

Tina is not as harsh in her conclusions about band teaching because without the free loan of an instrument from Slaithwaite's juniors she would have had no chance of learning. She had regular lessons with the band as a child and as a returning adult had also sought private tuition to reacquaint herself with the instrument. As for myself, I started playing at the age of seven and for many years had weekly tuition under the auspices of the local authority. A casual disregard of the need for practice was one bar to progress, a cornet that emitted sounds more typical of malfunctioning plumbing was another.

My road to success was inevitably closed for repairs, hence a thirty year detour away from brass bands. The unfortunate legacy of this is a muscle memory that instinctively "screws on" the mouthpiece. As any cornet player will tell you, the more you screw on the mouthpiece the more likely you are to screw up the music. But it's not always been like that.

Depping for one band, I was presented with a solo cornet part for the *Star Wars* theme. Someone had scrawled the injunction "screw it on til it hurts" under the reprise of the main trumpet theme. Faintly, right at the bottom between the two lines of the library stamp is written the name M. Murphy. For many beyond the band world that was the moment when, leading the trumpets of the LSO, Maurice achieved immortality.

Tonight, I didn't think I did too badly, Tina, too. "I thought you were sounding alright on your own there with that test piece, tonight. It's a shame no other bugger turned up."

Pennine

At home on Sunday evening, we have friends round and watch a programme about Huddersfield made in the early 1970s. James Mason fronts a documentary about a nostalgic visit to his hometown. As to our friends: the husband is Huddersfield born and bred; the wife a refined product of the home counties. When the video finishes, *Youtube* immediately brings up a recording of Marsden Band playing the march *Honest Toil* one Whit Friday in Delph. After thirty seconds or so there is a polite hesitation. "Can I ask you a question? Do you actually choose to listen to this? ... You know, for pleasure?"

I reply, "How do I even begin to answer a question like that?"

I tell Geoff about this before the rehearsal, he stands in silence for a moment or two. "People who don't come from round here, they really don't understand, do they?" as if I have exposed a fundamental moral failing, as if I've told him my friend can't read and write or doesn't know how to use a knife and fork. From an ironic, post-colonial perspective, is this the sort of feeling Dr. Livingstone experienced as he ventured onto the Dark Continent? Yet, I am inclined to take issue with Geoff; is he just a little parochial or overprotective in his response? Does the music belong exclusively in these valleys?

If you were to take a pin marked "brass bands" and stick it in a map it would probably skewer Huddersfield. Yet with a span from the extinct tin mines of Cornwall to the shut shipyards of Glasgow (via all points in between) the brass band is a national institution. A truly mind-boggling record supporting this view can be found online in Gavin Holman's directory, *Brass Bands of the British Isles*. Arthur Taylor suggested that the presence of the most prestigious competitions in Belle Vue, near Manchester, had a geo-magnetic pull that placed the brass band heartland in the north. I'm tempted to see it the other way round, I think the North attracted the contest.

—

In *The North-South Divide*, historian Helen M Jewell writes of the North as the top half of an ancient fracture. The geological spine of the Pennines cleaved lush, lowland, arable pastures from coarser upland grazing.

In *Looking North*, Dave Russell defines the north of England as the counties from Cheshire and South Yorkshire onwards. Tom Hazeldine suggests that this marks a boundary for different styles of production, the dividing line between the Victorian world of smaller midland workshops and the region of larger factories and industries.

Significantly, the mining areas were much more widespread. This aligns with Jewell's view that it is not the North/South divide that should be considered but that between the South and the periphery: Cornwall; Wales, and; the rough north. In England, the North exists in its own right but also, and often antagonistically, in relation to the South. The North/South divide is a physical fact but also a political one that found its most malign expression in the years following the Norman Conquest of 1066.

William I ordered the Harrying of the North in 1069, this was a scorched earth offensive to remove the last shreds of resistance to his new regime. It had the effect of creating a tabula rasa: eradicating historical systems of regional rule and redefining a large country with one strong centre of power (and little in the way of regional competition). Thereafter, London became the incontestably dominant and undisputed administrative and economic centre of the country. It developed a comfortable girth of home counties and settled into a thousand years of relative stability.

In *The World we Have Lost*, historian Peter Laslett noted that around 1700 the population of London was over 500,000. The next biggest cities, Norwich, Bristol and York had populations of between 25,000 and 30,000. By comparison France was more balanced with eight provincial cities with a population of over 50,000. In England after the three cities mentioned above there were around ten other centres with populations of up to 18,000. Below these Laslett notes that Lichfield, for example, had a population of less than 3,000. This economic power imbalance wasn't disturbed until the Industrial Revolution, the historical moment when the North and especially Lancashire finally came into its own.

The Industrial Revolution was the collision of four elements. The first, according to historian Alan Macfarlane in *The Origins of English Individualism,* was that England had well-developed traditions of individual private property and wealth long before the other major states of Northern Europe. Historians regard this individualism as the motive force of capitalism and the entrepreneurial spirit.

Second, and perhaps the most pressing, was the need for a ready supply of cheap energy. From time immemorial Britain had been powered by trees, at one time there were rather a lot, but by the end of the seventeenth century most had been felled. Fortunately, Britain was blessed with an abundant store of a superior fuel.

By the seventeenth century, there was a well-established coal mining industry (in the Newcastle area in particular). However, there were problems to overcome in exploiting deeper reserves and promoting coal as a properly national fuel source. The first was how to stop the pits from flooding, and the second was how to move the coal to the places where it was to be used. Before the industrial revolution, coal from Newcastle was delivered to London over the waves: sea coal..

The third element in this picture, as far as Lancashire was concerned, was the slave trade and the wider subjection of the British Empire. Slavery provided a constant supply of cheap cotton from across the Atlantic; territories like India provided protected markets for the finished cloth.

Having said that, during the Cotton Famine caused by the American Civil War, many Lancashire textile workers explicitly supported the Union even though to work they required cotton from the Confederacy. In *The Making of the English Working Class,* E.P. Thompson notes that the Lancashire mill workers saw themselves as the slaves of British industry and so in a comparable situation to the cotton pickers of America's deep south.

The final part of the puzzle came in the form of technological innovation. The pre-eminent character in this picture was James Watt who at a single stroke (or two if you wish to get mechanical) provided: the means to drain the deep mine workings; move the heavy black stuff from the point of extraction to the place of combustion; and ultimately the power to drive the factories. We should also remember Hargreaves and his Spinning Jenny and Crompton and his Spinning Mule, the machines that laid the foundations for the mass production of textiles. This is often depicted, with some justification, as proof of British world-beating ingenuity.

The argument that the Industrial Revolution is a product of English exceptionalism is challenged by Lewis Mumford in *Technics and Civilization.* He suggests it was the relative underdevelopment of the North that created the conditions for the Industrial Revolution. Mumford explains that other regions of Europe (areas in Holland, Germany and Italy for example) were much more technologically advanced at the time. Counter-intuitively, this created vested interests that opposed or resisted any economically challenging innovation.

Prior to the industrial revolution England was importing technical expertise from abroad, notable examples are the Dutch engineers who drained the fens and German miners. A number of later innovations credited to English ingenuity had in fact been tried years before elsewhere, such as the cast iron bridge (Italy) and the railway track (Germany). In contrast to mainland Europe, the relative historical underdevelopment of northern England meant that the main source of resistance to new technology came not from powerful financial interests but from the workers: the Luddites. Labour was much easier to suppress than capital and so new technologies were able to flourish.

After the brief Luddite interlude there was no further opposition to the full development of the textile mills in their heartland of the West Riding valleys and the Lancashire plain. Manchester in particular was transformed and became Cottonopolis. It evolved into a northern powerhouse with financial clout, if not great enough to threaten London, then sufficient for it to sit up and take notice.

If only for economic reasons, Manchester would have been an attractive place for brass band competitions, but there were cultural reasons too. In *The Northern Question,* Tom Hazeldine observes that Manchester, the South Pennines and the adjacent West Riding were not only significant for the economic activity that was taking place there, but also the political and cultural.

If any place could stake the claim to be the radical heart of Victorian England it was this region. Manchester was the city most closely associated with the Chartists and their unruly grand-daughters, the Suffragettes. Nearby Rochdale still proclaims itself the birthplace of co-operation and trade union membership was at its highest in these areas. This radicalism was supported by a tradition of worker education that emerged in the early decades of the nineteenth century. In her classic description of the *Mechanics' Institutes of Lancashire and Yorkshire*, Mabel Tylecote notes that the most powerful examples of these were in the Manchester area and West Riding towns such as Keighley and Huddersfield. Against this backdrop of popular education and radical self-organising it is only reasonable to expect a corresponding cultural ferment. Physical geography also played an important part.

The topography of the industrialising South Pennines created a patchwork of adjacent settlements large enough to have independent civic identities. In the Calder Valley, for example, there is a string of tarnished pearls: Todmorden; Hebden Bridge; Sowerby Bridge; Halifax and of course Brighouse. High on the hill, Queensbury may also wish to throw its hat in this ring. The Holme Valley has had bands in Honley, Hinchliffe Mill and Holme itself, even in settlements that don't begin with H. Slaithwaite and Linthwaite were the standard bearers for the Colne Valley.

The hub to which all these spokes joined was Huddersfield; the town was the turning point of a dynamic cultural wheel. Such a well-connected and close proximity allowed the cross pollination of bands: the transfer and sharing of musicians, knowledge and expertise due to neighbourliness and migration.

In Victorian times it was accepted as a matter of course that most journeys were by foot and anecdotes from the early days of Meltham Mills band suggest that at least one musician walked to rehearsal from Lindley, over five miles away. John Sykes' reflections on Slaithwaite life suggest that many people grew up with the expectation that they may have to move for work. Economic migration was often a necessity and so the "comer in" has always been a fundamental part of Pennine life. This is a trend that has now taken on a radically different character than it may have had in 1860. I mean, back then it was simply impossible to find a decent pilates class this side of Harrogate. Nevertheless, it is easy to imagine a mobile strata of society drifting between the towns for work.

The Pennine settlements mentioned above all supported public subscription bands, by far the most prevalent type. In the present day this is likely to mean that members pay a contribution to the band, but in Victorian

100

times the public supported their local bands with annual contributions in the manner of a magazine subscription. The successful factory bands, such as Black Dyke and Meltham Mills, also gave the South Pennines a powerful boost in establishing well-resourced ensembles. Meltham had the financial clout to bring in both John Gladney and Alexander Owen (initially as their star cornet soloist) from over the hill. Edwin Swift was a home grown product of the Colne Valley. It was inevitable that such a dense foment of musical activity should produce its own exemplar. All three talents circulated extensively within the West Riding and beyond.

Whilst the focus here is on brass bands, the strength of other musical traditions (such as choirs) should not be ignored. Choirs may have flourished because of the same factors, but an interweaving of complementary strands must have added to the strength of the overall musical fabric. By the 1890s there was a network of male voice choirs in the valleys around Huddersfield and these were often complemented by ladies choirs. Just as the band tradition has Black Dyke Mills so the choral tradition has the world-famous Huddersfield Choral Society. There were also musical contests. Small ensemble and solo slow melody contests have been a mainstay of brass culture, and the Mrs Sunderland competition still has musical clout over 125 years after its founding.

In terms of inspirations for locating the most prestigious band contest in Manchester's Belle Vue: it was in the centre of that cultural axis between Manchester and the West Riding; and also at the heart of the northern rail network.

—

Geoff's comments about people who aren't from round here contained an element that transcends music and touches on a deeply felt sense of place. It may be that anywhere that has some current of historical continuity develops an aspect of community with a distinct understanding of itself. Geoff wasn't just touching on a sense of band culture but a sense of Pennine culture. The notion of bands and the towns of the South Pennines are included in the mélange of themes that constitute a cartoon northernness.

It is worth noting that in popular culture there have been many significant contributions to allow a broad definition of the North: the Liverpool of *Boys from the Blackstuff; Auf Wiedersehn Pet* offered a take on the North East; and then there is *Coronation Street*. The cartoon North is not a fixed notion, but I suggest it reflexively evokes images of the former coalfields and steelworks of South Yorkshire or the former weaving sheds of Lancashire (but oddly, rarely points further north or south).

The geology between these nodes is dominated by a coarse-grained sandstone; this blackened rock has somehow become a metaphor for the area. As a child it was always in the background of my life; I had a view of the dark outline of Blackstone Edge from my bedroom window. As a teenager I spent winter Sundays battling the rain over the bleak moors, the quartz in the rock glinting from overhanging outcrops.

Geoff and I are not the only ones affected by our geography. The profound link between people and place has obsessed a number of writers: notably Herbert Collins in the *Roof of Lancashire;* and more explicitly the poet Glynn Hughes in his reflections on tramping the moorland tracks and mill town streets (he were a comer in, too). Hughes named his book after the rock: *Millstone Grit.*

The Bible

Over Christmas I spent countless hours in devoted practice: laying incense at the altar; honouring the ancestors. Today is my first opportunity for solitary practice since then and I am about to see whether or not my prayers have been answered. I run through the last page of the test piece and my lip turns to jelly a line from the end.

Given the amount of time I have devoted to it, I would like to think I have mastered the art of practice - the evidence suggests not. I may be doing the same thing every day and expecting to get different results. On second thoughts, I am getting different results: I'm getting worse.

One problem with practice is that it is often judged on the amount of time involved, for example, half an hour a day. A cliché derived from American writer Malcolm Gladwell is that it takes 10,000 hours to master an instrument. Not having read his book, I can't say whether or not this generalisation is hedged in by some qualifications. I am more inclined towards the Bananarama hypothesis, "It's not what you do..."

Most teachers will identify problems with a student's playing in a lesson and set exercises for practice at home. However, they may not teach the student how to practise. In my limited experience there seems to be a gulf between the teacher's intentions and what your seven year old daughter does in front of the music stand. As for the appearance of practice advice in our band room, it's as rare as our contest successes.

In desperation, I am compiling a compendium of strategies to improve my playing. However, the brass band tradition seems to revolve around insights such as, "just blow the bloody thing," or "get some air into it." The latter point seems oblivious to the fact that the instrument is always full of air. Whilst good old British advice may be robust to the point of belligerence the Americans are a different kettle of fish. The internet is full of wild-eyed trumpet players insisting that they only use 7Eh3 mouthpieces designed by NASA for the Apollo space programme, man.

Unfortunately, the classic cornet study books, no matter how well written, seem to allow too much room for misunderstanding. Playing a brass instrument is a dynamic not a static process, it doesn't easily accommodate the frozen moment of words or still photography. A pitfall of tuition is that it is easy for a teacher to assume that basic techniques taught several months previously have been remembered and applied. A problem for students is that they might not properly understand the quality of their playing. There are ways around this.

According to Laurence Bergreen, in his later years Louis Armstrong recorded all his solos and listened to them as quality control. That sounds useful, I try it and suddenly realise that what I am playing is not what I think I am playing. Armstrong also offered medicinal advice and smoked "gage" before he played. He thought it was wonderful stuff but the Chicago Police Department begged to differ. I am unable to draw my own conclusions as they don't stock it at the corner shop. I also remember what 40 Senior Service a day did to my grandad's lungs.

I have sometimes wondered if I might learn something from other disciplines; athletes, for example, keep training diaries. They not only plan their training time down to the minute but identify the aspects of performance they will focus on, the exercises they will use, and then keep detailed records to track their progress. This sounds like it may be worth considering, I can now do twenty cornet dead-lifts and bench press a euphonium.

For those who need to see words on a page, Kristian Steenstrup seems to condense the most sense into the slimmest volume. He draws heavily on academic research, discussions with some of the world's best teachers and his own experience. He devotes a whole chapter to practise, his top tip is to work to establish and reinforce good habits at all times. Most notably he recommends *very* slow practice of tricky pieces; this is not a unique insight. The great French composer Saint Saens is said to have advised, "One must practise slowly, then more slowly, and finally slowly." Steenstrup also recommends spending no more than five minutes at a time on any piece or technique and lots of resting. I particularly like the sound of that last point. The title of this revelatory work? *Blow Your Mind.* Playing in a brass band may be an art but practising the cornet is a science.

—

Sometimes it is best not to approach a problem head on but in a round-about way: picking it apart into its constituent components or examining it from a range of perspectives. When all other options have been explored it is time to seek advice. I hope to learn from the masters, to claim the legacy of great musicians who have left a trail of notes for us to follow. I am leafing through a shelf of music books seeking inspiration and guidance. These volumes are filled with pages and pages of dots and lines: more dots than a case of measles; more lines than a naughty schoolboy.

I am coming to the conclusion that there is little point in accumulating these studies, methods, tutors, call them what you will. They contain useful advice but often fail to capture what it was that made the author excel. If these attributes are to be described then they can be contained in a few sentences. However, words struggle to capture the essence of experience, what mystics call the inner teaching. The reputation of the teacher relies on their wisdom; the progress of the student relies on its application. Maybe the quantity of books is too distracting, maybe I should clear my shelves and retain just one volume, or two: the Bible and the complete works of Shakespeare. Any brass player will be able to tell you who wrote the bible: Arban.

The Complete Method for Cornet was composed and collated by Jean Baptiste Arban in 1864. Arban was a pioneering Victorian cornet virtuoso. His main technical contribution was introducing the flautists "tuh, tuh" tonguing technique to brass instruments. Arban's book quickly found fame beyond his native France; the English edition notes the adoption of the Method by the British military music school at Kneller Hall. The Arban is the definitive volume of technical studies for all band instruments, everyone (in theory) uses it. It is possible to have lessons with some brass purists and only ever use this book.

The Arban is divided into sections exploring different aspects of playing: scales; arpeggios; double tonguing; triple tonguing and much more besides. Studies such as these help players develop their technique. This is why I am leafing through it today, trying to find exercises that will build my stamina for those demanding passages in the test piece.

It should be noted that the Arban is not just a book for developing players. Gardeners know that without constant attention an ordered landscape reverts to jungle. Experienced performers refer to the Arban so that the quality of their playing remains consistent. The lip deteriorates after even short breaks; the Arban keeps the lip in shape.

What makes the Arban exceptional is that it has an appeal that transcends mere utility, at least in the Boosey and Hawkes edition: it is a thing of beauty. The book is published in the imperial folio size and is about 1/2 an inch thick. This is a heavyweight tome that has destroyed many a puny music stand. The paper is durable, the pages are clear and legible and there is something harmonious about their presentation. It has the aura of a sacred manuscript, a holy text, another reason it is known as "the Bible". I could have it as my desert island book and endlessly browse; lulled by the order and rigour, it invites the reader to study and be wise. There are other versions, some teachers prefer the Carl Fisher edition but, honestly... The pages are smaller, and likewise the print, it's like drinking tea from a tin mug when you're used to fine bone china.

The bulk of the Arban is a disadvantage and I never used it as a child. Instead, we were recommended the Wright and Round method, an ersatz imitation offering some of the tropes of the Arban, pinched and pruned. In its favour, it was cheap and could be rolled into the slot in a cornet case.

It is not just the physical beauty of the book that secures the Arban's status and reputation. It allows for the whole range of musical ability to benefit, and some teachers argue that every exercise in it is worth playing no matter the level of your expertise. The scope of the book extends far beyond generic studies. Towards the back is another feature that confirms its biblical status, a sort of New Testament of brass.

Part III is introduced by *Fourteen Grand Studies*. Each study is at least a page long and features a particular area of technique; they are a constant presence in the syllabii of the higher exams for most brass instruments. There are many performances of the studies published on the internet. They clearly confound some very experienced musicians, but not the LA Phil's principal trumpet, Thomas Hooten.

The book is rounded off with the Eighteen Solos (*air varie*) that have retained their status at the pinnacle of the virtuoso repertoire for over 150 years. An *air varie* consists of an air, a theme, a slow melody that is then replayed through a number of variations. These emphasise different aspects of performance such as: finger dexterity; compound time; single tonguing; double tonguing; triple tonguing; and above all, stamina. On top of all that the soloist must still charm, dazzle and amaze, as Russell Gray demonstrates on his recordings with the Foden's Band. Gray claims he played the solos on Arban's own cornet.

Industry

Still in thrall to the Arban, I drive off to the extra Sunday rehearsal. Russell Gray plays *Fantaisie Brilliant* through the car stereo. The rehearsal starts at 11:00, an inconvenient time neither fully morning or properly afternoon. In the meantime, I have a rendezvous with Andy for a late breakfast.

As I head out of Marsden in the fog, I hear them before I see them: the revving of engines; the application of brakes; the honking of air horns. Parked up on the verges near the Motorman's café, polished grille chrome glints in the headlight's beam. The *marques* of the vehicles catch my eye, the logos of BMC, Commer, and, in tune with the music that fills the car, Foden's.

Embraced by the café fug, Andy and I reflect on the historic link between industry and brass bands. Sponsorship arrangements were not uncommon in the lower sections, but at the pinnacle of the tradition there were more than a handful of bands that could be considered as a division of manufacturing.

The most enduring works band was Black Dyke Mills, founded in the middle of the nineteenth century. Foden's band were a relatively late arrival, emerging shortly after the Relief of Mafeking. From the very beginning the firm's commitment to the band was absolute with top players headhunted with the offer of employment and accommodation. Foden's band quickly went from strength to strength.

The factory band tradition basked in an Indian summer during the post-war boom from the early 1950s until the early 1970s. An exemplar of this peace time optimism was the Crossley Carpets band in Halifax, starting in 1949 and folding in 1969. Like other big and brief post-war factory bands, such as Ferodo, it lost touch with the workforce and became too costly for the employers to maintain. Nevertheless, some of the famous works' bands endured beyond this point; Black Dyke were paying musicians wages to their key players well into the 1970s.

Contributors to Arthur Taylor's oral history of the movement, *Labour and Love*, argue that the intensity of the work environment and the frequency of rehearsals and performances brought the whole ensemble to a professional standard. It is difficult to contradict this when listening to recordings of Dyke and CWS from the late 1950s onwards.

The embedding of bands within large industrial concerns cannot be dismissed as a mere marketing ploy. Arthur Taylor provides strong anecdotal evidence of the passionate devotion of employers to their musicians. This was often a heady mix of paternalism and ambition and there was a spiritual intertwining of the fortunes of band and business. Consider Black Dyke: it is impossible to mention the mill without the music.

The status of bands within prestigious manufacturers consolidated their profile within the ranks of the skilled working class. The brass band had significance amongst the starched white collars in the drawing offices of high flying engineering firms such as Fairey's. But, the appeal was broad and stretched deep underground to the blackened faces and frayed blue collars of the miners in Grimethorpe. One of the clichés of British popular music is still the colliery band. Because of his background, I regard Andy as an expert on this corner of the brass universe.

Andy stares at a congealing egg, "I'm not sure how much the band was integral to the colliery," he pauses, "it was more an extension of the welfare club. The colliery as such didn't have any input as far as I could see. By the time I was playing in it, it was just another part of village life."

I tell Andy about my parents' experience and that in other industries major employers offered their workers a range of recreational and restorative activities that extended well beyond music. "My mum used to talk about how the social side was a fundamental part of working at ICI. She started playing tennis through working there. Even in later life she would be bumping into people she used to work with, it had a big effect on her life."

In their study of community activity, *Organising Around Enthusiasms*, Jeff Bishop and Paul Hoggett suggest that up until the 1970s the majority of sports fields were provided by large employers rather than municipal bodies. In Huddersfield alone, ICI operated a vast sports ground as did David Brown's Engineering. These helped consolidate relationships between workers and offered benefits to the wider community. This benign cultural and recreational relationship was living on borrowed time, a fact not immediately apparent as the post-war boom peaked in the late 1960s.

—

The clouds of the rising political storm began to gather far beyond the horizon, in America at the start of the 1970s. The first shock was America's decision to leave the gold standard and end the post-war consensus. Consequently, American economists started to think not just about a new role for America but new models of economics.

America's most influential economist at that time was probably Milton Friedman. In a famous article in the *New York Times* (*The Social Responsibility of Business is to Increase its Profits*), he argued that business had only one purpose and no other: to generate dividends for shareholders. He said this could, and should, be done by any (legal) means necessary. For him there was no social, ethical, moral or other purpose beyond this bleak diktat. By leaving all decisions to the market we would truly know our own morality and set our ethical course through the power in our pockets. This was a radical challenge to the benevolent paternalism supported by the likes of David Brown's and ICI.

By 1979 Britain's economy was steadying but this was not enough to save the incumbent Labour government. The incoming administration, inspired by Milton Friedman, pursued a monetarist policy of high interest rates. Many businesses quickly found the cost of borrowing became unaffordable. Two things happened: the first was a huge wave of business failure; the second was the ascendancy of a species of investor known as the corporate raider.

Corporate raiders bought up struggling or undervalued companies, sold their assets (buildings, machines, etc) and pocketed the profits: this process was known as asset stripping. Notoriously, the traditions of the company in the community or the welfare of the workforce were irrelevant to these buccaneers. The asset strippers' legacy was that businesses became saleable commodities as much as they were productive units.

One school of thought suggests this moment was a long time in the making and was part of a larger picture of British decline. In *Going South,* Larry Elliot argues there were problems with the British economy from before the first world war.

In *The Rise and Fall of the British Nation,* David Edgerton suggests a contrary theory. It is his view that Britain had surged ahead in the wake of the Second World War. Any decline was a result of a natural process of losing market share to reviving competitors, such as Germany.

The State We're in was Will Hutton's assessment of Britain at the end of the twentieth century. It was intended as public advice to Tony Blair on his journey to Downing Street. Hutton suggested that the roots of Britain's economic decline lay in the investment traditions of British capitalism: the financial system tended to pursue high, short term returns from speculation; but was reluctant to support the longer-term, lower yields of industrial development. These traditions were also related to the worldview of Victorian *laissez-faire* capitalism.

A culture of private investment had clearly prospered in Victorian times, but Britain's imperial character encouraged City investors to place their money to the best advantage in a global context. The metropolitan heart of Britain saw itself as the centre of an empire rather than a mere nation. Investment was not considered on a local, regional or even national level as a matter of course.

Martin Weiner suggests City interests had at the very least ambivalent attitudes to industrialisation. They found it distasteful because of the damage to and pollution of Britain's green and pleasant land. Likewise, they were uncomfortable in the presence of the gruff industrialists who lacked the cultivation and manners expected in polite society. With hindsight, it is perhaps no surprise then that the economic tribulations of the late twentieth century had their most dramatic expressions in the British periphery. This was particularly true of the North.

In *Regional Policy in Britain*, Paul N Balchin observes that as early as the 1920s, governments were seeking ways to redress the imbalance in the North/South economic divide. However, this disparity was compounded by two important trends which emerged in the 1960s: deindustrialisation; and the early stages of globalisation, in the form of the genesis of the multi-national corporation. During this period, industry began to decline in the

South as well as the North. However, in the South, industrial decline was outweighed by new forms of economic activity in the service sector.

Another aspect of Britain's economic problems was the relatively adversarial quality that characterised labour relations, particularly in heavier industries. A decisive opportunity to heal this division also came at the end of the 1960s. Unfortunately, the TUC failed to back Labour minister Barbara Castle's *In Place of Strife* initiative. Instead, they cemented a rift between the unions and their preferred party of government. Within a few years the most powerful trade union, the National Union of Mineworkers, forced the Conservative Prime Minister Edward Heath to ask, "who runs Britain?" He was told that it was Harold Wilson.

Heath may have been out of power but his back-benchers took their time to plot a comprehensive revenge. This came in the second term of Margaret Thatcher's reign. An unforeseen effect of this was to recast brass bands as a historic and nostalgic musical phenomenon courtesy of the poignant cinematic masterpiece *Brassed Off*. The 1984 Miners' strike was an economic and social disaster for many communities across the north of England and beyond. Their experience was starkly at odds with the boom times in the City of London.

—

Pursuing an idea, I ask Andy, "Do you think closing the pits created the opportunity for dynamic economic renewal?"

He spurts a yard of tea across the table, "You mean was the pithead turned into a gleaming glass tower at the centre of global finance? Mmm, Perhaps not. Put it this way, I was on my way to university when the strike was on the cards. I didn't look back. My sister still lives there. God, if you thought it was grim in 1980..." He gathers his thoughts, "OK, the colliery's gone and there's trees on the slag heaps but where the pit head was it's just steel sheds. They're even bleaker than the winding gear."

I ask him if he supported the strike.

"I went to the picket lines a few times. But, Scargill was an idiot, he refused to build the alliances that would have supported us. Plus, he couldn't accept the fact many mines were living on borrowed time, the coal would run out at some point. At some pits, in effect, it already had. It was just madness to think all the mines were going to stay open forever..."

I probe further, so does he think the government was right?

"There needed to be a plan for coal but that wasn't what they were after, they were just out for revenge for the defeat of Heath. They wanted to crush the NUM. I mean, we were well and truly shat on..."

—

Modern Britain had built its sense of self on being the great imperial power and the great industrial nation. The Empire had to all intents and purposes disappeared by the early 1950s. However, at the end of the 1970s, Britain could still claim a seat at the top table when it came to industrial might, that was to end.

Manufacturing's contribution to the economy fell from 25% in 1979 to 10% in 2016 and the numbers of those employed fell by two thirds to around 2.5 million. Not only that, but as corporations consolidated they tended to concentrate their white collar core of head office functions, research and development in the south-east and blue collar functions of assembly and warehousing in the regions. This further reinforced the trends of wage imbalances that had concerned governments back in the 1920s and 30s.

Balchin shows that by the mid-1980s, government began to accept de-industrialisation as a fact of national life and abandoned attempts to rebalance the economy back towards the periphery. A new phrase began to be whispered in Whitehall (most famously in a spat between the Home Secretary, Willie Whitelaw, and Michael Heseltine with reference to Liverpool): managed decline. (https://www.bbc.co.uk/news/uk-16361170)

The emerging picture was inauspicious for brass bands as the tradition was embedded in the community fabric of the industrial regions. Brass band music is ultimately, to borrow a phrase from Miles Davis, "social music".

The founders of, say, Foden's would have been focussed on making trucks but would also have been making a statement about their place in their community. The term "building the business" would have had a very physical as well as economic meaning for the Edwardians and Victorians. To reinforce this point, the Black Dyke mill buildings are still the most impressive architecture in Queensbury. By way of contrast the businesses of the 1980s became increasingly focussed on the abstract generation of profit. This meant they no longer viewed the possession of assets as being essential to their core purpose.

The new business position was to divest liability through subcontracting, this became known as outsourcing. Wherever possible the workforce was placed at arm's length and the British workplace is now characterised by time limited contracts. With the rise of agency working, businesses may not even have direct responsibility for the people they employ. Workers may find that they are not entirely clear who they are working for. All of this may seem quite a long way from the simple experience of playing in a band, but everything takes place in a context.

Fish live in the context of a river, but if the river dries up or becomes polluted, that context has changed and if it changes drastically enough it may no longer be a suitable habitat. The political changes of the 1980s represented a rupture with the world that supported works brass bands: businesses were operating in a febrile and uncertain economic environment; the workplace was losing a sense of cohesion and consistency; and the new business models meant that it would become impossible for managers to justify a factory band to shareholders as it would have an adverse effect on dividend payments. Even without the political agenda of the 1980s the works band may still have been an endangered species.

By the late 1970s, the model of the Foden's style family firm was on its way out. Many large family firms were eviscerated by corporate raiders because they had been quietly ceding ownership through share sale; the BAFTA winning BBC documentary series *The Mayfair Set* examines this issue and the Hollywood blockbuster *Wall Street* dramatises it with explosive effect.

As mentioned earlier, where businesses survived they were likely to be absorbed into larger concerns with head offices in London. Head office managers were unlikely to have links to the communities of their regional branches. The formation or maintenance of a factory band would be irrelevant to the business. Without a passionate advocate there would be no-one to promote or defend a band.

The factory hemmed in by terraces and back to backs was also becoming obsolete, the growth in urban traffic made them unsuitable destinations for HGVs. The 1970s had seen a boom in motorways, link roads and bypasses; these became the nodes on which to build retail and office parks, distribution hubs and low rise industrial sprawl. They were out of town, on the urban periphery, as were the new housing estates with a car in every driveway. Not only was the world of work being reshaped but the link between work and home was transformed so that for more and more people it was no longer on the doorstep.

Those new houses were more expensive than the stone terraces and were being paid for with two incomes; the workplace was becoming more diverse. This in turn led to pressures to change the nature of relationships in the home. A former police officer told me that when he joined the force in the early seventies there was an expectation that there would be participation in some form of recreational club, in his case the Police band. The pressures from the changing domestic environment meant that employers could no longer enforce these demands.

Whatever the pros and cons of the changes of the past fifty years, there is one incontestable fact: there are no more works bands. There are also no more colliery bands simply because there are no more collieries. Fortunately, the collapse, destruction, or fracturing of many great manufacturing names (Foden's being a case in point) did not immediately undermine the profile and popularity of brass bands. The link to industry continued but this was more commonly in the form of the sponsorship and naming rights that will be familiar to football fans.

Many of the great manufacturers may now be almost forgotten but the bands they created have transcended their moribund commercial constraints. Sensing no possible identity beyond the industrial and musical, they retain the factory names in perpetuity.

—

We drift between these thoughts and the sports pages of the Sunday papers propped in front of us. I push the breakfast round the plate and check the time. According to my watch I have more than enough time to finish up, although I am not sure whether or not I want to. Andy gets quickly to the point, "Are you going to eat them sausages, or what?"

The Motorman's doesn't beat about the bush with its menu. For example, the sausages are sausages, not locally sourced, nor artisan, not from this farm or that butcher. This is not the place to eat if you want to know more about your sausages. A word of advice: if you need to know more about your sausages you should not be eating sausages, believe me, you should not be eating sausages. I reply, "I haven't made my mind up, I mean, do you think sausages really qualify as food?"

Andy snorts, "What are you on about, get 'em eaten. I worry about you, next thing I know you'll have turned bloody vegetarian."

Buoyed with an optimum ballast, I am bemused to see so many cars parked outside the band room as I am at least fifteen minutes early. Or, as I am about to discover, thirty minutes late. This morning is the cornet sectional and as I enter everyone else is tearing through the third movement.

James looks at me and I start working through the options for a flippant excuse. This process is halted when I see someone else is sitting in my chair and for a moment I lurch towards paranoia. Keeping my head in check I perch on the end of the row and assemble the cornet. Without a warm up it's very difficult to make a meaningful contribution but I at least try and look like I'm playing. I just about bluff my way through.

A little later, as the rest of the band wander in, there is a reshuffle of our newly completed front row. I stay put on the end and Sue moves down a seat to join me. Russ, the newcomer, will support Katie at the contest. I may be being harsh but the last ten minutes have not provided a compelling argument for Sue to lose her seat, but she says she is relieved to have a little pressure taken off her.

As the full rehearsal kicks in, Sue and I realise the extra body has allowed James to hatch some plans. Pencils out, we are relieved of rather more duties than we would like. When it comes to contesting, everyone can expect to be told to leave out particular sections or in some cases have their part played by a different instrument. Some conductors have a reputation for rewriting and rescoring the whole piece.

This morning we are dismayed to learn that after the third bar we now won't play for about half a page. How should we take this? With subtle sarcasm, obviously.

The sopranos

Winding our way around the stone-flagged passage we are serenaded by a shrill blast from beyond. A heavenly boiler blows its gasket. Pausing, reforming, it ascends an altissimo scale. Mirroring glances incline our heads, back, sideways. Squinting down our noses we affect knowing postures, Holmes and Watson with a vital clue. Tina offers a pronounced wink, "'appen..." she says in a Yorkshire woman's version of a mock Yorkshire accent. I tap my nose with my right index figure, "'appen," I reply with the Lancastrian equivalent.

Hurrying, we are eager to share our barely suppressed excitement. An excitement that is only heightened after confirming the sop seat is occupied by someone who both looks and sounds like a soprano cornet player. James sits by his side, sharp pencil lines underscore the points requiring particular attention.

Big Michaela dominates the centre of the kitchen counter, we sidle either side. Poised to share a thought with Mick, her palms compress the Formica counter. In preparation, he has braced himself across the back cupboard, primed to jump aside the moment Michaela takes aim with her index finger.

Pow! "What's 'e," the finger recoils as the thumb jerks just as violently to her shoulder, "doin'," deep breath, "in 'ere? Eh?"

Tina and I each take a step back and exchange terrified stares across Michaela's broad back. Before we can quite adjust our metaphorical frames of reference from Baker St to the Wild West Jack has sidled over.

"Hold on, Michaela. I don't think we need to go charging in at the deep end here. I know you and Nick have had your differences..."

"Differences?! I don't call being too drunk to play, "*differences*". He's a bloody liability!"

"Look, I know he's a risk, but, there's a time to let the water go under the bridge and start with a clean sheet and let bygones be bygones. Everyone deserves a fresh start. Anyway, we've been looking for weeks and he's the only option. We can't go to the areas without a s'pranna."

Steam seems to burst from her ears but we also sense that whilst her indignation is real she has accepted this *fait accompli*. Michaela has presented this small tableau to dramatise her views, the audience has appreciated the quality of her performance: we have got the message. Drawing herself up to her full height, she huffs and heads for her chair. The rest of us remain on tip toe, breath held then slowly released to the count of ten.

"And... relax..." Our eyes swivel left. "I don't find that particularly amusing, Chris," sighs Jack. "Well, you couldn't expect anything else, really, could you. She was hardly going to be running slow motion across a sunlit meadow to receive his fond embrace." Jack shakes his head and trudges to the waiting chorus sitting by the barn doors.

"He sounds alright to me..." says Tina.

"It's not what he sounds like tonight that's the problem," replies Chris, "it's what he sounds like on a Saturday that's the problem."

"What do you mean," she asks, "does he turn into a pumpkin on Friday night, or what?"

"Summat like that." Mick, sensing it is now safe to return, joins us with his elbows on the counter.

"The problem is, he can play his instrument but he can't handle his drink. He's straight in the pub on a Friday afternoon and that is pretty much that for the weekend. God knows how he gets to work on Monday morning."

"There's always a chance he's mended his ways," I offer.

"There's a difference between chance and favourable odds and as things stand there's more chance of Town winning the FA Cup." Tina and I consider the implications of Mick's resounding vote of confidence. We turn our gaze to the stand and hear the big notes ring out, in time, in tune. We are reassured. With a sound like that what can possibly go wrong?

Literate

"What are you doing?" asks Sue.

"Just getting that opening note sorted," I reply.

"Well, you seem to be making very heavy weather of it."

I explain, "I'm just thinking about what Geoff was saying about producing notes."

Sue leans over and interrupts Geoff who is blowing through his solo entry. "What's that Sue?" he asks.

"I said, what have you been telling him now, more of your strange ideas? You know he can't think and play at the same time." She turns back to me, "Now stop obsessing and just read what's written..."

We talk about reading music but that first dot never says "once upon a time..." It always hangs in space waiting to be identified, like a distant planet. Once it is located the rest of the constellation can be placed around it. For pianists and guitarists, the note is never in doubt, just press or pluck and play, but for many brass players without the gift of perfect pitch there can be a spasm of anxiety. This is often heard if a band tunes up and each player produces their solo note. There are often little wobbles if a note is lipped into pitch like a wind-up gramophone returning to speed.

Once the skill of musical literacy is developed the extent of association and automatic action is quite astonishing: how without conscious thought, valve combinations are pressed and an appropriate pitch produced at the sight of the instructions. Unfortunately, out of the flow of performance, amateur musicians will often find it difficult to accurately pitch and describe rhythm without their instrument to hand. The physical interaction with the instrument is an integral part of our experience of music and we struggle to understand or reproduce pitch and pulse without that tactile foundation. The instrument becomes the gateway to the music.

Preparing for the first note is like the dive into a pool, the moment before the swimming starts. As with swimming the dive into the music is prefaced with a deep breath. In performance the first note has to be perfect and confident to allow the rest of the music to follow on, belly flops are to be avoided. Once that is out of the way the rest might be threaded into place more or less automatically, given the complexity of the music and the skill of the musician. Pitch is not the only issue to address and James decides that we need to practise some of these other skills this evening.

Our conductor raises his hands and we start number 43. "No. Stop, try again. It wasn't good enough, we need to come in together." We start again and he stops us. "No. We need to breathe together before we play and I can't hear that. I should be hearing a big breath all around the room. I'll give you four in and I want you to count it, one, two, three, breathe." We silently count as instructed. "Better. You all came in together that time. This time I want you to focus on dynamics, let's bring it down a bit."

At the end of the verse we get some confirmation. "We came in together, the dynamic was better but there were some ragged moments. I can tell some of you weren't counting through the long notes. We shouldn't be guessing. This time we'll just play each note as a series of staccato quavers." He taps out the quavers and we play along.

"Good. Now this time I only want to hear the first quaver of the note. I'm going to give you four in and you've got to keep it together in your heads. You're on your own, I'll be listening. Ok. One, two, three, breathe." In my head I have, Pom t t t Pom t Pom t Pom t t t T t Pom t Pom t t t Pom t t t Pom t t t T t t t... and we play together, the notes landing in unison in the sparse surrounding silence. "Good, now let's do the test piece." I fold the pages out onto the stand.

The presence of sheet music is a mixed blessing. Some people get so used to reading the dots that they struggle to play from memory, even simple things they may play every day. There is an irony in this since such intense familiarity with a score will enable musicians to drift through it in an unthinking, unreflective, even unconscious way. Yet, remove the paper and they are lost, they have no memory of the music. A neurologist might have something to say about how this reflects the creation of specific pathways through the brain.

This musical literacy shapes the brass player's experience and understanding of music. The performances rely on musicians interpreting, "reading", a set of symbolic instructions from sheets of paper. This contrasts with non-literate musical traditions, such as the blues, where a set of chords are learned and applied to a variety of songs.

Musicians who learn and play aurally, by ear, will have a very different understanding and experience. For example, it is highly likely that most of Louis Armstrong's musical education was from the aural tradition. This would explain why at times he used valve combinations that would be anathema to formally trained cornet players. His sense of time is also radically different from formal musicality; he clearly didn't practise with a metronome.

At root these unwritten, aural, folkish traditions rely on known chord sequences. Songs are built from patterns and blocks that can be rearranged, run together, repeated or omitted as the need arises. They are driven by melodic phrases, rhythms, grooves, vamps, riffs: *ostinato*, as it is known in the formal musical world. This solid foundation allows musicians the opportunity to extemporise and improvise over the top. The whole ensemble may stretch and bend the music as long as there is an implicit understanding of where the beat lies. Musicians from similar traditions meeting for the first time will understand how to fit into their new circumstances: this can be clearly seen in music as different as jazz, doo wop or punk.

Having said that, it is easy to overlook the link between improvisation and the development of classical music. Some of Beethoven's late piano works (especially the *Hammerklavier Sonata)* reek of improvisation - likewise Chopin's *Nocturnes*. The Beethoven piece in particular would seem to be a kindred spirit to some of Keith Jarrett's improvised recordings.

The reason we view the pieces of these distant masters as texts to be reconstructed is that the only way they could record the sound for broadcast in their day was to write it down for others to play. If they had lived two hundred years later, would they have just recorded and not transcribed? If they had lived two hundred years earlier their musical ideas would have only been able to live in the memory and performances of their protégés.

In *Brass Roots,* Roy Newsome suggests that a good number of early bands, especially those emerging from church music, may have learned to play by ear and might not have been able to read sheet music. It may be to our detriment that the brass band completely abandoned this tradition and instead turned to the page, but the interpretation of dots on paper is not the only way in which literacy has been fundamental to shaping brass bands. Literacy created the culture that brass bands emerged from.

As music has two traditions, so has language. In *Orality and Literacy*, Walter Ong shows that prior to the introduction of literacy societies transmitted culture through word of mouth: this is known as the oral tradition. Stories and information were learned and memorised using melody, rhythm, rhyme and repetition. The story fragments were rhapsodised, as the ancient Greeks would have it: they were stitched together. This is also an important element of musical improvisation. Apart from expert improvisers, who are able to immediately produce their musical thoughts as sound, most musicians learn fragments in a variety of keys which they then stitch together into solos. I had first-hand experience of observing this in action helping a local street band rehearse for a community parade.

The main problem with the street band was having to learn my parts. These were begrudgingly transcribed onto scraps of manuscript for the likes of me. They consisted of an A part which was repeated until someone decided we needed to head into the B part. At some points we would lay off for solos. It wasn't always solos, some more experienced members would have a back and forth musical dialogue – or was it an argument? Either way they seemed to know, understand or anticipate each other's phrases; this sense of musical dialogue is comparable to the verbal process.

Orality lives through speech but literacy can only exist through a system of visual symbols such as letters or pictograms. The first alphabet was the cuneiform system of Mesopotamia, invented around 5,000 years ago. It took much longer before records of what might be considered literature were developed, and longer still before this was available for anything approximating circulation within a society.

Initially, the written word created new possibilities for memory and communication over distance and time. It also allowed the development of records of events and circumstances. The earliest written records were inventories of cattle: stock control. Not everyone welcomed these new developments. Socrates, the great Greek philosopher, is only known to us because of his dramatic appearance in the writings of Plato. He was deeply troubled by the potential consequences of this new technology, specifically, that storing information in written form would have a detrimental effect on the capacity of memory. His caution resisted the possibilities the new technology offered.

The profoundest social impact of writing is its effect on language and thought. Writing enabled the introduction of complex clauses into sentences and an expansion of vocabulary. This in turn gave rise to nuance and subtlety and allowed the invention of oratory: elaborate and persuasive public speaking. Not that we should assume that oral cultures are without powers of verbal persuasion. Nor should we forget that orality has its own form of thoughtful trickery, the riddle, however literacy offers other possibilities. By storing information for easy retrieval, analysis and re-ordering, literacy enables linear, abstract and categorical thinking: it allows the development of reason. Literacy also confers a type of immortality on the author of a text.

A text, any piece of written or printed words, creates a permanent record of an idea or discussion and thus gives it enduring life, immortality. The debates a text provokes are never finished, they can be returned to, revised or contested infinitely both in the mind of a solitary reader and as a silent representative in, say, a student debate. The ultimate response to any text is the production of another text which in its turn may stimulate further debate, and so the conversation continues through the ages. This creates an accessible, reflective, literate tradition with a body of work: a canon.

The experience of language and literacy can be compared to that of music. The building blocks of popular aural musical traditions are analogous to the mnemonic systems used to build the epic ballads and sagas of Homer or the Vikings. Indeed, the bards may have only been able to memorise the words if they were embedded in musical forms, reintroducing and reinforcing that link between music and language.

The development of musical writing after the Renaissance allowed for expanded and digressive structures with greater opportunities for nuance, detail and the introduction of unusual and unexpected elements. It also allowed the precise coordination of parts necessary for the development of the choir, orchestra and, of course, brass band. Literacy allowed the development of books of musical theory. The recording of musical ideas in written scores allowed composers to understand how their predecessors created particular effects or to improve on the deficiencies of their forebears. Beethoven's music could never have emerged from an aural culture and neither could that of brass bands, but that is not the end of the matter.

If there are two distinct traditions that we have constructed for the composition and performance of music, there are two distinct ways in which we appreciate it.

—

At some point after Matthew Arnold had pronounced on the nature of culture (which for Arnold was about immersing ourselves in "the best that has been thought and said") an observation was made that those things that were not necessarily of the best were still appreciated and part of our lived experience: they were part of our culture.

To avoid cultural contamination there came a parting of the ways between the high culture (experienced in great works of literature and great orchestral works) and the low culture of penny dreadfuls and the music hall. In music, this was manufactured by the introduction of new rituals of seated stillness and silence in concert halls, a marked contrast to the raucous atmosphere of the popular music hall.

Matthew Arnold's view of high culture was very much literary, incorporating poetry, the great works of philosophy and, as he never wholly escaped his Anglican roots, the Bible. High culture can be comfortably extended into other areas of the arts, in music the great Germans are obvious exemplars. The defining features of high culture are complexity and ambiguity: these suggest intellectual rigour, emotional challenge and a willingness to avoid simple morality and neat conclusions.

The term low culture, by implication, covered everything that high culture left behind. It would now include pop songs, genre fiction, blockbuster films and the shows of Andrew Lloyd Webber. Low culture is typified by its directness and accessibility, it is expected to place no intellectual burdens and make no excessive demands. However, that is not to say that the creation of low culture may not require considerable skill or that it may not communicate some significant truth to its audience.

Acute observers with a sense of cultural history are able to gleefully put a variety of spanners in these works by making some simple observations.

For example, within the world of literature Shakespeare is now regarded as one of the summits of high art. However, in his day the Globe theatre was open to all, it was truly popular theatre. Whilst his productions would have been patronised by the great and the good the stalls would have corralled the great unwashed. It may be no coincidence that in agriculture stalls are places for keeping animals.

Some sociologists think the high culture / low culture split represents a class divide. There is merit to this argument: much of the classical repertoire was commissioned by rich patrons; and some writers argue that the behavioural codes of the concert hall were designed as exclusive markers of social class. However, this isn't entirely convincing.

My paternal grandmother (who died at the end of the 1970s) is an interesting case in point. She worked as a cleaner and lived on the same council estate in Middleton (near Rochdale) for most of her life. There was a small record collection in her sitting room that included the opera Carmen, Chopin piano concertos and classical overtures by Rossini (Thievish Magpie) and Suppe (Poet and Peasant). For the visits of her grandchildren there were pop songs and Prokofiev's Peter and the Wolf. I did not consider this exceptional and would have expected something similar of any older relative or family friend with a record player.

There is a symbolic value in this anecdote since high culture suggests broad intellectual horizons, however, under no circumstances would anyone describe my grandmother as an intellectual or ascribe to her any intellectual ambition. The presence of that music in her home represents an open door to other possibilities and a willingness to engage with them. It also demonstrates an assumption that high culture is the right and inheritance of all strata of society.

From the mid-twentieth century, low culture became entangled and intermingled with terms such as mass culture and popular culture. This was because the way most people experienced it was through mass media: magazines; radio; the cinema and later; television. This mass culture aimed for a level which would appeal to the broadest audience.

20th century mass media created a popular culture (in the sense that it was consumed by the general population), but it didn't focus entirely on the low end. The BBC in particular had a long-standing commitment to broadcasting high culture. Even when it only had one or two television channels it would still programme classical music, ballet, Shakespeare and more at peak viewing times. These performances had a wide (if not always large) audience. A notable example of this cultural mixing was the popularity of Peter Greenaway's impenetrable high art film *The Draughtsman's Contract*, commissioned (I understand) to launch Channel 4. Conversely, those with high brow interests may have enjoyed the *Morecambe and Wise Christmas Specials*.

It is appropriate to make the distinction between high and low culture not in assumptions about the social class of their aficionados but the impulses that drive their creation and the quality of the demands they make. This fits in with the model of two modes of thinking popularised by Nobel Laureate Daniel Kahneman in his book *Thinking, Fast and Slow*.

"System 1 operates automatically and quickly, with little or no effort and no sense of voluntary control.

System 2 allocates attention to the effortful mental activities that demand it, including complex computations. The operations of System 2 are often experienced with the subjective experience of agency, choice and concentration."

High and low culture can be said to appeal to different facets of our nature. System 1 is happy to hit the floor when David Bowie insists "Let's Dance". System 2 may be reluctant to let its hair down without giving the matter some serious thought. Brass bands have always filled an unusual niche in this divided landscape playing anything from Abba to Wagner in a single programme.

At this point it is worth a quick glance in the rear view mirror. Coleridge proposed cultivation as a solution to the spiritually destructive influence of industrialisation, it was a broadening and sharpening of the mind and a refinement of sensibility. This enabled the student to engage with Arnold's proposal for self and social improvement through high culture: to become cultivated. Cultivation was at root a form of education, and entailed the development of a set of (System 2) mental skills and attitudes. The capacity for these may be innate but their mastery is only achieved through application and effort.

The need for cultivation had to be articulated because the nineteenth century lacked a coherent education system of the type that was established in the twentieth. The people who engaged in the nineteenth century workers' education movement had a clear understanding that it was a force for self-improvement and social emancipation.

However, there are those, such as Marshall McLuhan, who argue that there was a deeper reason for the rise of education and the pursuit of high culture. They suggest that the thirst for culture was not a consequence of economic and social conditions but of developments in technology. The technology in question was literacy.

Rooms

Test pieces demonstrate the band's collective poise and dexterity, revealing whether or not it can play with conviction and precision. Any decent test piece will encompass the full dynamic range, with a special injunction to play softly, sweetly and smoothly. But, when the music explodes the band will need to contain the forces of its nature and not merely blast and blare. On the contest stage the band knows it needs to produce a sound to fill the hall. A thousand seat venue can be a daunting challenge, the band needs to be confident it can summon the full dynamic.

Playing boldly in a large hall is one thing, but bands rarely rehearse in halls. They are more often found in much smaller spaces: Wellhouse in their chapel basement; Upperthong in our converted barn. Necessity is the mother of invention, beggars can't be choosers and I have also rehearsed in a primary school pre-fab and the billiard room of an old mansion. The rest of the mansion was converted into flats some time ago; I've noticed they always seem to be up for sale.

Nowhere was smaller than that old con club cellar, like the living room in a terraced house. Domestic details confirmed the effect: a small tiled fireplace with its mantelpiece clock. Lower cornets and trombones spent their evenings with their backs, quite literally, up against the wall. Some bands, however, live in luxury. Slaithwaite rehearse in their band club concert room. As for Dobcross, well, it's like the Palace of Versaille.

It is not just the size of the room that is an issue, even more important is the acoustic. At one extreme are "dead" rooms, some professional recording studios are designed to be dead. They have special panels to absorb the sound and stifle echoes, this allows the sound to be isolated when recording. A dead room can be very disconcerting for a band used to receiving some returning sound. The band can suddenly feel that it is fighting to be heard, but this is only one extreme. In November we played a contest in Rochdale Town Hall, it has a somewhat resonant acoustic. As we sat down to play I was convinced I could hear the last echo from the previous year's performance still bouncing off the bare walls.

There are ways to dampen the sound of the band and the smaller the band room the more necessary this becomes. Carpet tiles, fibrous ceilings, asymmetric walls and, in the case of Upperthong, judicious use of heavy curtains. Although in our case I am not sure if they are there to ameliorate the acoustic or just to block the vicious draughts that stab like daggers from the prevailing winds.

The acoustic environment can have a profound effect on a band's understanding of its sound. To play in a foreign space can be deeply unsettling for amateur musicians; familiar points of reference can suddenly disappear and players may feel confused and cut adrift. At times we need to be shaken out of the familiarity of the band room. Playing the music in a different acoustic will force us to rethink what we are doing and experience the piece as if for the first time.

—

Five miles out over a frozen moor and we are still searching for the village hall. *En route* we speculate as to whether anyone else will be there, they are. In the front seat, two silhouettes are wrapped in a spiralling cloud. Bright orange coals swing to and fro. Victorian detectives trapped in their own Whitechapel pea-souper, or maybe alien fireflies unable to leave their protective capsule. Somewhere to our right is the tinny thump and rattle of recorded music. Out there in the dark, a car is cocooned in its private test piece appreciation.

Big Michaela slides the side door of her van and we leave the cramped car's cosiness to unload the percussion. Angular structures wrestle and resist our attempts to guide them to the double doors where we wait for the caretaker.

"You lot must be dedicated coming out here on a night like this. Don't mind the cold, I put the heating on at five so it should have warmed up nicely for you." She unlocks the door then flicks the switches, looking round to check each group of lights come on as expected. Satisfied she turns to leave, "If there isn't anything else, I'll love you and leave you. I'll be back at nine."

Chris shoots a plume of condensed air and watches the cloud hang in front of his face, "Ooh, it has warmed up nicely for us." No-one takes off their coats. We might want to hide from the cold but there is no time to hang around. Within minutes Alan and Jim have half the stands built. Doreen is assembling the percussion and Sue and Tina have moved the chairs into position. Towards the back of the room Geoff is caressed by coils of cables as he sets up recording equipment; the laptop's glow throws his face into goulish relief.

Taking his seat, Andy peers at the music. Leaning back, he wrestles with his collar and bow tie to ease the constriction. James feels if we dress for the occasion we can generate a contest mentality, preparing ourselves for the moment we finally walk on stage. This obscure venue is supposed to have an acoustic similar to St. Georges Hall.

We may not be the only band experimenting with different acoustics. In the village this week I noticed posters for concerts in their respective churches by both Marsden and Slaithwaite. With just a fortnight before the Yorkshire areas what's the betting the test piece features in the programmes?

There is an unsettling start to the evening. James has been busy rewriting parts and these instructions are handed to those allocated new responsibilities. Paul is delegated some technical passages; he blinks, peering at them like a mole exposed to sunlight. He has a go, his fingers flailing like they've encountered a new Olympic discipline.

After the hymns and a quick test of the delegated duties we prepare for the first run through. Everyone leaves their seats. Andy lines us up at the side of the hall, "We'll have percussion and basses at the front. Let's see, back row I'll have you here, third cornets lead. Horns, trombones, bari, euph, then front row."

James takes over, "I want everyone standing until we're all on, then we sit down together. When you sit down I want to see instruments on knees. Cornets, hold the instrument in your right hand bell end down. Trombones rest your slides on the floor. Everyone else, hold the instrument as you would but keep it on your knee. Then I'll come on. When I raise the baton I want everyone to come to attention and I'll give you two bars in. I want to hear that breath on the last beat, I need to hear it from the whole band. Have we all got that? Once we start there'll be no stopping." He looks over his shoulder, "You can start the recording now, Jack."

Jack looks up, "Righto", he peers at the computer and jabs a finger, "It's recording now."

We walk on, sit down and wait. The concentration is evident. We watch as James raises his baton, the instruments follow. He mouths the beats as he waves his right hand. The first bar is excellent, but as the opening phrase fades out Russ falls off his notes. James scowls. The euphonium solo starts, the note splits and then all sound is lost. The horn part in the second movement is brash and it is tempting to assume they think the term *piano* refers to a stringed percussion instrument. And on it goes until the third movement which becomes a cross tempo free for all, we don't even finish together.

An embarrassed silence follows, James rubs his hands through his hair as if he has just cracked his head. Cringing glances shoot around the stand. Sue whispers, "third section here we come."

"Did you get that?" James looks at Jack who is pecking at the laptop like a confused pigeon. Geoff leaves his seat to inspect the screen. He stops the recording and a tinny echo of the opening bars wafts in our direction. "Yeah, it's all there."

James sighs and strikes out for a higher morale. "Ok, that's set a benchmark for the evening. We have to improve on that and we will improve on that. What we have to remember is that we were always going to be thrown by the room and the acoustic, that's what we were expecting. Let's not beat ourselves up at this point." Although I get the sense that he would clearly like to beat somebody up, but who? There are so many worthy performances to choose from, surprisingly, not Nick's. Our most recent addition sounded on top of his part as he belted out the soprano line.

The next three quarters of an hour are spent examining the more sensitive wounds from the first outing although there isn't time for reconstructive surgery. James gives the impression that he could go through the piece bar by bar an hour at a time, but he has to let it go. As nine o'clock approaches we pause. "Ok, let's have ten minutes to let our lips rest and then we'll have another run through."

We leave our seats, there is an osmotic diffusion from the square of stands to the fringes of the room. Those with foresight search out flasks of tea, others swig water to wet their mouths. An anxious preoccupation damps the small talk.

The hall clock directs us to convene for our entry to the imagined contest arena. In silence we line up and reshuffle into order. James looks to Jack and brings his finger down. Jack looks to the laptop and presses a key. Jim takes the lead and we file on in rustling readiness for James.

—

In the car afterwards Tina confides, "I don't see how we can even go on stage sounding like that, are we going to have to withdraw, or what? We're sounding like a sack of shit ."

I have no answer. We are running out of time and I can see no remedy for either the deficiencies of my own playing or the failures of the band.

Community

Spending three nights a week playing with one band might suggest that spending a fourth listening to another verges on masochism. Given how close to the areas we are I am chalking this up as research; what Bee really thinks about the idea I don't know. As a night out it is at least convenient, the parish church is only ten minutes walk from home *and* we'll be back for *Match of the Day*.

Usually, anything that fits within the category of entertainment involves a journey. The nearest cinema is over six miles away and most music or theatre is at least five. The village is not entirely without local amateur productions but for various reasons I have been reluctant to attend, perhaps for the same reasons that people seem reluctant to attend band concerts. The Pennines have fostered strong amateur traditions of drama as well as music and some nearby settlements have their own theatres. This suggests that like brass bands amateur dramatics achieved a quality of performance that could attract an audience of its own and was, if not exactly professional, still pretty decent. I get the impression that nowadays these venues too are struggling for audiences. In their study of community organisations in Bristol, Paul Hoggett and Jeff Bishop suggested that amateur audiences are built on the strength of social connections.

Our primary form of social connection is the family and those with a large extended family may not feel the need for much in the way of a social life beyond this. For those from more compact homes, the foundations of the social world may be built on neighbourliness: a sense of goodwill to and concern for those who live nearby. In a report for the UK's National Centre for Social Research (NCSR), Swales and Tipping confirmed neighbourliness is still an important value in national life. They suggest it is enhanced by economic prosperity and education and undermined by poverty and insecure tenure.

Friendship may arise out of neighbourliness, but this particular quality of relationship might also emerge from sources such as school, work or a shared interest. Family, friendship and neighbourliness are the foundations of community, but community is more complex than this.

In the internet age community is increasingly associated with shared interests and shared opinions. One of the conveniences of the internet's so-called communities is that they can be easily adopted and just as quickly dropped at the moment some discomfort, difficulty or offence is encountered. Flesh and blood communities involve encounters with a variety of perspectives, temperaments and manners. They demand engagement with those we may find difficult or unsympathetic as well as those who are congenial or simply delightful. Community demands the ability to learn some degree of tolerance and understanding, to set aside differences to achieve a common goal and to defer one's own needs so that others might benefit.

In day-to-day life there are many incentives for the development of community, these are often derived from necessity. The NCSR observed that children are the factor that is most likely to draw adults into attending community events and retirement the biggest spur to involvement in voluntary activity. It might be suggested that community is lacking to the extent people feel they can best address their needs through private means. Or worse, that through lack of education, knowledge or sheer poverty they are unable to combine with others to mutual advantage.

It is a dark thought to consider that attending a brass band concert may qualify as some form of community duty or obligation. This evening I wonder if this is how Bee views our outing. Whilst she has contributed to some sublime performances, she knows that I have endured some of her choir concerts as a form of selfless sacrifice (we don't talk about *Ein Deutsche Requiem*). However, she is too gracious to pass judgement on my band concerts and I'm not sure I could handle the truth.

There is a case that, at least in this area, brass bands have managed to bridge that audience gap between serving friends and family and being reputable entertainment. It is not feasible that bands such as Lindley would have been able to justify their annual concerts in Huddersfield Town Hall off friendship alone. Notions of tradition, quality and some love and understanding of the music and its circumstances must also be a part of the picture.

Most people manage to badger three or four friends to whatever production they are involved in but I know most of mine see brass bands as terminally naff. I hesitate to suggest that a band concert might be a way they would wish to spend their Saturday night. If sociability is still strong then it may be that theatre or live music is not something that people feel fits into their idea of leisure beyond trips to major theatres in big cities. On the other hand, it may be that contemporary television and other media set such high production standards that amateurs seem hopelessly gauche by comparison. This has not always been the case, and in the 1970s much of the BBC drama output was filmed on sets that had a decidedly cardboard quality; at times the entire budget of Dr Who seemed to have been squandered on tin foil and plastic pipes.

Leisure and entertainment is increasingly promoted as a private and personal choice. Even when shared with friends, I notice my leisure time may be more likely to be spent at home. Some friends with larger houses have begun to host smaller acoustic concerts in their living spaces. These are wonderfully sociable and may be financially beneficial for performers but might also be eroding traditions of public performance by bringing it into the private sphere. This is not without precedent, if we take the medium of the cinema and its challengers, we can see that from the 1950s onwards the silver screen was fighting a rearguard action against both television and improved home comforts. Even so, television had very fixed limits to its repertoire. The internet is a different proposition, through the wonder of wi-fi it offers its distractions and stimulations right here, right now. It seems to have drawn its inspiration from *Dr. Seuss's Green Eggs and Ham*; "would you like it on a train, would you like it on a plane..." With so much choice at the fingertips why plod through the rain to hear someone wrestle with a little light opera in a musty church hall?

Churches have been an asset to bands, they have not only provided a venue but also an audience. Bands and churches share some common features, as well as offering social and cultural benefits, they place an obligation on their members and expect regular weekly attendance. Relying on a committed core of volunteers, they are self-organised and self-running. Beyond the religious or musical role there is a more fundamental and essential connection. Embodying a sense of continuity across generations, they play an important part in maintaining the identity of the places in which they are rooted.

Bands and churches have a broader influence. They are not just individual institutions in particular places but are part of nationally significant cultures and organisations lying outside the influences of government and commerce. This tapestry of independent representative bodies, which also includes charities and campaigns for social change, is known as civil society and is important for shaping the values and heritage of a nation.

Returning to the original focus, there is a crisis of membership (locally and nationally) for both bands and churches. To be graphically tactless about it, sometimes it feels as if we are watching our audience die one row at a time.

—

Churches aren't the only community centred organisations caught in existential crises. Performance venues such as civic halls, mechanics institutes and the like that were founded by public subscription in the Victorian or Edwardian eras are also struggling. Over time many drifted into council control or became supported by community departments and grant initiatives. With the withering of local authorities and the cutting of funding, many have been handed back to community groups who now find themselves with costs that are often difficult or impossible to meet through room hire. Unable to employ staff to run or clean the buildings, a heavy burden falls on the shoulders of small bands of volunteers.

Writers at the heart of traditional conservatism, such as Ferdinand Mount, are rightly supportive of the types of civil society and mutual movements that developed the community halls and see them as exemplars of self-help that the post-war welfare state undermined. This argument has much to commend it, however, these traditions were patchy in their impact and as a consequence throughout the twentieth century the state gradually expanded its role and influence.

137

In the years following the economic crisis of 2008, it was the possibly disingenuous and certainly less than half-baked proposition of David Cameron that if state support was withdrawn from public provision a new community and mutual effort would automatically emerge to replace it. Experience suggests any such consensus, for example on the need for communities to subscribe to the upkeep of public buildings, is far easier to destroy than to rebuild.

If we were to give him the benefit of the doubt, we might argue that Cameron was demonstrating a passing interest in profound ideas. In *Making Democracy Work,* Robert Putnam suggested societies where there is a strong tradition of community activity, where people from different backgrounds come together for mutual benefit, exhibit greater consensus on social and even political values. This might also be the basis of an enduring and resilient economic prosperity. In the 1950s Edward C. Banfield argued that a lack of this civic sensibility was an important feature of what he termed, in the title of his book, *The Moral Basis of a Backward Society.* Defining features of backward societies are a lack of public trust and entrenched poverty.

Over recent decades a range of concerns have been expressed about the state of community life, the most robust of these studies have been in the US. In 2000 Robert Putnam caused a minor sensation with *Bowling Alone,* drawing attention to the collapse of community activity in America. He explored a number of factors which may have contributed to this, including the improved career opportunities for women (since the voluntary labours of women have always been the engine of community life). In his conclusions he suggested the two most influential factors in this decline were suburbanisation and television.

In *The Corrosion of Character,* the sociologist Richard Sennett argued that changes to employment practices in the Reagan years had been bruising for many workers and that the increasingly precarious job market led to a retreat from public life into the safety of the home and family.

In *Diminished Democracy,* Theda Skocpol surveyed patterns of membership for national organisations with a strong network of local groups, in particular those with some focus on campaigning. She observed a steady decline in participation starting in the 1960s. She noted that people hadn't discarded their public concerns but suggested they were increasingly inclined to devolve these to managed campaigns with paid employees, what Americans call "non-profits."

There are no British studies of comparative weight to Putnam's and it would be complacent to assume that what is the case in America will also be the case in Britain. This is particularly true of Christian organisations which are more buoyant in America. To emphasise this point, in his social history of *Popular Music 1840 - 1914*, Dave Russell notes that the decline in the popularity of choral singing corresponds to the fall in church attendance. This is a pattern that has been persisting for well over a century. If we return to the point made by Richard Sennett, we can see that in Britain the period that corresponded to the Reagan years was characterised by an attempt by politicians to reshape public attitudes.

—

A change in values was promoted in the UK during the last decades of the twentieth century, none greater than those around the notion of service. There were two main influences that underpinned the shift. The first was around long-term trends in the national economy. De-industrialisation was shifting the balance from the making of manufacturing to the selling of services.

The second influence came from the way government interpreted its own purpose. Westminster became less disposed to see its role as the governance of society and more inclined to regard itself as the manager of the economy. Part of its new agenda was to oversee the provision of services that ensured the efficient operation of the economy. This could be seen in the creation of such bodies as utilities regulators and standards watchdogs; citizens (most famously rail passengers) were told to view themselves as customers of government services. The media and press celebrated these changes by referring to the government as UK PLC.

The government explicitly pushed for the values of business to displace those of public service. They understood no incentive or purpose beyond financial gain: pay bonuses replaced duty and vocation. Consequently, service was no longer help that you offered but a thing you bought or sold; service was transformed from a verb into a noun. These attitudes gained a foothold in civil society.

In the 1980s, what was at that point known as the voluntary sector, providing charitable service through volunteers, was encouraged to become a contractor to deliver types of social work previously provided by local authorities. The charities shifted from being run by volunteers to being staffed by employees. There was a consequent shift in administrative emphasis from the role they played in the lives of their beneficiaries (soon to be known as service users) to the income they needed to generate to pay wages and break even.

The shift in emphasis and values from the promotion of the public good to the generation of profit would have far reaching consequences, most egregiously, immorally and notoriously in the demutualisation (the so-called carpetbagging) of the building societies. These were originally prudent financial institutions owned by their members. The corruption of those building societies, in both senses of the word (that is, the drift away from their true nature and purpose and involvement in some more or less criminal practices) played an important role in the financial crisis of 2008.

The most significant summary of this new state of affairs might be found in a paper prepared by Matthew Hilton for the Cabinet Office at the time of David Cameron's Big Society. Hilton did his best to justify "vibrancy" in civil society, unfortunately his views on the health of the voluntary sector were undermined by the effects of the outsourcing of public services. His acclaim of high-profile campaigning organisations was undermined by their lack of active grass roots. The "clicktivism" they encourage might be regarded as the personal outsourcing of civil participation. On the other hand, he acknowledged the shrinkage of community-based organisations which might have historically expected direct participation from their members.

These last points would certainly seem to bear comparison with the American experience. Setting this aside, the idea of community and the ideal of community participation are still very much valued. For some people this is still best expressed by involvement in churches.

—

Despite the concerns voiced earlier not all churches are struggling and there are still popular forms of association, but the fundamental character of these is often different to that of brass bands and Methodist chapels. The successful churches are now most likely to follow the American business model. That is, to pardon the impending pun, that they offer religious services. They provide the religious activities demanded of their customer base in ways that fit the expectations of 21st Century consumerism. The organisational responsibility is part of a business that nevertheless may make relatively onerous demands on the congregation.

New community-based leisure activities echo a well-established entrepreneurial aspect of community culture, the essence of which is captured by the dance class in the film *Billy Elliott*. There are a variety of ways in which this sector has expanded. Considering services aimed at children and young people: the playgroup has been challenged by the play gym; the youth club by the art class business and; the youth band by the school of rock.

These private leisure activities displace their voluntary alternatives with glossier environments, individualised concepts and high fees. The thankless tasks of voluntary obligation are exchanged for waged labour. These new enterprises succeed by offering acceptable choices, in acceptable formats to people who can afford to pay for them. The financial transaction also deflects any sense of reciprocation or duty on the part of the customer. In a market society the question of what is available for those who can't afford to pay is one that requires no answer. On the other hand some voluntary traditions retain both status and popularity, consider the Scouts and Guides for example.

A contemporary aspect of leisure which maintains a self-organising tradition is the midweek running group ((book clubs could also be used as an example). This differs notably from the band format in that little organisation is required beyond agreed meeting times, participation is entirely at the whim of the runner. Attendance is based around availability and convenience, not duty and obligation, the association is ephemeral and can fade as fast as it first took flight.

If bands are adversely affected by these changes, then one approach might be to consider cultural camouflage and adopt some of the practices of the marketised world. Whilst I am a staunch advocate of the literal approach to names (who wouldn't be proud to play for Dodworth Colliery Miners' Welfare Brass Band?) a branding approach may be appropriate for younger age groups. An example of this is Wardle Junior Blast, though I hope they don't get the wrong idea about musical style. Village bands might consider employing a teacher to run junior bands along the lines of the activities mentioned above, but it would be unwise to ditch too much tradition. Caution should be exercised in developing a branded leisure experience

141

rather than a village band. An entrepreneurial figure might relish such a project if their income was related to participation and find new ways to promote brass music.

Some bands have experimented with different types of performance. In the contest format, *Brass Factor* was developed to mimic the *X Factor* television programme. Others have provided live soundtracks to films. I understand some bands have experimented with Karaoke nights; these require a skilled arranger in the ranks to adapt the repertoire. Another option might be a Strictly Come Brass to echo the continuing popularity of *Strictly Come Dancing*, this would be a return to one of bandings brass roots, early bands often accompanied social dances. Some of Upperthongs best jobs have been as the minstrels at the end of club Christmas dinners providing the accompaniment to rousing carols and renditions of seasonal pop songs.

One future for bands is that they play on their diversity. On the one hand they will continue with contests and concerts which provide the ensemble with musical challenge and audiences with performances of quality. This includes the "palm court" tradition of providing background music for public events like village fetes or the carnival tradition of leading processions.

Bands might wish to explore ways to involve their community in spontaneous music making; with the decline of church attendance the opportunities for public singing seem increasingly limited. Singing is an essential human experience and should be encouraged and available as often as possible. The decline of churches means that traditional hymns and carols are disappearing out of public consciousness. No matter what your views on religion, these songs were until very recently almost universally known. In that sense they are an important part of the legacy of British popular music and British popular culture.

Beyond these ideas, for passionate devotees of the brass band world there are two questions that are circling each other here: is this about a form of music or a way of life?

—

We take our seats in an empty pew towards the rear of the nave, our backs against the glazed wall of the new refectory. This late remodelling may have made the church more amenable to community activity, but I am pleased to see that many original features remain. Slaithwaite, like many Anglican churches in the area, has boxy wooden galleries to provide extra seating. Methodist chapels are notable for their rounded balconies, but they are of an altogether different type from the ones here which seem to have been plonked on top of a standard church plan. In Slaithwaite the roof void, instead of mimicking the vaults of an ancient cathedral, has a flat suspended wooden ceiling pocked with a patina of mildew from long winter weeks standing cold and empty.

It doesn't take us too long to realise that the two bands will significantly outnumber the audience. This rather dampens our expectations, fortunately we are soon shocked out of our stupor. Slaithwaite take the stage with vim and vigour, taking advantage of their conductor's virtuosity to add screaming trumpet lines to an up-beat Lionel Ritchie tune.

To my ears this is a band shouting, "first section here we come!" There are more shocks in store. They have some well worked light entertainment routines in their slick set and a marked absence of a test piece run through. Here is a band with two weeks to go to the biggest day of the year showing the confidence to take a chunk of time out of their preparations and enjoy themselves. A stark contrast to our schedule which feels more like Napoleon's retreat from Moscow.

Slaithwaite give an impressive display, but City of Bradford have star quality in spades - it is clear that this is a very tight band. At one point I find myself marvelling at the precise articulation of each note in some rapid unison runs. This is a marked contrast to Upperthong's current style, it seems to be a miracle if we play the first and last notes together - what happens in between is anybody's guess. On the strength of what I hear it could be assumed Bradford may have already booked their coach for the national finals - but this is Yorkshire...

As we step into the drizzle Bee is puzzled, "Some of the playing was absolutely superb, don't you think? They must all be music graduates if they're playing to that standard. What gets me is, why, if you've trained for so long to get so good, you'd want to play in a brass band?"

I summon previously untapped reserves of patience and understanding, "They might not see it that way. You could look at it that they're playing to the highest standards of the art form and that they might value that. It might even have been their *ambition* to play in a brass band."

"I can see that, but it's so... limited, isn't it?"

"What do you mean, limited?"

"Well," she gives me a sideways glance, brings her fist to her mouth and puffs out her cheeks, "Doo Do Do De De De Derrrr!" She looks very pleased with herself, "It all sounds the same, doesn't it?"

"Oh, Come off it. That's more than a slight exaggeration…"

"Ok, I suppose it is." We lapse into silence. "Oh, that hymn was fantastic, it nearly made me want to cry, the way they held that last note. It was so quiet but *absolutely* perfect."

As always, she manages to touch a raw nerve. If I hadn't joined Wellhouse all those years back I wouldn't seek out band music as recordings or live performances, although it has hardly reached the level of obsession, even now. As we talk around the subject it is apparent that there are parts of the repertoire we both admire; I love an epic overture and Bee is partial to a proper hymn tune. Unfortunately, both of us feel that there is a certain cheesiness in some areas of the canon. There are pop adaptations that make me a little uneasy and Bee has a violent aversion to medleys. Sometimes playing summer park jobs I pinch myself to check the Second World War has really ended. The more we talk it becomes clear that for both of us one of the issues is the timbral range of the unit.

Roy Newsome credits the limited versatility of the band sound as being part of the reason for a falling off of their popularity at the start of the twentieth century. As orchestras experimented with a broader palette, bands were restricted to experiments with the mute. No brass instrument can honk like a saxophone, either.

It seems we both have some reservations about brass bands because of how they sound, and they sound like…

—

A week later, I am in a club in Huddersfield to see Brassic Park, a local ten piece New Orleans Funk band. I've been told they're good and indeed they are. To my surprise their trombone player is familiar; Jake was the principal trombone at Upperthong before I joined. He left to study for a music degree and stayed on in Leeds afterwards. In recent years he has depped for us once or twice, even helping at the areas in our hour of need. I find him at the break and offer an Old Testament challenge. "Hast thou forsaken the one true faith?"

He smirks, "I did five years at Upperthong and loved it all, but..."

"But...?"

Echoing Bee's concerns he tentatively offers, "It has its limitations."

"What do you mean, limitations?" I reply, feigning incomprehension.

"You spend three months playing the same piece of music three times a week. Then you sit in an empty hall and play it to some old guy sat in a box. There's a definition of madness in there somewhere. It's a challenge at first, but there's a point when it becomes a pain in the arse: I think that happens sooner rather than later. "

I have to admit, "There is something in that."

He continues, "You can also spend your time aiming for a sort of unattainable perfection. You're always thinking, am I good enough or do I sound shit? So you never actually enjoy what you're doing. It doesn't matter what level you play at, bottom of the fourth section or Dyke. I bet everyone who has played in a brass band will know what I mean. And if you do let rip and enjoy yourself, you look up and there's the conductor staring at you."

I nod, sadly. There is more, "Basically, if you look here tonight, people are actually dancing and enjoying themselves. I've made loads of cock-ups tonight, but no-one gives a toss. We're not playing the dots, we listen to each other, we have solos. We improvise for God's sake. It's like the quality of the performance isn't judged on someone going, "that should have been an F sharp in bar 41". It's about the buzz, was it a good crack? Band and audience. It's about the relationship.

"If you play in a brass band how often do you ask yourself, what am I doing here? Why are the audience here? What does everyone expect? It's like there can be this moat between the audience and the stage. Sometimes it feels like everyone is going through the motions. Bands are important, but somehow they can't ask the basic questions about what they want from the music or what the music is for."

The problem here is not unique. Many young people who grow up in the movement are inspired to study for music degrees but then recognise there is a whole musical world that brass bands can't or won't embrace. Admittedly, there are significant issues around copyright and its effect on the expansion of repertoire.

Copyright permission now makes it very difficult for arrangers to produce copies of pop hits for bands. This is a problem that is perhaps not as insurmountable as some think. Most pop music is ultimately generic and in its contemporary incarnation has a set of tropes or forms such as ballads and anthems. Entertaining, generic pop style sets could be produced quite easily.

The brass band movement has always been able to respond to challenges and here it could look to its entrepreneurial publishing tradition. A competition might be organised to appeal to university brass departments with a challenge to produce a half hour entertainment set of pop themed music with a party atmosphere. The final performance and the quality of composition would combine to determine the winners. If four groups entered and this was run for three years, there would be twelve sets. A publisher could be given discretion to publish the best. The brief would be to produce simple but enjoyable ten-piece material in both a scored and head chart format to encourage new styles of music making within bands. Familiarity with written material may make it easier to take a leap into less structured formats.

It seems impossible to escape the fact that bands are wedded to the dots, they won't play anything unless it is written down in front of them. In his book *Musicking*, Christopher Small argues that this way of making music is very much an anomaly, both globally and historically. Small claims that in the Baroque period, Handel would have only given his musicians an outline of what they were to play. He would have expected them to use their own musicality to flesh out his ideas in performance. In turn his musicians may have considered it an affront to be given exact and detailed instructions. This tradition may have survived into Mozart's day but was broken in the nineteenth century. From that period until recently, there has been no expectation that classical musicians would have the ability to play anything other than what might be set before them in print.

Readers may recognise that the baroque tradition bears comparison with aspects of twentieth century American music. However, it was not found within the classical sphere but in big bands such as those of Duke Ellington and Count Basie. Their musicians would be expected to juggle the challenges of reading scores with improvising solos.

Unless musicians are brought up "bilingual", playing by ear and reading from instructions, it makes it very difficult for bands to embrace more spontaneous and unplanned music making. This is especially true when bands can't see how they might split their time between learning new skills and preparing for concerts. This all touches on a fundamental issue that is tearing at bands.

Jake felt the constraints of repertoire and performance style, but this is also a manifestation of the way bands are organised. Brass bands are the soundtrack of the industrial revolution. Instruments were state of the art precision engineering, the mass-produced music machines of the factory age. Organisation reflected the model of industrial management; the various departments, most noticeably the cornets, were subject to a strict division of labour. Second and third cornets are indentured labourers producing a steady supply of perfectly formed ums and pahs. This is musical piece work and the coarse hands of the lower cornets will never be allowed to touch the fine melodies of the artisanal front row. Production is supervised by a central overseer, the conductor: the final arbiter of quality control.

The conductor has mellowed from the tyrant of brass band legend, understanding the need for an affable style to make rehearsals as congenial as possible. Authoritarian attitudes sit uncomfortably beside the allegedly egalitarian tone of our times. Many younger musicians are likely to have an instinctive aversion to towing the line when the rest of their leisure is seemingly determined by individual impulse rather than collective obligation. We might also reflect on the way that working relationships are now expected to be more transient and transactional, rather than the job-for-life ideal of the twentieth century. There may have been a crescendo in management rhetoric around the ideal of the team, however Richard Sennett suggests this is best accompanied with a large helping of salt.

The traditional conductor focussed band is influenced by the orchestral ideal and reflects the desire of bands to be taken seriously as a high art form. As the orchestra and choral society become ever more marginal phenomena, bands may need to realign their thinking about what their musical role models might be.

Bands are on the whole friendly and collaborative groups, and most are governed by a democratically elected committee. These fall somewhere on a spectrum from being solid torchbearers of the band tradition to progressive representatives of the general membership view. But, because of the role of the conductor, the band rehearsal is not a negotiated collaboration in the way that say a small jazz group might be. As one conductor said to me after I offered an opinion, "What do you think this is, a democracy?"

Bands are caught between the desire to change, the understanding of the need to change and the gulf they have to bridge. They easily hide in the comfort of the familiar. In the meantime, a situation arises where young people develop their skills to a high degree then find the band movement restricts their ability to experiment and develop in new directions. Directions which for bands may provide lucrative sources of income; Jake tells me Brassic Park will get £1,000 tonight.

With a little more of a sense of adventure it is possible to envisage bands moving themselves into a position where they are an acceptable choice for wedding and other party entertainment, both affordable and local.

If bands are ultimately community music, they need to find new ways to serve their community: they need to make their performances enjoyable, for both band and audience; they need to make a band concert something that you would want to go to. Playing to an empty hall is of no use to anyone.

Bands may be wrestling with the need for change and the familiarity of staying put, but that is not to say that change will not come (or for that matter, that it is not already happening).

As demonstrated earlier there are a number of forces that created and maintained the band structure. They have a role to play in the continued health of bands, but bands must find ways of responding to the need for change. To drift to a more informal smaller group with ad hoc organisation might lead to new forms of community music but it would also signal the death of the band as it is known.

A large part of the future will rely on the band tradition of training and developing new members. Changes are most likely to come in developing strategies to retain them. To support this intuition, there seems to be a revival in youth and training band contests; these are better attended than they have been for many years.

Bands are likely to prosper over the next decade by making minor alterations to the tradition. From the outside they may seem to change very little but internally changes in attitude and organisation may be significant.

Culture is mutable and malleable; it is shaped by and in turn shapes society. A culture that cannot change is dead.

Bradford

The coach all but blocks the lane, its belly open to the barn. Inside the band room, the heavy curtains are withdrawn to reveal two dusty timber doors. Andy wrestles with the stubborn bolts; Tina and Sue remove the iron bar that locks the doors flat to the frame. We are marshalled to push like ancient warriors storming a city gate. "We need to get some oil soaked into those hinges," says Jim, as the screaming metal spits orange dust. Or, perhaps we are more like a Latin congregation bursting out of the cathedral to process their holy relics. Our doors disgorge polygonal percussion and the dark sarcophagi of the silver basses. In bible black blazers we execute the ritual manoeuvres. Our human chain feeds the rumbling beast; within the hold the driver tessellates his complex cargo.

Cars are still arriving. Karen pries herself out of a passenger door. Her husband takes her uniform, bag and case from the boot as she leans into the backseat child seat for a last goodbye. Those on the verge scatter as Cass drives at them full tilt like an extra from Death Race 2000, her fat tyres chewing the grass to mud. Taxis disgorge the chorus. They're all got up as if heading for a winter weekend in Blackpool, a place whose charms are closely aligned with those of our destination: Bradford.

Given that Bradford is less than twenty miles away it may seem a little odd that we are going to the double expense of hiring a coach and a hotel, furthermore we are all expected to contribute to costs. No matter the state of your personal finances you must never grumble about this in public. In the fullness of time it may be found that the fees paid up front by the committee don't match the receipts from the band; this will be simply stated as a loss on the event in the annual report.

Today's journey is a band tradition rooted in less mobile and more prosperous times. Paul tells me that when he joined, the Christmas carolling income was well in excess of ten thousand pounds rather than the two or three we might now expect. The areas was only one of a number of outings that were bankrolled by the band. At the very least there might be a trip to either the Butlin's Mineworkers' Festival in Skeggy or a contest in a Pontin's camp at Southport or Prestatyn. Our hotel stay has a practical as well as a social purpose, it gets the band together before the big day and instils in us a reminder of the need for collective discipline. However, it is not band morale but another force that shepherd's us onto the bus as a wall of snow drives in from the black hill beyond the fields.

The driver shuts the door and Andy patrols the aisle counting heads. Chairman Jack asks, "Are we all here, now?" Andy reports his findings and these match Jack's list.

"Where's Nick?" asks Karen.

"Don't worry," soothes Jack, "he says he's going to a wedding in Brighouse this afternoon and he'll be getting a taxi to the hotel later."

This news is not well received by Big Michaela who broadcasts her dissatisfaction to the neighbouring seats. "In that case we can say goodbye to us having a soprano cornet tomorrow, then."

Her Dad harrumphs his agreement.

—

We are not the first coach at the hotel and a queue is already forming at reception, but before we can be booked into our rooms the percussion must be man-handled into the reception hall. We have formed a consortium with the other bands here, we provide the percussion and they pay for the room which has been booked until tomorrow afternoon. The next twenty-four hours are divvied into rehearsal slots so we can all fine tune our preparations for the contest.

The young woman in the suit pauses her briefing as our clanking carnival crashes through the double doors. She has been insisting on a strict timetable for rehearsals. This ends too early in the evening for Andy's liking, "So, you're telling me that if you had a wedding reception, they'd have to stop the disco at nine?"

She is caught off guard, the messenger not the author of the policy. "Well, that's different..."

Andy doesn't think so. "How? Do they all put headphones on and dance in silence?" His arms allude to John Travolta and he mimes, "Night fever, night feevaah..." The receptionist is flustered.

Jack glides in. "Don't worry love, we know the score. We won't be blowing into the small hours, you can be sure of that. This lot'll want to be heading for the bar long before then."

As the receptionist retreats, Chris sidles up behind Andy. "You're a right wind-up merchant you, aren't y'?"

Unpacking upstairs in the lonely bedroom, I hang the uniforms then close the curtains on the sodium city. I change and try the bed. Retrieving a book from my bag, I while away the hour.

—

James arrives to a fanfare from Jim who is reconstituting a solo cornet line from Punchinello. "We're going to have fun in here aren't we?" he says to Chairman Jack.

"What do you mean?"

James instructs him to "Just listen," as the cornet's sound rebounds off the double height windows, the glazed doors, the bare walls, the parquet floor, the ornamental mirror, the moulded plaster ceiling and the cut-glass chandelier. Some bands specifically seek out sympathetic acoustics for the night before a contest and James now wishes he had done a little research too. He is also unhappy that we agreed to take the final rehearsal slot from 8:15 to 9:00. The band on the other hand have used the time to hunt down curries in the streets beyond the city hall. Jack had gambled that the timing would prevent a slide into the Wetherspoon's that obstructs the walk back. He hadn't bargained that some would never make it past its front door on the way out, he is assured it was purely the lure of the food.

151

As Jim begins to remember his melody, the percussionists unfold their plan and push the scaffolding into position. The warm ups from the rest of the band are initially restrained, cowed; we are self-conscious in the bright acoustic. Little by little we lose our inhibitions and get to grips with the passages that cause us most concern. Tap, tap. We are brought to attention by James who sets out the agenda for the next half hour, "Topping and tailing... focus on some details". As he swivels to his left he asks, "Where's Nick?"

—

The second section doesn't start until two o'clock this afternoon, so it is a surprise that most of the band are down at breakfast by eight. It is not a surprise to see the state of Andy's plate, the sausages are piled up like a scout camp fire. "According to him..." he says, pointing a skewered banger in my direction, "According to him, sausages don't qualify as food." Paul laughs and Andy looks over at my plate, "I thought you'd be on the rabbit food, isn't that more your style?" I butter another slice and avoid admitting to my childish fascination with the conveyor belt toaster.

It is hours until we play and everyone is tucking in. If we were on first thing we would be more cautious, in case a full stomach obstructed the free movement of the diaphragm. It is an age until we take the stage and our rehearsal is over the horizon at half eleven. After breakfast I feel the need to find a paper and trudge through the sleet into the city centre. The first building I pass is today's contest venue.

St. George's Hall has been a presence in the city for more than 150 years. It was built by public subscription, including generous donations from the immigrant wool merchants of the self-explanatory Little Germany district, to support the demand for a major concert venue in the city. The architects, Lockwood and Mawson, modelled it on the recent example of Liverpool's celebrated St Georges Hall. However, whatever grand ambitions architect and client may have had were constrained by the size of the site; the hall is squeezed onto the junction of two major thoroughfares. This conspires to reduce the grand impression it would otherwise impose on the city centre. By way of contrast, the City Hall opposite breathes freely in its own precincts allowing full appreciation of its palatial, Florentine ambitions.

St. George's is built in a neoclassical style, adopting some of the features of a Greek Temple - think of the Parthenon on the Athens Acropolis. The window heads on the other hand are rounded in the Romanesque style named after the inventors of the arch. The hall's Liverpool inspiration is surrounded by a colonnade; the limits of space in Bradford mean its pillars are embedded in the walls. These engaged pillars are an architectural reference to nature in the form of the tree trunk. The other style favoured by the Victorians, the Gothic, takes this symbolism one step further, and the crowns of the columns fan out into vaults reminiscent of a canopy of branches.

In recent years the development of cultural centres such as concert halls has been regarded as a marketing and branding opportunity for cities seeking a global profile. If the pun can be excused, concert halls have become instrumental. They are tools of economic regeneration intended to promote a region as a site for corporate relocation or tourism (for example, by hosting brass band contests). As such, the value of the building is judged not by what takes place within its walls or the cultural service to its broader community, but the money it can attract to an area from elsewhere.

The clamour for attention has resulted in cities recruiting internationally renowned architects and designers such as Norman Foster, Frank Gehry and the late Zaha Hadid. They have been employed to produce amorphous structures that appear to not just float free of their physical surroundings (they could seemingly be built anywhere) but also their social context and any sense of cultural continuity. They are like stuck records relentlessly screaming "NOW! NOW! NOW!" The architectural style, their aesthetic, isn't anchored to any allusions to their purpose or the history of the arts they may contain. This is in contrast to the popular Victorian styles which, in their veiled and perhaps unwitting references to trees, cannot avoid some association with the notion of roots.

As far as brass bands are concerned St Georges Hall has a solid link to our musical roots. In his book on Victorian popular music, Dave Russell cites at least one article from a Bradford paper remarking on the number of local bandsmen present at a classical concert. Working class musicians from Wyke, Saltaire and Queensbury would pay the high ticket prices in order to listen to and learn from the best musicians of their time. They would bring the same depth of appreciation to the music as their middle class peers; this is as it should be.

In *A History of Adult Education in Britain,* Thomas Kelly suggested that in their earliest incarnation, at the end of the seventeenth century, many public concerts had a definite educational purpose. A point of interest is that some of those concerts didn't happen in a formal concert hall setting but in the table and chairs environs of the tavern and the coffee house. This will bring a jolt of recognition to any band that has played in a working men's club.

St George's Hall might be presumed to be the home of Black Dyke in the same way that Huddersfield Town Hall has been claimed by Brighouse and Rastrick. It is instructive to note that the Brighouse tradition only began in earnest after the Second World War. Roy Newsome observed that during the Victorian era bands were far more often heard outdoors than in. Bearing that in mind, it can't be expected that St George's hosted many bands on stage in its early years. However, it is now, even if only for this weekend, the focus of the Yorkshire brass tradition.

Beyond the hall, in the lanes of the city centre, I am dismayed by the desperate rows of empty shops. Not just empty shops but, it seems, empty streets. Not just peripheral streets but some of the fine commercial buildings at the heart of the city. Many give the impression of having been empty for some time, others advise that they have relocated to the self-contained shopping centre beyond the back of our hotel.

I am not surprised by the state of Bradford as it's one of the poorest urban areas in Britain, of the 14 wards around the city centre 12 rank in the most deprived category. The topography of Bradford seems to exemplify a tussle between civic ambition and poverty. For the renovation of every mill of the grandeur of Lister's there are several cheap stone piles burning down on the evening news. Fortunately, even in its diminished state the city centre offers some hidden gems, and I flick through the paper in the formica-topped splendour of the Fountains Café.

Splashing back to the hotel, I slip into St George's Hall where Tina is mooching around the trade stands. "Have you heard anyone, yet?" I ask.

"I was just thinking about going and having a look, are you coming?"

We climb the stairs to a balcony where we are challenged by a steward. "You can't go in without a ticket." We explain we won't get our tickets until later because we are in the second section not the fourth.

We argue that we have tickets in spirit, if not in name. "It's not as if you're holding the crowds back, is it?" I ask.

"It's not as if we're going to be misbehaving," adds Tina.

The steward looks us up and down, "You never know with you lot, love. You might be groupies, it'd be more than my job's worth if you start screaming and fainting in the aisles." She kindly pulls the door open and there is a round of applause.

"Is that for us?" asks Tina.

We settle into red plush velvet seats and soak up the cinema hush. The heavy curtains are drawn over the windows and the meagre daylight is kept firmly outdoors; we like the feel of the acoustic. Tina looks in her programme to check the numbers on the stage - the band number and the running order. We realise we haven't got the running order and will have to take a guess at who is playing next, whoever they are they won't be in the prizes today. "The hall's good isn't it? I mean, you can hear the detail in the playing, there's no hiding your crimes from the adjudicators." I have to agree and hope no-one from the Crown Prosecution Service is in the audience when we play. The fourth section test piece doesn't inspire and we leave the hall after the second band.

As we reach the hotel, we notice Nick standing at the top of the steps. His left hand is in a trouser pocket; his right cups a fresh cigarette.

Tina says, "We missed you last night."

With an effort he suppresses an incipient belch, pushing it back to the depths from which it was rising. "Yeah, I know, I just lost track of time. You know how it is."

"Some people were worrying that you might not make it," I reply.

This is obviously unjustified as he assures me, "No, no, I had a quiet night."

Nick seems momentarily distracted. He looks over to the court house across the way and then at the ground; a curtain of vomit sluices across his feet. He turns his attention to Tina, "I only had a couple of bottles and then called it a day, I was in bed by half ten."

I am uncertain how to take this. At first I wonder if Nick is daring us to challenge him, that he is pressing us into a complicity where we reject the evidence of our own eyes. I discard the proposition as, to my horror, it dawns on me that Nick may actually have no awareness of what he has just done.

155

"Nick," I say as he continues to chunter on. "Nick!" I am emphatic and force him to pay attention to me.

"What?"

I look him in his glassy eyes, "You've just puked on your shoes." He looks bewildered so I repeat the statement, slowly this time. "You've just puked on your shoes."

His eyes reluctantly revolve to the ground. "Oh, shit!" He waddles gingerly down the steps to a grey puddle at the kerb and begins a penguin shuffle, dipping his toes alternately into the icy filth. Tina checks her watch, it is eleven. We exchange horrified glances and head to our rooms to prepare for the final rehearsal.

—

Jack stands before us. "The draw is at half past one and the first band will be on at two o'clock. If that's us we *must* be ready to register straight away. So you all need to have your uniforms and instruments to hand. We can't be hanging about." Geoff puts his hand up. "Yes, Geoff?"

He clears his throat, "I was wondering if we're going to have another warm up together before we go over."

Jack shakes his head, "No, there isn't any time for that and James's said that because of all the hanging around he doesn't feel there's much point to it, either. It's up to everyone to make sure they're warmed up before they get on stage." This touches on a problem with Bradford as a contest venue. In November, at Rochdale Town Hall, we had ten minutes in a warm up room before registration. There is no such possibility today and there is some concern that we will be going on cold.

Geoff replies, "Couldn't we just have a quick blow through here before we go over?"

Jack is rueful. "The problem is that we're sharing this with other bands and the first section bands have booked it all afternoon..." He lets the thought fall away before rousing us. "Righto, over to you James."

We skip through a couple of hymns and then run the test piece in order of its weakest links. "That's Ok, let's go to D..." We seem to let the rehearsal drift along its course; it is hard to truly gauge our effectiveness in this room. James wants to keep us in reasonable condition. "We won't touch the solos unless there is anyone who particularly wants to do theirs'..." He looks around the room, restating the question with his eyebrows. The soloists seem relaxed, unless they just don't want to tempt fate.

I do a quick internal check, how do I feel about this? I remember as a child, there were contests where the preceding weeks developed their own momentum. When it got to the big day everyone just knew we were going to do well. The rehearsal room would be animated with this knowledge and if we didn't get a good placing then we would feel robbed, cheated of what was rightfully ours. Today we feel flat; we lack a sense of anticipation. That feeling feeds off itself: when there is anticipation there is concentration; when there is concentration there is attention to detail. Suddenly, there is a loss of an awareness of anything beyond the music and there is what athletes call "flow".

In this moment we are nothing if not self-conscious and conscious of each other. When Nick ends a particularly long note with a belch it is a shot that's heard around the band. When James stops us a few bars later it becomes the burp that dare not speak its name. James wrestles with his anger and distaste, juggling this against the need to maintain equilibrium and concentration. I don't know if I hear the whisper of these words, or if they just push into the room under their own psychic force; to my left, behind the horns, Big Michaela is stifling a different type of eruption. "I told you this would happen." Then, more darkly and deliberately, "I'll kill him if he does that on stage. I'll ruddy kill him."

As the rehearsal ends Sue turns to me, "Can you take the music?" I reach for the sellotaped bundle of paper on the stand. It is technically a breach of copyright but none of us are using the original parts (these are being kept for when we play the piece again which for test pieces is usually... never). We magnify the pages on the photocopier for our feeble eyes or cut them up to produce a sequence that overcomes awkward page turns. Sue and I have obliterated whole lines with black felt tip where James has told us to leave off, added nuanced instructions at key points and scrawled sarcastic remarks for our own amusement. A few bars have been taped on here and there to help out the second cornets. The paper scrunches in my hand and I wonder where best to keep it. I lay it flat on the cornet as I lock the case, but first I remove the valves and slather them with oil.

We leave the rehearsal room and loll in the lounges of the hotel, making idle conversation as we wait for the draw. We are on number five.

—

After two, we all march down to St Georges Hall. I don't know if the gathering point is the artistes' entrance or a backstage maintenance door at the front of the building; what I do know is that the security are reluctant to let us in. After ten cold minutes, we are allowed entry, but only to queue again in a corridor that is one step removed from being a back alley. Another age passes before a procession to our next station of the cross. This low ceilinged, tight, white corridor at least has heat, carpet and light. It also has a poster of Engelbert Humperdink, every time we play here there is always a poster of Engelbert Humperdink.

"Engelbert Humperdink, eh?" says Jim, "I'm surprised he's still around. How old must he be now?"

Chris chips in, "He's probably saying the same about you, Jim."

Jim turns round. "Ged aht of it."

Nicola whispers to Cassy, "Who's Engelbert Humperdink?" She is wide eyed, half smiling at the oddity of the name, but also not particularly interested in learning more.

"A pop star," says Sue, "from the seventies."

"Pop star..." muses Nicola, as if considering an archaic term for the first time - as might well be the case.

"He was on telly, too, weren't he?" considers Tina. Sue says, "Sunday Night at the London Palladium," she almost sings the title. "Me mum loved him, she'd go, "ooh, he's very dishy..."" offering what may or may not be a close impersonation of her mum gripped with a late onset teenage crush.

Nicola looks up from her glowing screen and a tinny voice is swiftly joined by Tina and Sue, "Pleeeeeease release me, let me goooooo..." before they dissolve into hysterics. "What are you on?" asks Chris, in amused bewilderment.

"You actually listened to this?" asks Nicola, incredulous.

"I'll have you know that went to number one, young lady," replies Jim, archly exerting his seniority.

Nicola turns to Sue, "I thought pop music was, like, David Bowie."

Sue thinks and replies, "Well, he was big, but pop music was more mixed than that. There were people like Bowie, who was obviously very cool, and then stuff your mum might like." She slips into a reverie and wistfully turns to Tina, "D'you remember the charts? On Sundays we would always have the charts on when we were having our tea."

Tina perks up, "Oh, in our house we'd all be listening. Me and mi brother would be shouting at each other to shut up for the songs we liked..."

Sue adds, "Yeah, and slag off the ones we hated."

That is how I remember it, too, but nowadays my main encounters with what might be termed pop music occur in the aisles of the local co-op. I am disturbed by what I hear, although readily acknowledge this sample may be far from representative. After all, most pop music is forgotten and only a few highlights of any era are remembered. Putting that thought aside, I still can't shake a conviction that something fundamental has changed; the supermarket pop music seems gripped by a terrible, anxious emptiness.

—

Brass music and pop music don't immediately seem to offer too many opportunities for comparison. However, they both occupied similar levels of public awareness in their respective times, two periods separated by one century. Brass bands began to gather pace in the second half of the nineteenth century and pop in the second half of the twentieth. They both suffered decline in the early decades of the following centuries. One of the factors that undermined brass bands was the availability of recorded music. Understanding the forces that have impinged on the fortunes of pop may also give insight into the contemporary challenges for brass bands.

It is difficult to identify the nature of pop's crisis. It seems aware of what the historical forms are, some chord progressions, an alternation between verse and chorus, but it seems to paddle round a shallow pool of possible rhymes, rhythm and structure. It has been stuck there for some time. As for the substance - a sense of yearning, optimism or the tribulations of young love – this feels as if it is being delivered in direct translation from Latin or Sanskrit. It's as if today's performers are in search of the meaning of an obscure original text. This is in marked contrast to, say, the Motown girl groups of the 1960s. Who could doubt the innocence and sincerity of The Shirelles when they insisted, "this is dedicated to the one I love"?

If The Shirelles had an innocence in their music, it was surely a legacy from growing up in the shelter of Detroit's Beulah St. Baptist Church. A childhood spent in the church choir also taught the vanishing art of song. The gospel churches of America were an important influence for pop music, even as far back as the nineteen forties and fifties, their heritage is evident in styles such as Doo Wop. Doo Wop inhabited a shallow musical pool restricted by a very limited set of rhymes, rhythms and structures.

Doo Wop was just a phase, it was always just a phase. Pop music was marching on, exploring new territories. Now it feels like pop has reached its final destination and is just going through the motions, endlessly regurgitating and reconstituting its inheritance. It has lost its sense of purpose, its reason for being. It is playing out an eternal, final moment like the lead out groove on a worn LP.

In his book, *Music and the Mind*, Anthony Storr draws a distinction between pop music and popular music. He considers popular music to be within a nebulous category that might also be termed light music. This is music which may use instrumentation and compositional techniques similar to classical music but eschews the extremes of mood and tempo, the shocks and abrupt turns of its more cultured parent. These sharp edges are smoothed out to facilitate what at the extremity is termed an "easy listening" experience. In Storr's view, pop is by far the more rudimentary of the two genres. It is of interest to note that brass bands (having strong light music roots) have tried to square this circle by attempting to adapt to and accommodate the presence of pop.

The distinction between pop and popular music is not always clear. In those first decades of pop the popular music stylings were certainly not banished from the charts. Even in the sixties and seventies, singers such as Shirley Bassey would be backed by small orchestras and the music would be professionally arranged. In contrast to a number of her pop contemporaries, there was no doubt that Shirley could really sing.

One of the charges often laid against pop music has been about a lack of talent. This is somewhat unkind and disrespectful to the many gifted performers who have made it their musical home (a notable example being the jazz musicians who migrated to funk at the start of the nineteen seventies). Unfortunately, it is not a challenge to find instances where the accusation is justified.

Taking two of the most successful British acts of the 1970s: the evidence of live tapes suggests that Pink Floyd were at heart a pub rock band, albeit with one of the great guitar stylists of the decade; similarly, David Bowie's live tapes call into question his ability to sing. In the case of the former, conceptual thinking and intelligent use of recording technology created one of the most interesting pop records of the decade. In the case of the latter, there was a restless, mutating imagination at play producing a range of expressions of identity that were as equally important as the music; Bowie's vocalising was a point of reverence for his fans. Clearly, musicianship isn't all when it comes to pop. Having said that, Bowie usually used top session musicians in his recordings, and by the late 1970s so did Pink Floyd.

The popstrels of yore had a grounding playing covers of the songs of others in youth clubs, pubs and church halls. They could immerse themselves in a subculture with its own codes, mores and performance standards. Along the way they had to get a rudimentary grasp of their instruments, how to play in a band and also some idea of what made a good song. Looking in more detail, the bass player on David Bowie's album *Hunky Dory*, Trevor Bolder, was able to contribute a trumpet part due to a childhood playing cornet in his local brass band. Immersion in any musical culture gives a musician transferable skills.

Perhaps the beauty and purity of British pop was that it grew up in the margins. It was a musical culture young people created for themselves away from the formal musical world. However, for some, a formal training may have provided them with skills they could use elsewhere

With computer technology it is possible to bypass the loose apprenticeship of the covers band, a consequence of this is that the frustrations and compromises of collaborating with musical peers may be avoided. Composition and recording software can also remove the need for a budding songwriter to develop a feel for rhythm, pitch and harmony. Once the listener has learned to recognise it, the presence of the autotuner is inescapable in twenty first century pop vocals.

The pop pinnacle of computer manipulated music is the techno DJ. The beats and patterns have their own compulsion, but they belie the irony that, for all the sophistication of the technology and its promises of infinite flexibility, the genre has as many limitations as the brylcreemed Doo Wop quartets. Techno inhabits a shallow musical pool restricted by a very limited set of harmonies, rhythms and structures.

The great American producer Quincy Jones has observed that most contemporary pop music is based on repeating four bar loops. These don't even need to be the artist's own composition as they can be sampled, borrowed or stolen from other recordings. However, recurring patterns are not necessarily detrimental to musical style; in some circumstances they are an essential element.

Repetition is a fundamental part of much folkish music and one of the roots of pop music – the blues. Repetition does not in and of itself create banality. Listening to Chester Burnett singing *Smokestack Lightnin'*, the attention is soon drawn to the endlessly repeating eight note figure of the guitar. Between the singing and the guitar there is a mystery as to what draws the listener in, ironically part of that answer lies in the very nature of that twanging phrase.

Stevie Wonder noted, "just because a record has a groove Don't make it hit the groove". Burnett's guitarist hits the groove. The music is not restricted but liberated by the constraints of those eight notes, and the white British teenagers hearing *Smokestack Lightnin'* for the first time recognised this. They were in awe, the groove was beyond their experience, it came from another place. Chester's voice too, he was not merely a singer; his voice was elemental, it was like the baying of some wild animal from out beyond the Mississippi river. Chester may have been aware of that himself as he had adopted the stage name Howlin' Wolf.

Duke Ellington famously said, "there are simply two kinds of music, good music and the other kind ... the only yardstick by which the result should be judged is simply that of how it sounds. If it sounds good it's successful; if it doesn't it has failed." Louis Armstrong rephrased this with his customary mischief, "there is two kinds of music, the good, and the bad. I play the good kind."

If we take the example of The Shirelles and Howlin' Wolf, the essential ingredient for making good music would seem to be the immersion in a tradition, what jazz musicians called a scene, and to have a single-minded devotion to it. The gospel singers and the blues musicians had that immersion forced upon them for reasons of culture and geography, as did the members of Victorian brass bands.

If beauty is in the eye of the beholder, then the final judgement of the quality of music, of what is good, is made in the ear of the listener. I have no doubt there are devotees of contemporary pop who will attest to the significance of their music, how nothing else speaks to them in that way. Who would deny their experience? However, at a critical distance it is possible to raise a few questions and concerns.

The laptop superstars of today do not live within the narrow confines of a cotton plantation or a Baptist church, they are subjected to a relentless bombardment of stimulation from the internet. This deprives them of both a fixed point of reference and the empty time to absorb and contemplate the content of this electronic storm.

In an interview available on the Black Dyke website, David Pogson suggests that young musicians have too many choices and that it is difficult for them to allow their focus to settle exclusively on one interest or path. This is going to be particularly difficult for those constantly distracted by mobile phones. The mention of young people gives a clue to another reason for the failure of pop, for that anxiety echoing in the supermarket.

From its earliest incarnations pop was an essential element in the construction of that post-war marketing innovation, the Teenager. These were young people who were floating free of childhood but not yet harboured in the adult world. More importantly, they were also in possession of disposable income (or at least in the USA). They were given a uniform to buy (blue jeans), role models with interesting haircuts (James Dean) and a musical style to clearly differentiate themselves from their regular quadrilateral parents (rock 'n' roll). Music was absolutely central to the moment because it not only set the mood but allowed Teenagers to experience it in a primal way that went deeper than words, dancing.

Now those original Teenagers are mouldering away in care homes. They realise that not only do their children listen to the same pop music as their grandchildren, but they all wear the same branded nylon leisure wear. Teenage was a fast-track education in consumerism and its graduates never forgot its lessons. To put it more bluntly: we are all Teenagers now. This is the same as saying there are no Teenagers any more.

One of the founding purposes of pop was to delineate the commercial separation of parents and children. Now they are part of the same seamless consumer culture pop has lost part of its essence; pop can no longer be a primary shaper of a distinct youth profile.

When David Bowie died there was a tremendous intergenerational outpouring of public grief. In hindsight this was not just a mourning of the man and his music, but also a lament for a time when pop music had the capacity to shape the identity of the listener. This fraying of the link between music and identity has eroded the meanings of pop; as pop has been diminished so music in general has lost significance.

—

I turn to Geoff, "I expect you have an extensive collection of Engelbert Humperdink."

He takes me seriously, "Not really my thing."

I can't quite gauge what his extra-mural listening preferences might be. "So, what do you listen to?"

He thinks, "Classic American big bands, Count Basie, Maynard Fergusson..."

I can see that would fit with his attitudes but suspect these are later acquisitions rather than lifelong passions. "What about when you were a kid?"

He turns to me, "What, you mean pop music and all that?" He pauses, "I never really had much interest, it was always brass bands."

I tease him," So you were off to town on a Saturday morning tracking down the latest release from Rothwell Temperance?"

"No, I didn't really buy records. But I'll tell you what, they keep cropping up in charity shops and I just buy 'em all. Anything, any band. There's loads of this stuff when you get going, not just the big name bands either. Most village bands will have put a record out at some point."

I sense a touch of collecting mania here, "Are they really worth listening to?"

"Mmmmm. I'll admit there are a few that don't make it through the first side. Some of them are recorded in their band rooms and we know what a mixed bag they can be. But it's fascinating... Sometimes there'll be a piece that's fallen out of fashion and it might be the *only* recording of it anywhere."

"I can see that," I add, "and you've got an archive of band history. When it's all put together in one place it must give a sense of perspective, but on another level isn't it just like collecting beer mats."

He looks offended at the suggestion.

"What I mean is, there's this stuff and it has its own history but very few bands were making these recordings for posterity, it was just a very up to the minute thing to do. They were disposable. But does anyone even have a sentimental attachment to it?"

He thinks about it, "Well, if you were on it or a family member. It'd have some importance then."

"But isn't that just sentimentality or curiosity?"

He comes back at me, "that's what you were asking, but what's wrong with that?"

I am struggling to express something, "why is it that these LPs are mouldering away in cardboard boxes in junk shops and charity shops but some obscure rock album that sank without trace in 1973 will be selling to collectors for a hundred quid? I mean, if the music is poor and it's a cheap recording there isn't a lot to recommend it. By the same measure shouldn't at least the top end of brass band recordings be up for similar prices?"

Geoff doesn't follow my line and I suspect this is because at that crucial age he was immersed in the culture. Bands had a grip on him, that round of practising, contests, concerts and camaraderie was his world, whereas I was always looking out of the window, so to speak. I was susceptible to the enchantments and seductions of pop; pop records offered something more significant but intangible than a square piece of cardboard and a round piece of plastic. This contrast somehow devalued the band for me and framed it in a grey and less than glamorous light. If I was to hazard a guess at the cause of my confusion it is that pop music dazzled, beguiled and enchanted those who gazed upon it, brass bands obsessed those people who were immersed in them.

Pop was always an intensely commercial enterprise and it was the drive of the marketing that created its mystique. By the 1970s this had developed into a mode of expression that was an art form in itself. The most arresting and enduring piece of graphic art of that decade was the cover of Pink Floyd's *Dark Side of the Moon*, it was an enigmatic and elusive image of profound mystery and sophistication. In contrast, the covers of brass band LPs would have featured three rows of (usually) blokes in full regalia on the steps of a local civic building weighing up whether or not they were going to say cheese. There may also have been a trophy in front, the recording being a way to mark a contest triumph.

Some people balanced an obsession with pop with a dedication to brass bands, but the conflict between pop and brass bands boiled down to its essence is the difference between consumption and participation. For pop the greatest magic was found in the purchase of musical artefacts, by being on the outside looking in, for bands the greatest magic was being on the inside blowing. These two worlds were masterfully combined by the genius of Derek Broadbent and, love it or loathe it, the Floral Dance was an inspired and more importantly inspirational recording. If at the time (as noted earlier), brass bands were spreading their wings on the expansion of post-war music education, pop was soaring on thermals warmed by commerce and technology. According to David Byrne, in his book *How Music Works*, these were to prove to be fair weather friends.

The first major concern that technology posed to pop's income was the arrival of the cassette recorder and the home taping of records. However, contrary to expectations, the sale of recordings rose rather than fell. The next technological innovation, the CD, saw sales rise even further. At the height of CD sales (around 2000) David Byrne suggests that they were three times those of vinyl twenty years earlier but the fall from that peak was just as sharp as the rise. Major problems arose with the arrival of the internet.

At the same time as the internet arrived, so did both affordable digital recording technology and the capacity for computers to copy and duplicate CDs - known colloquially in the global village as ripping and burning. Websites sprang up that enabled fans to swap and share recordings, this meant that fans were able to get copies of CDs for free; needless to say this meant that both artists and record companies lost significant income. There were a number of legal battles around copyright infringement and some major file sharing and pirating sites were closed. However, this was not a decisive victory as record companies had not understood how the online world was evolving and were ultimately outmanoeuvred by tech entrepreneurs. As a result of these changes, music is increasingly listened to through streaming services such as Spotify. This is great for the streamers as it is a profitable business model; Byrne argues that for the artists it is not so good as they have been forced to cede access to their recordings for a pittance. As a consequence, it is increasingly difficult for new or emerging artists to make a living from their music and record companies are less willing to provide commercial breathing space for artists to develop their talents through unsuccessful recordings. For those artists attempting to go it alone the business models set out by Byrne are onerous and terrifying.

The story of culture on the internet has been about finding ways to make money out of selling entertainment, about how to put a turnstile on the product. There are two ways this is done: by selling subscriptions, or; by selling advertising space on free services. A mature phase has been reached and this has had radical and unforeseen effects. One notable example is the way in which traditional media outlets such as newspapers and the BBC are left with a falling and aging audience in the wake of the drift online. In my limited experience services such as Netflix are more likely to be younger people's first choice for screen-based entertainment than the BBC.

The internet creates two problems for music that are even greater than the squeeze on audiences and income. The first is that music is now one of a number of forms of digital, streamed media competing for time and attention and so will thrive according to how well it conforms to the formats of the platforms that it is presented on. For example, on Youtube the most successful material will be brief and have a strong visual component. It should be noted that music in this form is a video production of exactly the same status as a film of a skateboarding cat. Online there is no hierarchy of content as there was, for example, in the heyday of TV and radio. There are no slots when only specific types of music will be broadcast. Music is deprived of a context that will make it special, music is also deprived of our full attention as the web site encourages its visitor to always be looking at something else.

The second problem is that online there is no such thing as a shared cultural experience. User activity such as searches and viewing habits are monitored, not just by the website being viewed but often, by other websites that have been visited. This is done using trackers called "cookies", the online world is a surveillance society. The information "harvested" is used to understand the psychology, character and interests of the user and then promote "content" that will encourage frequent returns and longer stays.

This "personalisation" might be considered beneficial as the user is always being offered things that they like or may interest them. On the other hand, it avoids the challenge of the unfamiliar or unexpected. This means that if there is no conscious search for content in that territory a viewer will never encounter Beethoven, Black Dyke, Bowie, or for that matter Beyonce. However, if the viewer has friends who regularly forward and recommend videos of performing cats, they will see an awful lot of these and be recommended far more. If that sounds too sour and haughty then remember the reverse is also true. If your friends bombard you with videos of Beethoven recitals, they may be part of a vast conspiracy to deny you the opportunity to experience the pinnacle of human culture and civilization: the Roomba cat video.

No matter whether we are considering a diet of cat videos or Beethoven recitals, a state of affairs where internet algorithms are directing what is watched or read becomes a form of censorship. Technology determines what we see. The viewer is deterred from seeking new perspectives, music also becomes a solitary preference rather than a shared understanding. This can only lead to a narrowing of horizons not only for individuals but also for society. More insidiously, the more that culture and music are defined by their online presence in a virtual world the less people will understand them as social experiences in the material world - In Real Life.

—

If there is one forum that might be expected to broaden horizons it is the education system. Unfortunately, a number of factors are working against music in schools. An enduring lack of government support verging on sabotage is the most important of these. Broader social trends are also having an effect, for example, the decline in the popularity of the piano as parlour entertainment means that schools have fewer staff who can accompany communal singing - this is most noticeable in primary schools. The reduction in wide ranging instrumental tuition means that there are less likely to be school music groups such as orchestras to fulfil that role, either. What singing there is is likely to be accompanied by recordings and videos. It is now probably impossible to complete a school education without encountering *The Greatest Showman*.

The loss of musician exemplars in teacher and student bodies means that there is a loss of musical understanding, a loss of musical literacy within schools. With a loss of musical literacy also comes a loss of musical and therefore cultural history, of heritage. This is akin to the English curriculum ditching Shakespeare to focus on back issues of *The Sun*. As a consequence, music is likely to be understood, appreciated and experienced only in its simplest forms – contemporary pop songs. It can be no surprise that fewer and fewer young people study music to GCSE. If this sounds too gloomy then we might consider the examples of schools such as Wardle in Rochdale who continue to make remarkable efforts to reverse this trend. Their commitment to broadening the musical horizons of their students is exemplary.

The experience of the new, the unfamiliar and unexpected is one of the delights of music and I know I am not the only one who feels this. "Did, I tell you...?" I ask Geoff, "last week, there's this woman at work, Sarah. She usually has some pop music playing on headphones when she's typing. Anyway, it turns out she volunteers as an usher at her local theatre. As I was chatting to her on Monday morning she goes, "listen to this" and brings something up on Youtube. She says, "there was this brilliant band on at the weekend they were absolutely amazing. You've got to listen to this." She only pulls up a video of Dyke. She says, "What do you think of that?"" I add, "You've got to bear in mind that *no one* at work has any idea that I play in a brass band."

Geoff thinks about it, "There you go," he says, "people only have to be introduced to the music and they get it." He is suddenly distracted, "Karen, you need to take the weight off your feet. What must you think of us chatting away like this and you fit for floppin'?" he asks sensing her fatigue. "Here, sit on this." He upends his flugel case and pats the top in invitation.

"Are you sure?" she asks.

"Just sit down," he says.

Her relief is palpable. "There's too much standing around, I'm knackered," puffs Karen.

"Can I get you a drink?" asks Geoff.

"No, but thanks for asking," she pulls a bottle of water from her jacket pocket and takes a swig.

No sooner has she settled than at last we are ushered into the dressing room, like the corridor it is low ceilinged and windowless. We dump the cases, change jackets and ties and start warming up. Those with larger instruments test stiff lips on cold, clutched mouthpieces, it's the buzzing of a busy hive. The smaller instruments are plugged with practice mutes, a whining cloud of angry gnats. It is becoming difficult to move easily, the larger cases are stacked in all the available spaces. Soon it is time to move on to registration, we jostle out of the door and into the corridor.

"Hold on, hold on," it's Jack, "you need your tickets and registration cards." Registration strikes to the heart of the brass band tradition; it is apiece with that pernickety attention to detail that is represented by both the band uniform and the rigorous contest preparations. Every band member has a registration card. These are issued by the national brass band registry; they confirm which band you are a member of and that you are you by means of a passport photo glued to the central panel when the card unfolds. In addition to this detailed security information are stamps recording the contests in which you have participated, like entry stamps on a passport. The cards are held by the band contest secretary, although I suspect we have to retrieve Jim's from a special collection in the V & A. We pass the cards one to the other until we all have the right ones. We compare faces to see who actually resembles their photo. Andy is wanted by Interpol, Nicola won't get served at the bar tonight and I have hair.

The table in the registration room is staffed with three people: one to take the card and ticket and write the players name on a checklist; the next to stamp the card; and the third to give it back and hand us a wrist band. That is how it appears to me although I am sure I have misunderstood some of the minute details of the ritual.

The registration system has been in place for well over a century and it is there to stop that other great brass band tradition, cheating. It is an attempt to stop bands packing their ranks with foreign talent to trump their rivals on the contest stage. Whilst there is still skulduggery, to the extent that occasionally there has been police involvement, the principles are increasingly redundant. There are only a handful of bands who might gain any meaningful material advantage from cheating and ironically perhaps the most profitable event of the year (Whit Friday) does not require players to be registered with the bands they are playing with. For the rest of us it causes more problems than it solves.

I have yet to play in a contest with any band that hasn't had some staffing problems in the run up to a contest. The registration system has often prevented us from easily filling the vacancy. If a band is able to draft in half a dozen players to lift the quality of their playing for a contest this is usually no compensation for knowing that after the big day they will be back in a half empty band room. Whilst the case is still strong for registration in the top section the rest of us would probably be happy to let it go.

Back in the corridor, we are within sight of the rickety wooden steps that lead to the backstage area. We have been here hardly any time when a band comes thundering down. After they have dispersed to the dressing room we ascend to the backstage area. This is surprisingly spacious, probably to accommodate props and chorus lines for the quick changes in big shows.

We blow through our instruments and twiddle the valves ensuring they are up to temperature; our lips must also feel fresh at the moment we go on stage. The usher is alert and hushes us at even the sound of a strong breath. Some of the band make conversation with their eyes whilst others cock their heads to try and gauge the quality of our rivals. We believe it is better to follow a poor band than a good band as this may recalibrate the adjudicator's expectations in our favour.

Applause bursts into the space as the stage doors open and the last band wander off. At last, it is our turn.

—

The plan was that we would line up, basses first, then percussion followed by trombones, baris, euphs. horns, front row and back row, sop in last. We'd take our seats and patiently wait for James, instead we shamble towards our fate.

In the wings screeds of velvet and black disappear into intense, vertical light. We wander onto the stage dazzled, strangely stranded on a desert of bare boards. The merciless sun beats down hot upon us. We seem to lose our footing and stagger thirstily towards the oasis of chairs and tangled stands in the middle of the stage. I sit and smooth the creases from the music which has become frighteningly invisible in the inescapable glare.

I glance around the stand; some share anxious advice or blow yet more air through to stay warm. The percussionists drag and clank their kit into place – everyone apparently sets up differently. Mutes rattle on the stage floor. Some of the larger instruments are upending their bells and pulling slides, obsessively chasing every last drop of condensation from the tubes. When James finally arrives, we notice him as we may a distant acquaintance in a crowded pub.

Our conductor raises his baton and my attention sluggishly coalesces in his direction. Who is he? What am I doing here? There's something important I need to remember. Yes, how do I breathe? Pull in the abdomen, push out the last breath and let go. All of a sudden breathing is no longer easy, I feel strangled by the shirt's tight collar and tourniquet bow tie.

My eyes are caught in the space between the folds of the creased, bleached sheets and the tip of the slender white stick that is rising all too quickly above Sue's head. Some people have had their instruments in place for several seconds, their eyes glued on James. Those who have been squinting at their music are now gradually swivelling towards him. They are almost too late - we are in.

I blow that first note, confident, in tune. No sooner has it left the cornet than I feel I am in a monstrous practical joke; the room has taken the sound and swallowed it whole. For a spasm I feel like I am playing solo. I look around expecting to see the rest of the band rolling around in mirth, not believing that I could fall for that old trick - but we are all playing, intensity furrowed on every forehead. The acoustic has taken me by surprise, as it does every year.

A relatively simple opening, but one of the hardest bars of the piece. Hitting the first note cleanly, perfectly pitched, no split, only one of the bands has done that. And then we're into the piece and can relax until the first major challenge - that high A trill for two bars towards the end of the first movement.

Around me the creaks and groans of a badly tied structure prevail. There have been some contests where one player has made the conspicuous error that loses us first place. Today we are in an egalitarian mood and spread the faults evenly across the band. Even so, some of us still manage to rise to meet the demands of the day; Katie gives a superb cornet solo, the best she has played it. I get through the trill and then it is the dash to the end of the movement.

The second movement wobbles to its feet. The horror, Geoff scuffs his entry. Tina chips in with a well phrased, warm baritone solo. Neither she nor Katie will be mentioned by the adjudicators who don't like the liberties taken with tempi throughout this movement. Nick defers his death sentence with that long note. It is not the best he has played it but it is more than acceptable within the context of our performance.

Finally, the third movement; we gallop through it like stallions that have crashed the stable door. Sometimes we are neck and neck, at others the cornets lead and the trombones stumble, the euphoniums rally and the basses flag. The website *4barsrest* notes the errors are too frequent to ignore. Oh dear, oh dear. At least we end the last chord together.

There is applause and the odd cheer thanks to our loyal support. James invites us to stand, we glance around nervously. I gather the sheaf of sellotaped paper off the stand and check I have my mute. Sue defines the path I follow as we shuffle and scuttle off stage. James reaches the doors first and shakes hands, thanking us for our performance as we pass. It is difficult for us to meet his gaze and he to meet ours. We thunder down those wooden steps past the waiting band, whirl through the changing rooms and head for the exit. Slaithwaite wait at the tail end of the corridor, the afternoon's closing act.

Geoff and I escape into the city centre and grab a quick coffee. He is wrestling with his conscience over his flawed solo entry and cannot be consoled. Within the larger context it was negligible, but Geoff has his standards. I try to give him a realistic sense of perspective, "Look Geoff, if your performance deserves this level of punishment, I should be on death row."

We return to the theatre to catch the last two contestants, one of which is our neighbour, Slaithwaite. They are confident, polished and precise, everything we weren't. As they leave Geoff stands to clap them off, tears of pride streak his cheeks. Slaithwaite were his band, he was there for forty years, only leaving to care for his dying Father. That bond endures, it is deep and eternal.

Now begins the wait.

The hall gradually fills as earlier competitors return from the bar. There is a lazy hum of speculation and anticipation. Eventually an official from the area committee takes the stage to introduce the proceedings, they are followed by the adjudicators and some band reps. There is still a while to wait for the results. First come thanks for volunteers and some long service and other awards. The minor prizes are brought to the fore, Youngest Player and other low-level awards are handed out. Prizes for soloists are held until last as they surely give an insight into the final placings; it is at this point the adjudicators step forward.

The judges begin their presentation with comments on the technical challenges of the piece and how these were overcome (or not). There is a general comparison with other area contests, they take particular care to say that the standard was higher than over in Lancashire since they wish to leave the hall with the good will of the crowd. And finally, and finally the moment arrives to announce the top six placings. Being a realist my heart sinks ever further the nearer we get to the top spot. The minor placings don't contain any names that interest us, the embarrassment comes as we approach the denouement. Slaithwaite are second, Geoff says, "Surely we haven't won?" I shoot a sidelong glance, fearing for his sanity. The winner is announced and Wakefield cheer loudly.

The mark sheets are collected from the front table. We gather round, desperate for a peep. First we read the comments then we look at the placing - not a surprise, we are rock bottom. The adjudicator's remarks, clear and courteous, skewer our conductor like a specimen butterfly. Crushing, I expect James will now resign. The past six months have been pinned on the minimum of keeping us a second section band; we have crashed through the floor into the third section in a fashion that could hardly be less dignified.

Despite the result our mood is surprisingly up-beat. Deps Nick and Jenny are thanked for their assistance, maybe they will become permanent fixtures. Nevertheless, as we mill around and pore over the adjudicator's remarks, I sense a storm is brewing. Michaela and her Dad may have reluctantly commuted Nick's death sentence (I suspect they aren't minded to grant a full pardon and notice that they are the only ones who do not thank him for his help). With their fury thwarted I sense they still need some form of physical outlet for their frustration at our predicament. On our perimeter lurk the dark silhouettes of two Aztec priests. Veering away from Nick they can be heard mumbling, "... he said he was going to keep us in the second section. Now, look at this shambles..." They are scouring the hall for their human sacrifice.

I had not counted James with any great powers of prescience but luckily or skilfully, at this point he is nowhere to be seen.

3. Whit Friday

1978

Cold air rolls down the steep slope from the dark hill behind, scything through the thin polyester of my purple shirt. Hugging myself and stamping flat feet, I perform a shuddering, ritual dance to invoke the return of remembered warmth. Crouched beside me, a thin boy curls in a tight ball, he sucks absentmindedly on his mouthpiece as if on a giant teat.

Down to my right, in the library entrance, signing on sheets are packed into carrier bags, tables and chairs folded and stacked. Volunteers in car coats and cagoules share a joke as the librarian opens up.

Beyond the library, across the road, the low stone doorway to The Bull's Head is still a melee of drinkers pushing for last orders. Cheers erupt as a glass hits the pavement pursued by a double encore of mocking and scolding.

Towards the river, the sodium lights' golden glow gilds the revellers on the street below. Swaying and staggering they struggle to find their feet; chattering voices scamper through the night air. Our road has vanished beneath that formless flux and there appears to be no route to march. We remember the last band disappearing into this foment some time ago; since then, our concentration has crumbled.

In front, a girl swivels; she shoots coy glances at a back row boy. Her fringe swishes like the curtain call in a west end show revealing eyelids that dip like leaves in rain. Someone behind me is joshed and teased by his mates, but the cold numbs most of us into static silence.

Shouts from the front ripple row by row, time to get in position. Chorus-line girls, right hand on their neighbour's shoulder, space themselves across the street. Aligning with the backs in front, I eyeball side to side, shuffling uphill then down. The tired or gormless are chivvied by mother hens.

Someone blows a whistle urging us to approximate attention. The drum gives the beat and we present lips to mouthpieces. Six bars later the lead board marches off; we follow on - left foot forward, or is it right? Skipping in indecision, I glance at the feet to either side as they disappear into darkness. In the end I give up; circumstance has reduced us to a sluggish shuffle.

Progress is slow through the throng. The chalked name registers, local kids, and the crowd roars beer-breath boisterous against my tender cheek. Strong hands pull the too drunk back from collision. The Chieftain bobs in and out of gilded focus at the end of my cornet, God only knows what sound is coming out.

Forging ahead like an ice breaker through the cracking Antarctic shelf, the crowd opens, peels around us then closes as if we were never there. Somewhere near The Swan, the drum gives two taps, then three; we finish the phrase and pull the instruments from our lips. Marching a few steps more, we clutch close the coppery coils.

Pushing and weaving our way into the tenebrous lane, we slowly, skilfully pick a course through the crush. Nudging elbows, jigging pints, we incur brief wrath but also receive sustained encouragement. There is just the beer light to guide us outside the entrance to the club, that and the final line of a contest march tangled in the trees.

Agile stalkers, we deftly thread our way through the press, squirming and squeezing past the applause for the finishing band and onto the stand.

The stand is a patch of tarmac road between the club and the Methodist hall sketched out by strings of naked bulbs. An adjudicator waits within a large caravan sheltered in the shadow of the hall; for a brief moment it is the centre of our attention. Returning to our task, we pause to get our bearings, then: head for our places; nudge out our elbow room; shuffle into line; step back; and reluctantly break our focus to make way for the straggler heading to the gap in the opposite rank.

The conductor's hands describe two converging arcs. We waddle closer in like penguins bracing for winter. This is how we will play: tight; together; intimate; intense.

We are silent, waiting.

The PA announces the band number and the name of the march; everyone but the adjudicator knows who we are.

All eyes are on the centre and our breathing is shallow, pensive. Air is blown through cornets. Valves are reflexively fluttered. Water keys are opened and vigorously fuff-fuffed. I jig from left to right assessing sightlines around the purple monoliths blocking my view.

The whistle.

There is a noticeable dip in volume from the close crowd, even so there are still shouts for quiet. As the last band of the night, we should be accorded a few minutes of valedictory respect.

Two palms rise in the centre: cornet up.

A hand, fingers raised, is presented to the three sides of the band: two bars in.

The baton is held aloft, the focus of all eyes. That slender stick attacks the air, one, two, one. It is raised again, big breath. It drives down hard. Daah dede Dahde Dahde duhdedede dah Daah... and the opening fanfare has passed.

I take the mouthpiece off my lips for the first cornet solo, I don't play again until the bass solo - bars that will haunt my dreams for decades to come. After the drama we creep quietly to the section's final climactic phrase.

The trio opens with the second of the cornet solos. I knuckle down to a bout of delicate um pahs with the older boy on my right. Each of us takes a turn through the piano repeats. Nudging me with his elbow, he indicates he is passing on the duty. We double up for the run up to the end of the trio. This is finished in a sort of breathless horror as we realise we have to start from the top, full force, once more.

Staggering through the opening section again, I succumb to a mounting and debilitating fatigue. My lips turn to rubber; it can't be over soon enough.

In the end it is over all too soon. As the baton describes a closing circle, I realise that Senator has finished for the last time. Even so, we keep the instruments in place for a few more beats, as if there is an unscripted bar of final silence. We attend to the chords decay as if to a catastrophic vibration in fragile glass. The impact of that last note must remain intact.

Tremendous applause, cheers all around. But even as we turn to look and drink it all in there is less to see.

The crowd is turning, departing, retreating back down the lane. Grouping into reflective twos and threes we slowly follow in their footsteps. After a cautious assessment of our performance, not our strongest (since it was the ninth of the evening there was no way it could ever be), our consensus is that it was good enough. As it turns out we have underestimated the quality of our playing; at the next rehearsal we will be told that on the night we were judged

179

to be the best youth band. We will also be told that we have made history as the first youth band to win the prize for best local band. Some bigger noses will be put firmly out of joint.

By the time we reach the high street it has already emptied. Only the slumped casualties of the tenth pint and the walking wounded of a hard day's drinking remain. The band trudges through a different village, one that is reluctantly, slowly sobering.

Whilst no-one was looking, Whit Friday drifted off into the night. It faded like the land of faerie and closed to mortals for another year. Having only passed through thirteen years, that seems like eternity to me.

Nostalgia

There is a spectre haunting this book, the spectre of nostalgia. Any project of sentimental significance must be driven by it at some level.

Nostalgia was a disease invented by the Swiss doctor Joseph Hofer in 1688. The name is derived from the Greek words *nostos,* meaning to return home, and *algos,* pain. The term described a physical condition Hofer observed in Swiss soldiers, symptoms included: nausea; lung problems and even cardiac arrests. Bouts of nostalgia were triggered by familiar sounds such as alp horns or cow bells.

As nostalgia became fashionable and the diagnosis spread across Europe, a notable group of sufferers were Scottish soldiers rendered maudlin and lachrymose by the sound of bagpipes. I find the sound of bagpipes brings tears to my eyes too, but perhaps for different reasons.

It is generally considered that nostalgia was the catalyst for the emergence of another sensibility, that of nationalism. Nationalism found its first expression in the writings of Johan Gottfried von Herder in the second half of the eighteenth century. The boundaries of European states at this time were nothing if not fluid and so his was a sensibility of culture: of language and music; of heritage and geography – it was rooted in experience. Herder's nationalism was not political in the sense we might understand it today.

Isaiah Berlin credits Herder with a populist perspective; he coined the term *Volksgeist* to invoke the "spirit of the people", the sense of a collective identity. His celebration of the particular is found in movements promoting the preservation of song, dance and national costume. The national language campaigns in countries such as Wales and Scotland owe a debt to Herder. Likewise, a concern for identity propelled the Brothers' Grimm to collect their folk tales and fairy stories.

In England, at the turn of the twentieth century, musicologists such as Cecil Sharp became worried that industrialisation and urbanisation were wiping out traditional folk songs. Later in the century there was a fascination with folk culture as a "true" and authentic alternative to the synthetic culture produced by the mass media.

For Herder, nationalism was originally an idea about a people, their history, the place they inhabited and the way of life they had evolved.

As European national borders became settled, particularly in the twentieth century, nationalism often became an idea of a political identity rather than a cultural one. The nadir of political nationalism was obviously Nazi Germany. It is worth noting that the Nazis were aware of the cultural aspects of Herder's thought and incorporated the idea of *Das Volk* (the people) into their ideology. However, Herder's nationalism was decidedly un-militaristic. This may be because living at the time and in the places he did, he understood all too clearly the destructive consequences of war and the trauma of military occupation.

Herder's writings were matched by a complementary perspective in the thoughts of an English writer of Irish heritage, Edmund Burke. Burke laid the foundations for an English notion of culture as tradition and developed his philosophy in *Reflections on the Revolution in France*. This was, as the title makes clear, an analysis of the possible outcomes of the French Revolution, but it was also a defence of what Burke saw as the English way of life. It is because of this that Burke is considered by many to be the father of Conservatism.

Not everyone shared Burke's horror at events across the channel, some were delighted at the havoc it would cause the old enemy, others were envious. Many public figures of the day celebrated the revolution because they saw it as creating the model society of the future. The French Revolution was the mature political expression of the age of reason, the so-called Enlightenment, the movement of science and philosophy that was sweeping 18th century Europe.

In the immediate aftermath of the French Revolution, Burke made some bold predictions. He was concerned that by completely sweeping away a whole regime, and replacing it with a new one, the French were losing traditions and skills of governance that had taken centuries to evolve. This was famously summarised as "We are afraid to put men to live and trade each on his own private stock of reason; because we suspect that this stock in each man is small, and that the individuals would do better to avail themselves of the general bank and capital of nations, and of ages."

Burke suggested it would be impossible to expect a completely new regime with new institutions to spring up, step into the breach created by the revolution, and smoothly govern such a large country. He prophesied that there would be much bloodshed, later borne out by the Terror, and that this instability would lead France to war with its neighbours, which also ultimately proved to be correct.

In opposition to the radical re-creation of society that was taking place in France, Burke set out to defend tradition. Jesse Norman summarises this in his biography of Burke:

Society was the product not principally of reason but of affection, built up from below: "to be attached to the subdivision, to love the little platoon we belong to in society, is... the first link in the series by which we proceed towards a love to our country and to mankind," And its domain, its sphere of moral concern, was not a person, or a group or class, or even a generation, but the social order itself, persisting over time. Society was "a partnership not only between those who are living, but between those who are living, those who are dead, and those who are to be born."

It is easy to take Burke's position as a manifesto for forelock tugging deference. He was indeed a staunch defender of the institutions of church and monarchy, in England of course these were and are still inseparable. However, as Terry Eagleton points out, he was a prominent critic of the English occupation of Ireland and vehemently denounced the atrocities committed by the East India Company. He also realised that the style of rule in the American colonies was indefensible and likely to lead to a revolution. At home he argued that the institutions of governance and tradition needed to be flexible to allow for renewal. Nevertheless, there were limits to the flexibility of the English establishment; it would spend the next century and a half fighting a sometimes bloody rearguard action to resist campaigns for universal suffrage and the dignity of working people.

Burke argued the social order needs to be felt in a meaningful way in daily life - in what he termed "the little platoons." This is an argument for a deep sense of culture, but this sense of culture can only have meaning if it is part of the habits of a community. Culture is pretty thin if it merely boils down to how you travel to work, the programmes you watch on TV or how you cook your potatoes; a culture needs cultivating.

According to Isaiah Berlin, Herder's beliefs, like Burke's, ran contrary to the grain of his time; he didn't believe in the type of grand universal ideal that had driven the French Revolution. He also believed that different cultures and different societies could be governed by different values and principles but the fact that these may not be compatible was a reason to respect the experience of others rather than reject it.

If Herder was transported to the England of the twenty-first century he would be looking for the ways in which historical patterns of regional culture and experience were being expressed in the present. Burke would be looking to see how the spirit of the nation manifested in the little platoons. Both would have good reason to regard the receding of the industrial identity of the North as a moment of crisis.

If national, regional or social identities are threatened or lost people will seek to mend these gaps in forms of culture – this might be done individually or collectively. In *Nostalgia and Anthropology* David Berliner suggests that nostalgia usually traps the nostalgic subject on one side of a historical break. Bearing this in mind, perhaps it is no surprise that political nationalism has become a seductive means of plugging the cultural or psychic holes left by the changes in society over the past half century. It goes without saying that political nationalism should be treated with caution. It has the knack of rousing passions, therefore it needs to bear little relation to lived experience nor, it must be said, to actual historical fact: the emotion is everything. This symbolic manipulation is nothing if not nostalgic.

—

In *The Future of Nostalgia*, Svetlana Boym considers the two roots of the word nostalgia. Restorative nostalgia is rooted in *nostos* and seeks to rebuild the lost home. Ironically, she suggests that restorative nostalgics don't identify themselves as nostalgic as they are busy restoring their version of the past, perhaps making America great again. Reflective nostalgics, rooted in *algos,* wallow in the ruins; they wistfully mourn a past age. In England the leading exponent of this form of nostalgia is Iain Sinclair who returns to a vanished London in the pages of books such as, *Lights Out for the Territory* and *Hackney, That Rose Red Empire.*

Modern nostalgics are children of the clock. Time is no longer the cyclic procession of seasons and years that would have been the world of the medieval peasant; a world that always returned to the point where it began; an organic world defined by natural processes.

Nostalgia only exists when time has been mechanised: measured out into tiny packets and distributed along the finely calibrated track of material progress that starts in the past and ends in the future. We place ourselves on this timeline and stand in the station looking up and down the track, waiting for events to arrive or watching their tail-lights recede in the distance. For us time is linear, hurtling forward like an express train. As such, nostalgia is not a regret for lost time but a form of anxiety, a panic attack caused by our alienation from natural, organic, biological time. Nostalgia is the natural condition for those trapped within the mechanism of the clock.

If nostalgia is usually framed as retrospective, a longing for the past, it should also be considered with its opposite, a concern for the future. The future is always uncertain and is an ideal territory on which to focus apprehensions and anxieties. At the moment, there seem to be a lot of them to choose from which leads into one of the pitfalls of nostalgia, catastrophism. My own views on the state of the brass band movement have been heavily influenced by the catastrophic school of thought, with at least some justification.

The subjects of nostalgia may be real, however, it is a project of the imagination not of hard history; it is a reconstruction of situations, memories and desires. For the nostalgic the past is a place that is fixed and no longer amenable to change, manipulation or the gross uncertainties of the moment. Nostalgia is a model railway of the soul where the trains always run on time. The subjects of nostalgia are random, arbitrary and personal. It is always partial and incomplete, bringing some elements to the fore whilst conveniently and carefully forgetting others.

If the past is another country it is one I have no particular wish to return to; I protest that I am not nostalgic. This is a memory from around the time I went to primary school. It takes place about half a mile from Rochdale town centre where the road has been excavated to allow traffic to pass beneath an ugly, box railway bridge...

–

It was late in the afternoon on a heavy grey, wet, winter day, and as the bus approached the bridge there was a sort of eclipse. The black sooty walls closed in on each side and the leaden viaduct devoured the top deck. This should have been a brief transit from the light, but as we emerged from the shadows the darkness seemed to return as the midnight filth of a smoking mill reared up to our right and a dark wall loomed on the left. This claustrophobic vision of unrelieved hell somehow came to embody an essence of permanence and solidity for me. It was possibly the most unequivocal thing I had ever seen, it's a shame it wasn't beautiful.

A few years later the mill was demolished and the site redeveloped with low rise industrial sheds which were both insubstantial and inconsequential when compared with their predecessor. The road was diminished by the loss of the mill and the area as a whole seemed to lose structure and focus. The mill was cheap, ugly and unremarkable and, apart from the sense in which it has been remembered here, is neither missed nor mourned.

As a snapshot of Rochdale this tableau seems unfair, although it will satisfy anyone who feels there must be a touch of grim northernness in a book about brass bands. To show the best of Rochdale at that moment it would be better to turn the bus around and head into town. A few hundred yards back, at the junction with Milnrow Road, was the splendid Odeon cinema. Originally the Rialto, and opened by Our Gracie in the late 1920s, it was everything a cinema should be with its tiled façade and gilded, plaster-moulded interior.

Carrying on downhill the bus would pass Hills Economy Stores, already struggling to compete with the underwear at Marks & Spencer's. Glancing across the road as it joined Drake Street, there was the stolid and substantial Deco-ish frontage of the Rochdale Observer. Close by was the Victorian elegance of a glass arcade: the entrance to Iveson's department store. Further down, opposite the junction to Water Street, the Champness Hall.

The Champness Hall is worthy of a brief pause as it is a significant site for my childhood memories. For many years it hosted a variety of competitions in the always well supported Rochdale Music Festival. The festival was held close to the February half term, and if the heating was not at full capacity the greedy concrete floors sucked any warmth out of both the room and its occupants. Not that most children really noticed because as performers moved to and from the stage everyone else in the room was caught in a whirlwind of glee, running from aisle to aisle and row to row to gossip with friends. These days off school performing with bands, choirs, orchestras and other ensembles were an event to be savoured for which the music played second fiddle – unless you won!

There was something special about these moments; for a day or two each year kids who might not have given each other a second glance in the school corridor were bound together in a higher purpose. Ironed white shirts and tight-knotted ties, polished shoes and fresh haircuts all trooped on stage for five minutes of intense concentration and a burst of applause. The fact that I was able to take so much time off school is an indicator of the scale of involvement of young people in music making within the Rochdale borough at that time.

The Champness Hall also served as the town's concert venue for most forms of music since the main space in the town hall was essentially an empty box with the acoustic of a public lavatory. Indelibly stamped on my memories of the Champness Hall are its unforgiving seats and interminable renditions of the Messiah.

Back on the bus, it seemed that Drake Street's destination was the ABC, the largest of the town's cinemas. But it avoided this conclusion and instead swung left into South Parade stopping at the front door of another department store, Howarth's, offering passengers a view of the town's banks.

I was told that for many years the main bus and tram terminus was on the Esplanade, a vast open roadway cum sprawling civic square between the town hall and the Portland stone elegance of the central post office. Next to the post office the cenotaph gardens were finely framed by the Victorian library and art gallery.

These open spaces were concealing the town's dark secret, the River Roch, which runs through the valley bottom between the hills and slopes on which Rochdale rests. This accident of geography cleaves the town and historically prevented the creation of a coherent centre. In the early twentieth century the river was culverted to develop routes for the new tram network. As the Esplanade petered out of town it could look over to, as no-one in possession of a functioning vocabulary would ever describe it, the verdant sward of Dane Street, home of Rochdale Cricket Club.

Running off South Parade is Yorkshire Street. Visits to town at this point would incorporate a trip to the wooden stalls of the nearby outdoor market, I can't remember much about the adjacent indoor market.

The markets were the true focus of the town: an eddying pool where the road flowed in from South Parade; a lagoon of commerce that caught the pedestrian cascades washing down the hill.

A little higher up Yorkshire Street was the butcher's shop. After queuing for meat, I would be offered a sweet and a pat on the head by the jovial proprietor, we would see him the next day in church. After a while our visits became less frequent and I divined from my mother that the butcher may have harboured devices and desires in his own heart of a wholly unchristian nature.

Further up Yorkshire Street was the essential destination of Cheetham Street. For a penny in the slot in the toy shop window an electric train would complete its mesmerising circuits: disappearing into tunnels; crossing over bridges and cruising through a trim station. Things didn't stay that way.

The council initially retrenched the town centre by demolishing the markets and assenting to an unlovable concrete shopping precinct hosting a new covered market with fibreglass stalls. This quickly came to resemble the set from a dystopian science fiction epic, although Michael York and Jenny Agutter never chased each other across its brown tiles and into Top Shop.

The recessions of the mid to late seventies saw the shops I have mentioned wither and contract. The early eighties saw them all off and the derelict Rialto "accidentally" burned down to be replaced by an MFI flat pack box. The ABC has become a Wetherspoon's and many of the banks have been converted into wine bars of varying viability. The fortunes of the cricket club sank lower than those of the town's football team and the pitch has been carpeted with the car park of an ASDA supermarket.

Drake St is now fronted by the battered steel shutters of empty premises, charity shops and the inevitable rash of takeaways. The Rochdale Observer seems to have been pulled into this whirlpool too, its offices and printing hall long since abandoned and plastered with the plywood sheets of the emergency glazier. There is one note of optimism, the Champness Hall is in the hands of a community trust and renovated to a high standard. It appears to be a far more comfortable and inviting venue than the one I remember from the 1970s.

The decline of the town centre economy was contrasted by the ascent of the motor car. In the late 1960s, to accommodate increased traffic, a dual carriageway had been cut across the top edge of town amputating Falinge and Spotland, where my grandmother lived. On the other side, the banks of John St were washed with the alluvial debris of a concrete cascade that powered down through the traffic lights and pushed its tide up Mellor St. The two routes converged to cauterise the top of Yorkshire St.

The logic of the car dictated that parking and shopping should be indivisible; successive developments have attempted, and largely failed, to consummate this union. Unfortunately, planning laws and the credit boom of the 1980s created more lucrative opportunities in the out-of-town supermarkets and megastore sheds - not forgetting those later alien crash sites of retail commerce such as Trafford, White Rose and Meadowhall. The other factor affecting the fortunes of Rochdale town centre was the pull of the bright lights of Bury market. For those with only a hazy grasp of the geography of South East Lancashire, Bury is a small town near Heywood.

—

The ghosts of Rochdale town centre may make a textbook case for nostalgia, but it is only a general context for my memories rather than their essence. This is to be found on the street, in particular that generic Northern or maybe urban trope of the open road where children could gather and safely play. We were rarely disturbed, only occasionally stopping our games of rialio and chain tig to make way for whirring milk floats or weary bin men.

My first experience of sociable play was in the street. As I got older our territory expanded into games on school playing fields, forays onto neighbouring roads and explorations of Racky's pond in the gardens of the demolished manor on Broad Lane. I also encountered the young arsonists down the road and was instructed in the techniques of fire raising on the waste ground at the back of their houses. As primary school ended the adventures ranged further afield, across busy main roads and onto the canal towpath.

As a teenager it was interesting, as well as economically necessary, to walk everywhere. I became attuned to the fine details of Rochdale's urban landscape. Features of my regular routes included: the bowling green on

Sedgely Avenue; the view of the Edwardian primary school down Clarendon Street; the cobbles of Watkin Street; and the ginnel between the two with the alsatian that bit one of the twins. I always made a point of stopping at the window of the antiquarian bookshop on Oldham Road, an establishment that was far too exotic for its location; its very presence seemed like a spur to self-improvement.

Acting as informal way-markers were the canal bridge on Well i' th' Lane and the mature trees in the avenues of homes fit for heroes off Milkstone Road. Somewhere near there I'm sure there was a mural by Walter Kershaw. All were on my route to Tuesday night band practice.

These impressions are certainly not startling and will have no significance for any but those with some link to the area, but the landmarks, observations and incidental memories gave my walks a rhythm and structure and even an emotional course. It became possible to become lost in thought and be well advanced on a journey before I became fully aware of where I was.

The walks became a matter of muscular reflex as much as mental mapping; there is a sense in which I embodied the place in which I lived. If I experienced a physical identification with my neighbourhood through solitary walking, I experienced a social connection by walking with others.

I would never have considered it this way at the time, but the institution with which I had the most enduring contact was the local church and its Sunday school. Many of the other children there would be familiar from school, even if they were not in the same class or year group. Whilst they may have been familiar, the only contact I would have with most of them would be for that hour on a Sunday morning.

As I got older the Sunday school sessions would dovetail into the church services. The congregation always seemed to justify the capacity of the building, even if it was never packed to the rafters. Although there was one day when it always was because we combined with the local Methodists. They not only filled the gaps in the pews but the standing room too, any space left over was for the banners. I remember this clearly because one year a shaft of light cut through the gloom, illuminating the embroidered lamb.

On these days, the service in church was brief because out on the streets the procession would be broken with stops for hymns and prayers. I can't remember the exact route but recall walking down Oldham Road. Later we stopped on Turf Hill Road so the curate could climb a telephone box to deliver his sermon.

As a child I might have held one of the guy ropes for the larger banners. When I was a little older, I might have been playing with the youth band from the local middle school.

Some elements of the parade were not strictly religious. I seem to recall every year a different girl, with her retinue, was appointed as Queen of the May.

This annual procession was not a trivial event. In the terms of Euclidean geometry, we could be said to be describing our world. As a church we were marking and celebrating the significant points of the parish boundaries. By describing the physical world we were also describing ourselves as a religious community and as a specific part of a broader secular community.

This tour of the parochial perimeter seemed an emphatic way of saying, "This is who we are and this is where we belong". This was one moment when, like in a drawing by William Blake, the clouds parted, the sun shone, the world was illuminated and the cosmic order revealed.

This was Whitsuntide.

1992

"One becomes aware of the collective frameworks of memories when one distances oneself from one's community or when that community enters the world of twilight. Collective frameworks of memory are rediscovered in mourning."

Svetlana Boym

The psychologist Lev Vygotsky stated that meaning is not generated by literal memories but by an interplay of symbols. But symbols are not just words and images, there is a more powerful symbolic language. Visiting a frail and fading Uncle recently I asked him what he did all day long and he said he looked out of the window. I asked him what he thought about, and he said, "Music".

—

My first bout of brass band nostalgia occurred one gloriously blue June afternoon in 1992. Family friends had moved to Dobcross and we were invited over for Whit Friday. I was keen to go as I realised it was nearly fifteen years since I had last been to the contest. When we arrived, I was thrown into confusion, everyone wanted to hang around in the kitchen talking. It didn't seem to bother them that the bands were already playing on the green, there was no urgency and maybe no understanding. I was in a dream, shouting that the house was on fire, but no one could hear me.

I wandered into the village alone. Grimethorpe took to the stand playing *Knight Templar*, it was early in the contest and the performance was close to perfect. I was deeply affected; it was overwhelming, like trying to look at the sun, beautiful but unbearable. I could hardly contain the emotions but didn't understand what they were. Brass bands were something I had left in the past...

Morning

Even though we had known for months that Katie was not available, Chairman Jack had not given up hope the band would make it out on Whit Friday. With three weeks to go the coach company put their foot down and said they wanted the booking confirmed. Since there were no other options for principal cornet, Russ had disappeared after the areas and Sue and I aren't good enough, we had to face facts. Plus, there were also a euphonium and a trombone to find. The final announcement in the band room split us between relief and disappointment: between those for whom Whit Friday was a drag and a chore and those for whom it was almost a raison d'etre.

At the end of rehearsal, I mentioned my disappointment to Alan, not realising that he had played with Brownhill in their last period in the championship section. He told me he still had links there, understood they needed a cornet or two, and would put me in touch. This would give me a Whit Friday in Saddleworth with a Saddleworth band; at that point I didn't really understand what that meant.

Alan was sympathetic when I talked to him about it weeks later, he said, "If you haven't played with one of the village bands you just don't understand the sheer enormity of it." Enormity, mmm. In the years since then, having had the opportunity to do Whit Friday with other Saddleworth bands, I also came to appreciate that a day with Brownhill was a case apart.

The contest starts in the afternoon, so I have taken the precaution of booking a day off work. This might be overly cautious, but I want to avoid a last-minute rush and panic. In recent weeks authoritarian traffic exclusion signs have sprung up on all the roads into Saddleworth; a visitor to the area may be forgiven for assuming it is about to be put under martial law.

A week before the contest, I phone Malcolm, the band secretary, to confirm arrangements, "You'll need to be at the band room by eight thirty at the latest."

I'm confused. "That won't give us much time at the contests, will it?" This is when I realise the scale of my commitment.

"No, eight thirty in the morning."

It seems I have left it a bit late to say I had only been expecting to turn up in the afternoon.

By the time the big day arrives I have a better idea of what's in store. I've read through both Alec Greenhalgh's definitive history of Whit Friday, *Hail, Smiling Morn,* and Henry Livings classic account of Dobcross Band, *That the Medals and the Baton be Put On View.* Livings was the band secretary for many years and describes the origins of the village's contest in 1968. It was a means of healing a rift between the various churches and the band. The United Effort organises the walk, the afternoon recreations and the contest to this day.

Brownhill village holds many similarities with Dobcross; it's built on a hillside with a central green reached by narrow snaking lanes. Their Whit Friday follows a routine common to most of the local villages. It is customary to begin the day with a short service in the square above the green, but not this year. Instead, the congregation is packed into the church hall to avoid the appropriately biblical deluge.

St Thomas's church hall hums with hymns from the youth and senior bands, homilies and prayers from the clergy. As always, the bands play the Saddleworth hymn *Silver Hill* and remember those who have departed in the past year. With the fading of the closing prayers, we brace ourselves to face the sodden street, reckoning without divine intervention. As the hall doors are opened to inspect the weather, the storm hesitates then loses confidence. Instead of the deluge there is drizzle.

The band sergeant insists, no matter what, we will march in uniform not raincoats, "We'll worry about the consequences afterwards". But those who expected to be drowned are dry. If the sun is still a long way off at least there is the glory of *Hail, Smiling Morn* [arr. W. Rimmer]. The steep streets are tramped up and tramped down to drum up the procession.

The character of the village shapes the character of the morning; the spirit of other villages is also formed by their own particular geography. My favourite memory of Uppermill is an essential Whit Friday one: lining up in formation on the wide open, early, empty street; the band waiting for the snare and bass drum to strike up the kindling cavalcade.

If the tramp round Brownhill seems a bit of a hike whilst blowing it is harder on the lips than the legs. Even after half an hour on third cornet I am wondering how I am going to blow a note in the evening. Walking, we welcome more people to the parade from churches and houses. The top Methodists give respite with their faff and kerfuffle manhandling prams and pushchairs onto the road. Soon their banners billow aloft, like galleon sails striking out for adventure.

It is with relief we pass the Duck and descend to the Fleece, turning to march on towards the Huddersfield Road. There is welcome discord approaching the roundabout as our sound clashes with the bands arriving from Dobcross and Diggle. At last, we are a proper procession.

Railway arches frame our progress confirming us in our roles and tradition; we enter the ritual moment as others have done before us for a century and more. Under those vaulted, damp stones the drummer beats the skin with vigour; we fill our lungs and blow for the echo passing to the marching lines behind. Children shout to hear their voices reflected, giving their gift to those who follow.

Approaching the first houses of Uppermill, the river becomes a torrent seeping from the road; lapping up the pavement it merges with the clapping spectators. Slowing, feeling the press of the crowd, our flood is backed up against a great dam wall. I take a breather. As far as the eye can see are people packed like the dense crowd breaking away from a football match. And now we can barely shuffle.

Turning to each other, we joke about the state of our lips: how our comrades, their lines finished beyond fatigue, have saved the later marches from collapse. We berate ourselves for the perennial error of belting out those first marches for the sheer exuberant hell of it and leaving nothing for later. The open air always tricks me like that.

Becalmed in a benign sea, we watch the opposing bands from Greenfield and Uppermill forge their path down the spillway to the park: a shallow river falling off the weir. Inching forward, we are recognised by the crowd and cheered. Suddenly, there is space, there is room to march. We are on the quarterdeck once more, lifted to a fuller and brighter sound than we believe our bruised lips can blow. Squeezed through the gap, pushed down the slope, the wave breaks in the park where we finally stop, leave our instruments and find a cup of tea.

—

The service in the park is the real heart of Whit Friday. Whitsun was, along with Christmas and Easter, one of the three principal festivals of the Christian calendar but over the years it has lost prestige. It is a British term for the feast of Pentecost, ten days after Ascension. Pentecost marks the point where the Holy Spirit descended on the disciples, gifting them all the languages of the world to go forth and spread the gospel. This is why Pentecostalist churches prize their congregants speaking in tongues.

Pentecost is sometimes called the birth of the Church and became known as Whit Sunday in Britain. It is not entirely clear what the origins of the term are. There seem to be correspondences to terms for the festival in Norse languages and also suggestions that it is a corruption of the word wit (as in wise). Some suggest that celebrants wore white vestments on this occasion: White Sunday.

Whit Sunday is the principal day of Whitsuntide, the Whitsun bank holiday traditionally followed the day after. Because Whitsun relates to the religious calendar, and not the secular, the bank holiday occurred in different weeks each year [a movable feast]. In 1978 the secular holiday was formalised to occur at the same point, towards the end of May. The religious festival still shuttles along stops between mid-May and mid-June.

For much of the twentieth century, the Whitsun festival was celebrated across the British Isles in the form of street parades. An internet trawl will produce local history archives of monochrome street parades from anywhere near the turn of the century until the late 1960s. The majority of those processing would have allegiances to churches and local societies; the earlier photos often show crowds lining the streets. These may have been religious events but they clearly allowed communities to celebrate their territories by parading through the significant thoroughfares and, as in my childhood experience, circumnavigating the parish boundary.

According to David Tipper and Hannah Haynes in *De Balderston II,* prior to the establishment of the church in my childhood parish, members of the local community would have headed to Rochdale parish church for the town's Whit walks. It was not just large settlements that celebrated the festival in this way. An excellent visual document of a Whit walk in the 1950s is found in the film archive of Miss Lucy Fairbank of the Colne Valley near Huddersfield. She shot clear footage of the Wellhouse Methodist walk being supported by Linthwaite Band, Wellhouse qualifies more as a hamlet than a village.

Saddleworth is unique in holding out with the Friday processional tradition. Some neighbouring areas have reluctantly conceded to modern demands and retreated to the Sunday; local bands are recruited for these walks too. Alec Greenhalgh reports that in the 1980s Saddleworth was put under pressure to follow suit but held its ground. The push for change has been led by the increasing congestion caused by the car.

It feels to me that in many ways the car has become a restriction to mobility rather than an aid - spend some time on the M62 around 8:00 a.m. and see if you agree. Whilst motorway madness may be familiar to many, the car has pernicious effects closer to home. Streets that have become car parks are no longer suitable meeting places and playgrounds. There is something fundamental to community identity to be able to collectively claim and celebrate a place by walking through it together in a conscious and deliberate manner.

The value of the Whit tradition goes beyond the chance to process through streets with banners and brass bands. Henry Livings and others mention how children might get new clothes for Whitsun. They might visit their neighbours in the hope of a compliment and a penny or two, cementing or antagonising the relationship with those who lived next door. Whit Friday supports other activities and traditions; in Dobcross, for example, the community doesn't just parade, it often rounds the day off with picnics, sports and games. All these require coordination and organising and no doubt a small army [of, presumably, women] to butter the sandwiches and bake the cakes: the United Effort.

As the Whit Friday evening contests have become more international [even attracting bands from Australia and Japan] some of the visitors have been invited to join the morning celebrations. However, it will be one of the local bands that process to Uppermill park that plays the hymns for the service. Even the most devout members of the other bands will not be hanging around to appreciate the mellifluous tones of their rivals, not when the Con club has just opened its bar. Whilst the pursuit of refreshment will be paramount, anyone with a local banding history will be looking for familiar faces in the crowd.

After the service it takes over twenty minutes to get the procession out of the park. Dobcross consolidate junior, training and senior bands into one seamless crimson crocodile for the journey home. Brownhill are envious of the scale of their parade, even though we have had a good rest, I am not convinced we have fully recovered from the earlier march.

Fatigue tips music out of liars and there is a bobbing in the ranks. The rearguard swoop and stoop to collect the hymn books and march pads which are passed up the line to their embarrassed owners. Seniors are reminded to curb the expletives, there are children present. All the bands head for the railway viaduct, Diggle, Dobcross and ourselves then head on home but the others double back. This means that not only is there the joy of the blast under the arch but the opportunity to test your musicianship in a band collision.

The fun for the bands this morning is that at the moment of acoustic combination it is impossible to separate the two marches. The skill is to keep count so that at the point of separation your band is still playing together.

After the viaduct the bands can finally down cornets and walk to the solitary beat of the bass drum. As we near the top of the long lane leading into the village centre, a march is chosen and we play the procession to the band rooms. With a second wind and the walls of the houses pressing close, the village vibrates to our rich resonances - as it has done on and off for the past 150 years.

The band falls out and we amble along to dump uniforms and instruments. I feel a tug from this profound immersion and wonder if I am wallowing in nostalgia. Perhaps, but on the other hand, perhaps not, because my youthful banding experiences were not in this village, not with this band. They did not so tightly bind music, people and place. Of those walking with me most have a Brownhill connection: some have moved here bringing accents forged south of Watford; others were born or raised in the village or have risen through the ranks of the youth band; there are some willing helpers who have travelled further than me this morning. Whilst this is a regular job for an established band, there is no-one I chat with who is not at some level in awe of the significance of what we are involved in. I can't shake the thought that this is the epitome of village banding.

Throughout the day I catch myself thinking about the events from one remove. I compare what's happening with how I would like some idealised memory of the day to be and it is almost as if I become an actor in a drama about Whit Friday. I imagine what theatrical grand conclusion it might lead to, the irony is that I know how it will end and that it will be worth the wait.

Evening

It's a late Whit Friday this year and those early clouds have parted. Everyone has spent the past fortnight glued to long range weather forecasts. Until yesterday they had been dominated by black clouds and heavy raindrops, but with a deft swerve the worst has moved elsewhere. The breeze has now dropped and the temperature risen to that region of the thermometer marked perfect. Soon, the afternoon is rolling on, the first of the evening contests begin at four.

Swifts scream over the square. We loll insouciant against walls and railings, tipping our caps to rakish angles (we are the only band out tonight who still wear them). Someone wonders if Brownhill is twinned with North Korea, or Norman Wisdom. If we were conducted by Sergio Leone we'd be hunched under ponchos and sombreros, haunted by a line from a lonely harmonica.

Giant snail shells, crumpled tubas, sit upturned on the cobbles and setts. Of all band instruments the basses seem to lead the hardest life. As a child it was rare to encounter any that were perfect and many looked as if they had been beaten out of a junior metalwork class. Whilst bass players are the butt of band jokes, some mitigation should be allowed for the problem of manoeuvring delicate instruments through difficult spaces, such as a coach gangway.

Greenfield

Basses at the front, cornets at the back. Instruments and supplies are stashed under seats. Home bakers have brought cakes, the family minded sandwiches and picnics. Idlers or opportunists discuss plans for refreshment stops. There is beer on the bus, a bad sign.

Brassed Off has reinforced the Whit Friday reputation of the boozy band. I see no reasonable objection to the occasional swift half during an extended wait, but a clear head is essential for a classy performance. If drinking is the primary objective, it is much better to soak up the atmosphere as part of the crowd. A few big drinkers in a competitive band can make it a frustrating night for their comrades. Someone proudly shows me a sports bottle full of gin and tonic; my heart sinks.

Our itinerary has been mulled over for several weeks. Even so, dissent and dispute persist in debating the best route, best starting village, must visits and must avoids. Some consider the classic crossing to start in Lees, on the outskirts of Oldham, followed by a drift across Saddleworth for a Denshaw denouement. One of the problems with this is that the evening may begin with a huge logjam followed from village to village.

On a day like today Lees will have a strong crowd for the street march, starting the evening with a rousing cheer. This was not the case on my last visit, a torrential downpour had driven everyone home. Another reason to start in Lees is that the chippy does a very fine rag pudding.

Whatever is announced, the route is always provisional and subject to on-the-spot change. Jean and her daughter Lola, our excellent principal cornet, seem to be the undisputed captain and sergeant major. Nothing moves without their say so.

This year we start at Greenfield and miss out Top Mossley. According to Alec Greenhalgh, Mossley was one of the three original contest venues. As the contest has become increasingly popular it has been split in two between Saddleworth and Tameside. Tameside takes the historic contests of Mossley and Stalybridge, Saddleworth the status and the scenery which attract most of the best bands and the biggest crowds. Tameside's lower profile means bands competing on that circuit don't have to waste too much time queuing.

At 3:30 Greenfield is uncommonly quiet, if we returned at seven the Chew Valley Road would be packed. Whilst the tactical start here is sound it is a waste of the best street march in Saddleworth. Starting outside the Con Club is a long straight road that takes the band into the *trio*.

Street and contest marches are printed on an A5 card: part one, from the top; halfway down is the second part, the *trio*; at the end of the *trio* is the *D.C.*, *da capo*, to the top; and the first part is played again. At other contests, notably Lydgate, the band is lucky to get past the end of the first line.

Even though we arrive half an hour before the start, there are five bands already booked before us. Over the rooftops, from waste ground, distant car parks and the entrance to the park the robust passages of famous marches ring out. With time to kill we take a cue from the early arrivals and have a last look at the test piece. Ahead of us in the queue are local rivals Uppermill, packed to the rafters with championship deps; we applaud them as they set off. When it is our turn, as a local band, we are accorded an especially warm welcome from the thin throng in the curb-side deck chair encampment.

Of the two marches the bands will play tonight the street marches are the easiest: less technically demanding and at a slower tempo. The solo cornets grumble if the melody rises above the stave as this is more taxing than the lower range. *Army of the Nile* hits top B within the first few bars, that's asking for trouble; many bands omit the first phrase of that particular march.

If a band has strength in depth in the cornet section, roles may be reversed; the lower cornets might play the solo parts to save the front row's lips. Some principal cornets might not play a note as they march down the road. At times it can be tricky marching and playing, if the breathing is mistimed the player can be left sitting on a reservoir of bad air or gasping for breath. The movement and the road surface can combine to make the sound, how to put it, a bit wobbly.

Many of the marches betray military leanings, *The Chieftain, Death or Glory, 1914, Standard of St George*. Others have more ruggedly romantic connotations such as *Slaidburn* or *Westward Ho*. Tonight we play *On the Quarterdeck* by Kenneth Alford who also wrote many of the marches listed above.

Alford was the nom de plume of Frederick Joseph Ricketts, a director of the Royal Marines Band. His composing heyday spanned from the start of the first World War to early in the second. Ricketts' most famous march is *Colonel Bogey*, later adapted as the theme tune to the film *The Bridge on the River Kwai*. *On the Quarterdeck* is in 6/8 rather than the usual 2/4 which gives it a certain swagger.

Whilst the Greenfield street march is not to be missed, the glorious spring afternoon transforms the contest arena into a very English paradise. Saddleworth Moor is the often forbidding but now beautiful backdrop, the foreground a lush, green park. In the middle-distance children chase or pester parents for a taste of the cooking meat whose greasy smoke drifts by our noses. Beyond is the cricket ground with a good and lively crowd: the smack of leather on willow; the shouts of raucous appeal.

Sheltering under the horse-chestnut trees, we wait to be called in front of the occluded adjudicator in the curtained caravan. We follow on from a Swiss band, cuckoo clock precise with step change dynamics through a crescendo, *piano, mezzo piano, mezzo forte, forte.*

The Greenfield contest is not our finest moment. It is a greatest hits of musical mistakes: hesitancy; rushing; poor dynamic control; split notes; missed entries. Everyone is of a mind to chalk it up to experience as a test piece test run, this is only allowable if we learn from those mistakes.

Delph

Approaching the Yorkshire aorta of Uppermill we head to Delph (although Saddleworth is really in Lancashire). The contests have closed the area to road traffic with the exception of buses, bands and the emergency services. For a moment it seems that our safe passage is not a foregone conclusion; coaches are being rigidly marshalled through a militia checkpoint in a failed state. Jean acts as our translator guide and sets off to talk a way through. We don't have to wait long until we are waved on.

Delph disappoints. Anticipation had pencilled in a generous wait: half a pint of mild in the band club; black peas in the Methodist hall. That rarest of Lancashire delicacies is always slathered with a powdering of pepper and a torrent of vinegar. Black peas add a particular piquancy to one of the best band atmospheres to be found on Whit Friday.

Unfortunately, there are only three bands in front of us; we'd better get our skates on, it will soon be our turn. Indignant, I am almost minded to submit an official complaint. I am not alone, others have also banked on Delph as a refreshment stop. Ushering the band into line Lola tries to fob us off with the lame excuse that we will be able to fill up elsewhere, I for one am not convinced. Putting the grumbles to one side it is always a pleasure to play in Delph.

Next stop Denshaw.

Denshaw

Denshaw is a late-comer to the contest circuit. This may be because the village is too small to provide the close squares that are a charming feature of Delph and Dobcross. It has its fans though, particularly from the Rochdale area; it is peripheral and not subject to the roadblocks of the core villages. Amongst the crowd are my parents, we are in and out so quickly that I have no time to say hello. Even without their feedback I feel our performances are starting to improve.

Coach

As the coach rises above the bowl of Saddleworth I feel the first twang of the full Whit Friday effect, a subtle temporal dislocation. The early start is catching up and I feel a twinge of fatigue. We have been on the road for what seems like hours; I check the time: six o'clock. I protest that it has to be later than that, six o'clock is well before the start of any long night out; Whit Friday is nothing if not a long night out. The castle of concentration crumbles and I enter an unfocussed drift.

"Everyone out!"

Lydgate

The Lydgate contest is based at the back of the vast car park of the vastly extended White Hart pub, weddings a speciality. At last, we are told there is an hour's queue so we can take time off; two of us go and find a quiet room in the pub.

After a while I wonder if we are taking too much of a risk with this extended break. I have anxious visions of being stranded without a coach; no-one else is in sight and my phone is locked in my cornet case. I stumble out of the pub, in the middle distance a band in scarlet uniforms is playing our tune. Oh, dear! The march is so short it's hardly worth bothering with, " I was saving my lip for the contest..."

—

Three bands await their turn on the stand. I am accosted by Super Sue, since Upperthong are having the night off she's come as a spectator. She noticed my absence from the street march, wags her finger and gives me a stern stare. Enquiring about our test piece, I tell her *Knight Templar*, the definitive contest march, written by George Allan.

Allan was a classic example of the amateur autodidact in the mould of Edwin Swift. His day job was painting railway coaches in the works at Shildon, County Durham; he moonlighted as a musician and composer. Allan wrote over seventy marches and the address on the top of a band copy of his march *The Wizard* suggests at least some were self-published.

Marches played on the stand on Whit Friday are known as quick steps because they are played at a fast pace (116 -120 BPM). Most adhere to the

206

2/4 march time and are expected to be played straight to tempo, but they also have almost symphonic ambitions.

The notion of a brisk contest march might summon the brilliance of the works of Sousa but Sousa's marches, whilst challenging, always retain a drum driven sensibility. British contest marches do not and will include a range of moods and styles; the nearest stylistic comparison is the overture. Contest marches test the full range of the ensemble's technical abilities and expose the skills of each section within the band.

Most marches have a strong opening phrase followed by the quiet of a cornet solo. This leads into the first bold repeated passage which will demand some dexterity from the front row and a good deal of rhythmic and harmonic foundation from the rest of the band. Another quiet section, then a loud repeat before the *fine*: the end of the first part and ultimately the piece.

As a front row cornet player, it is impossible not to feel some degree of pressure from the technical demands imposed in the louder passages. However, the expectation is to back off rather than blast forth, it makes crisp articulation easier and also saves lips. Another reason to ease up is that one of these passages is always known as the bass solo; the bottom half of the band is going to go for glory.

Tonight's march is true to its title; *Knight Templar* includes a fair few heraldic flourishes. George Allan's other truly great march, *The Wizard,* has motifs that suggest flashes from the mage's wand. Both have passages with bold rich chords that encompass the breadth of the band. Allan's *Wizard* should not be confused with the street march by William Rimmer.

William Rimmer is Allan's strongest competitor for the contest march crown and *Ravenswood* is the closest rival to *Knight Templar*. *Ravenswood* is also a much harder blow. I fancy that I can always spot a Rimmer march, his complex cornet passages seem to have something of a carnival quality. The most famous example of this is in his street march *Punchinello*. Of his other marches: *Honest Toil* feels more like forced labour; *Viva Burkinshaw!* places a heavy burden on the principal cornet and so is an easier ride for the front row. I quite like *The Cossack,* too.

The rope is unhooked and we are waved in front of the caravan, we don't disgrace ourselves.

Scouthead

We climb higher expecting inclement conditions; Scouthead is notoriously cold. To be precise the contest is Scouthead and Austerlands.

Austerlands rolls around my mind making connections with Austria, Australia and austerity.

When the A62 was a nineteenth century turnpike road it ran through Slaithwaite as Austerlands Road; the name Austerlands can still be clearly seen on the remaining milestones. Oldham library has a wonderful wall-sized photographic panorama of the town under construction in the late nineteenth century. This makes me wonder if in Victorian times Austerlands was the more important place.

Scouthead and Austerlands is a medieval fair ringed with tents and marquees, but no flags fly. Instead, heraldic banners and coats of arms are emblazoned on the breast pockets of challengers jousting with the sounds of metal serpents. They compete gallantly for the favours of the one whose face is concealed behind gauzy curtains in the royal box.

Underfoot, persistent rain will rapidly turn the contest arena's heavy clay into a sticky bog. Memories of my visits here are marked by slithering and sliding in slick mud then shivering against the onslaught of driving storms. However, tonight it is positively balmy. Tropical? steady on! But I almost expect us to be garlanded as we form up on the road.

No queue, straight on; we settle on the stand. Leaving the other cornets, I nudge next to the basses to get a better view of the conductor.

Stuck out on my own on third, my part is more generally rhythmic. There is nothing tricky to play but I need to avoid rushing to help the more complicated parts keep time.

Halfway through our performance, halfway down the page, I become aware of the occasion, the surroundings and my reflections. I have missed the repeat, lost my place and lost my concentration. I take the cornet off my lips, look for the next landmark and wait for the band to arrive so I can pick up. For anyone with a few years banding under their belt it is probably impossible to get lost in *Knight Templar*, it is a form of reflexive knowledge like the automatic responses of breathing: you can do it in your sleep.

The *trio*: a change of key; a change of mood. This leads into the second major quiet section of the piece, a quartet based around the euph, rep, sop and principal cornet. The back row has to get out of the way as much as possible; the adjudicator will be looking for the ensemble skill in managing the dynamic range. This passage has a mix of technical phrases and slower melodic episodes to expose the sweetness of the soloist's tone. One more big blow before the *trio* ends with a hymn-like chorale, descending to a deep reflective peace. Back to the top and the heraldic charge.

Afterwards we contemplate beer tents and burgers. Lola and Jean point to the coach...

Friezeland

The sound of a horn, the belch of diesel. I start to feel a certain irritation at the excess, the insanity, of a hundred coaches spending the night driving around these narrow lanes.

Weariness creeps amongst us. Most of the band are slumped on the church wall with instruments at our feet; jokes and conversation ride an ebb tide. Jean and Lola command a tight huddle to debate the next moves in tonight's odyssey. We consider the voyage to Ithaca; Brownhill must be reached before the clock strikes ten.

"Wakey wakey, look lively. Friezeland could be our big chance of a prize." It is only for third section bands and below.

On the stand, at last I feel the fatigue kicking in, holding the lip so the notes don't wilt. As the light begins its long, crepuscular fade and the midges move in, the music pulls me into its structure: the cornet solo; the bass solo; the *fine*; the *trio*. These five minutes become their own compelling universe, but this is not particular, it is common to every contest march. Our brief eternity contains a clue to why music has a role in most religions. Marches have their own unity, anyone who has played in a band will tell you of how they might start humming one march intro and then end up in an entirely different bass solo. This is deep stuff absorbed at an impressionable age.

Uppermill

Again, we find ourselves in Uppermill, on the street, signed in. Four bands in front of us and an hour on our side, have we got time? I think we have. But, the band that has just formed up doesn't leave, not now, not in five minutes, not in ten. By the time two bands have moved off we only have half an hour left. We abandon the plan, we need to get a move on. "Everyone back on the bus".

On departing, the reason for the delays becomes clear: the street is packed with drinkers. I quite enjoy marching down a boisterous street, but there is a difference between boisterous and boorish and the scene we see from the coach window has very little to do with music or any form of cultural celebration. It seems to be the antithesis of the morning's crowd, its evil twin.

Out of all the villages, Uppermill should be the crown jewel of Whit Friday night but it seems to have lost its grasp on the evening tradition. This is definitely not due to the efforts of the no doubt, selfless organisers; the village has been overrun. The battle for the park, a magnificent grass arena for a band contest, was lost in the late 1970s. The routed musicians have retreated to a corner of the car park behind the high street. The bands do their best here in this beleaguered redoubt.

Brownhill

Ten to ten, at last we are back in Brownhill. Cresting the top of the lane, we disembark. It is dark and the smiling morn is long gone. Deciding that since there will be a long wait until we play, I head down to the green and soak up the atmosphere. Nudging into the crowd, I assess a couple of bands. The lure of Whit Friday is strong: one has come all the way from Cornwall. After a while, I wander back up the hill.

Youth band parents have claimed the band room; visiting competitors pack the bar. We stake out our space at the stage edge.

The mood soon sags like a collapsing air bed. Ties are loosened and instruments rested in open cases. Some eye up the never shrinking bar queue, others find a table and unwrap their final sandwiches. The concert room is like an airport lounge when the night flight to Malaga has been delayed.

After twenty minutes of this purgatorial slough, I decide I need a little information and visit the registration desk. There are ten bands before us; we will probably be setting off at 11:30. I should have brought a sleeping bag.

The band club is a flat beach at the end of summer when all the slow waves are spent. This listless lacuna leaves me wishing we had stayed at Uppermill and maintained the contest momentum, but orders are orders.

After an hour of watching the slow hand clock crawl there is a ripple, a murmur. The youth band are on their feet and marshalled to the door. Checks for music, instruments, absent friends and they are gone.

Next, nudges amongst the seniors, the slow rise from armchairs. Figures of authority stand to command attention at the head of the drinker's tables; conversations are broken and directions given. We pillage the stage for jackets and caps then retrieve our instruments.

Whispers of breath blow warm air into cold coils; a few arpeggios test the lips. Those with lax deportment are taken to task over skewed ties and hanging shirts. We drift into the still warm night; the car park wall provides rest and support. Down the hill, a sudden cheer like a Wembley winner: the youth band have arrived on the green. Two bands later it will be us.

The night turns, the listlessness lifts; a busy bustle fills the road. Neighbours standing on doorsteps chatting, winding down the day, offer us their curiosity and attention.

Sorting out our order, straight lines, horizontal and vertical, take shape up and down the road. Even though in the dark no-one will see us, it somehow matters most of all at this moment. We pledge that, "This time we will play it right", a forlorn hope as half of us have left our head torches in the club. Too late now...

Calls for discipline align our focus. Shaking ourselves into concentration, rolling shoulders and shuffling feet, we practise the stances of performance. I tut-tut the opening phrase with tongue in mouthpiece.

Someone shouts "Ready." We stand straight and, chin up, look forward, holding our instruments close in front. Listening into the sudden silence... Tap tap. One, two, three, pause. One, raise the instrument. Two, place on lips. Three, settle, pause, breathe. Play. Dehrehreh Deh, Dehrehreh Deh, Deeya daya deh, Pom. We march, hopefully left foot forward, down the lane.

Between the tight walls of the houses, from streetlight to streetlight to streetlight, we remember enough to keep the music moving. The sound may be ragged but the blowing is joyous: we are the sailors reaching harbour; the wanderers coming home. Regardless of the quality of our performances of the evening, at this moment we ride on a tide of triumph.

We receive our welcome as we descend to the green. It is now a sacred grove of light-strung trees: trees that have been watching over the bands for the past sixty years. Forming into our horseshoe, we focus the gaze of a hundred faces on the street and on the slopes, in bedrooms and in yards. The kind weather has kept a crowd until the end.

Silence sweeps the village for the last time as we take the stand. Collective concentration is brought to bear, our final preparation to enter the temporary eternity of *Knight Templar*.

Shepherded by the sheepdog baton, the conductor corrals our eyes. For a moment we are aware of our breath and how this must be marshalled one last time. He allows the breathing of the band to rise and fall until it seems we inhale and exhale as one dynamic organism. We prepare to blow, then we're in...

Conviction and significance is a little stronger in every note than in any other performance of the night. With the awareness of the day's end there is a desire in each of us to hold onto these last embers.

Phrases are animated as we sculpt the sound. Occult hairpins and mystic italics burn the page, illuminating the spiritual life of this sacred manuscript. We perform a ritual invocation of the spirit of music. Even the most cloth eared, the most tone deaf, the utterly unmusical cannot escape the call.

Warm acclaim rewards the closing phrase, but before any sense of finality can consume us, we are joined by two more bands in their red coats and white shirts. Seventy-five musicians crowd round those trees. White lights glint on brazen bells.

Hymn sheets are handed out and for two verses we give wistful and melancholic thanks for the day thou gavest, Lord. The first firm, the second diminished to a quiet quartet.

But the basses cannot let go and hold a profound, insistent, swelling drone like the throbbing of a mighty engine. We wait and look towards the centre, eyes on the conductor. He stares back, confirming the connection with his players. When the bond is solid, he sweeps us into one final impassioned blow. This time we struggle to see the music due to a damp distortion of vision.

The last of the hymn balloons and billows towards the stars.

That's it. I look at the woman next to me, we raise our eyebrows and shrug. It's over. Parents are collecting children. Music is returned, marches and hymns to separate hands.

I would love to stay a while longer, but there is no reason.

Strolling back to the band room, I collect my case and coat. I hand the band jacket, cap and tie back to Jane in the storeroom door and am unnecessarily thanked for my help. It was more than a privilege, so much more than a privilege.

I am looking for my car somewhere down on the Huddersfield Road as the church clock strikes midnight.

4. British Culture in Uncertain Times

Introduction

When I started writing the book it had the initial premise of being an inquiry into my motivations for playing in a brass band. Ironically, the urgency of that question has receded because the more time that is spent immersed in a cultural activity the more it begins to shape identity.

Over time the accumulation of and devotion to routines and rituals produces its own forms of meaning. I have a much deeper commitment to my own band, and the art form in general, than I would ever have imagined when I began playing with Wellhouse all those years ago.

An important part of that commitment comes from developing a deeper understanding of the history and traditions of the brass band movement. This is reinforced by an understanding of the significance of the region I grew up in, and still live in, to the development and maintenance of that tradition. I think of brass bands as pennine roots music.

Since the book has followed the tribulations of the fictional Upperthong Band, there also needs to be a concluding statement: about its current condition; how it has survived Covid; and how it is facing the future. But there are also other issues that need to be addressed.

The book has been a process of personal reflection, but it has also been an opportunity to explore larger themes of identity and culture. Some of the initial queries were answered along the way but there are still some loose ends. In particular, in the wake of Brexit, there at least needs to be some comment on the culture of British politics. This is fundamental because the nature and health of the political system has an influence on what might be considered the national character. In turn, politicians' own understanding and experience plays out in public policy towards culture: both how it is defined and how it is used. This in turn influences the everyday culture of British life, shaping attitudes, sentiments and experience.

The astute reader will have noticed that Britishness is something that so far has not been clearly defined. At times there may have been a secondary obfuscation with the terms English and British being interchanged, seemingly at random. This is a problem because without an understanding of Britishness there can be no definitive statement of British culture, or English culture for that matter. There are also some other problems that arise when attempting to make statements about culture. Culture is not static; culture is a process. British culture is not something that can be understood in the moment; it needs to be considered over time. But taking the long view, it is still possible to see if some underlying principles can be identified.

Brass bands are useful in helping us understand British culture because they have surfed the changes in our society for nearly two hundred years. In that sense they help define Britishness as an urbanising and urbanised culture, as over that period that is where the population has been increasingly concentrated.

As cultural organisations, bands have evolved to accommodate developments in music technology and musical taste. They have also survived some very significant social upheavals. They therefore represent a reservoir of cultural knowledge for us to draw from. The book ends by considering what brass bands have to offer British culture in the twenty-first century, the wisdom they may hold for us in uncertain times.

Why do I play in a brass band?

The answer to my initial question now seems fairly banal; joining the band was a means of assessing and reconnecting with the culture of my childhood. The primary attraction has probably been the belonging, the collective commitment underpinned by trust and obligation - but the common purpose is the music. The determination to create something meaningful in the here and now has made it far more than an exercise in nostalgia; playing in a brass band is a vital undertaking, a living project.

Against all expectations the book wasn't done and dusted in twelve months, it may have started before Brexit but it wasn't finished until after Covid. For those who followed the progress of Upperthong Band through the disaster of the areas, this leaves the question of what happened next.

It is no surprise that James was replaced, although not before having a go at getting the band back into the second section; in fact, no-one left immediately. After the disappointment of the result there was a surprising lack of rancour; Big Michaela managed to make her peace with Nick and in turn he sorted out his drinking. Things settled down and we plodded on until Covid hit.

Many feared that the Covid hiatus might be the death of the band. With no compulsion to practise, playing deteriorated. Those first few months back at rehearsals were beyond dire, but then, slowly, things began to change. The old familiarity returned and we realised that no-one had disappeared; the band was back together and we felt good. Not only that, but under the baton of a new conductor we began to improve and not only that, we began to believe in ourselves.

In the run up to the first areas there was a mood of optimism in the band room. This was partly inspired by the knowledge that whilst we had remained intact many other bands hadn't. There was no delight in the misfortune of others, even if there is still some sense of rivalry between bands and conductors. Ultimately, we know that all bands benefit from a healthy environment, from a deepening rather than a shrinking pool of potential members. Hearing that a band was withdrawing from the areas, or worse that it had folded altogether, was a cause for sadness rather than celebration. Even so, we couldn't help feeling the odds were tilting in our favour – but our optimism wasn't purely based on the problems of others.

As the weeks went by, no-one suggested we were going to win but we all knew we were going to be happy with the performance. During those rehearsals Nick's soprano solo took on an almost talismanic significance. He nailed his part within the first fortnight and every time he played it from then on that sound seemed to say, "good things are going to happen".

On stage, one Saturday afternoon in early March, our soprano sang out like a lark, filling the hall with soaring melody. When we swooped into the test piece's final movement, we knew we were flying: we had the wind beneath our wings, so to speak. In advance of the result, Nick collected his award for the best soloist. Suddenly, we dared to dream.

Upperthong: champions! It was a tremendous feeling, our supporters cheered and grown men cried.

If winning was a collective triumph, it was also a personal success of sorts. In the pub afterwards the conductor leaned over, "I was expecting you to cock it up today... but you didn't," which must qualify as fulsome praise in anybody's book. My personal odyssey to musicianship was clearly tacking in the right direction, buoyed by the band's rising tide.

If the victory had one supreme meaning it wasn't about the defeat of other bands, it was the confirmation of that buzz in the band room: it was about the pride of being in the band. But this book was never just about being in a band. The Brexit moment had spurred an inquiry into Britishness, into the nature of British culture.

National Culture

Since the Brexit referendum, the debates about British culture and identity as being something separate from that of Europe have understandably receded. However, the legacy of Empire is still a sore point.

The British Empire ended in the decade after the Second World War and as a result Britain's profile slowly diminished. Unfortunately, rather than herald a national revival on the international stage, Brexit has pushed it closer to the wings. Even more alarmingly our political parties seem to be producing leaders that reflect this increasingly stunted status and the fact that a character such as Boris Johnson should become Prime Minister is a cause of concern for his party as well as the nation at large. It is not as if there were no warnings as to the limits of his abilities. Johnson's immediate predecessor, Theresa May, appointed him to the post of Foreign Secretary for the explicit purpose of demonstrating his unsuitability for public office. Her lesson went unheeded and Johnson became leader of first party and then country. The question remains as to how this could possibly happen, part of the answer to that inquiry is found with Jeremy Corbyn and the Labour Party.

Political parties have been an important part of national traditions for several hundred years. They can be seen as cultural because they represent sets of values that encompass all corners of society. They may also have traditions and symbols that bind their membership and followers, such as the red flag of the Labour Party. The current state of British politics can be read as a failure of culture, because, as institutions, the main political parties have proved unable to both maintain deep traditions and develop the talent within their ranks to create a process of renewal. To appreciate this properly it is necessary to have at least a basic understanding of what the parties have traditionally represented.

The Labour Party was founded as the parliamentary representative of socialists and the trade union movement. As such, its purpose was to improve the pay and conditions of working people and create a more fair and equal society. This purpose was expressed in support for public education, housing, health and welfare systems. The Labour Party explicitly used the tax system to redistribute wealth. At times Labour brought into public control utilities and services that were of national importance such as power generation, water, railways and even major industries such as coal and steel. This process was called nationalisation and historian David Edgerton argues that in the post-war years it was the Labour Party that invented the idea of the British *nation*. The Labour Party could be seen as a challenge to the traditional order as represented by the Conservatives.

The Conservatives were the party of the establishment, a term first used in the twentieth century to represent a closely bound elite network at the top of British society. This was a particularly male network. Members of the establishment were expected to have attended public school and from there proceeded to elite universities. Many moved into the officer class of the armed services, London law firms and the judiciary, financial interests in the City or careers in the higher echelons of the civil service. The English gentry and nobility were seen as bastions of the establishment and the Church of England its conscience. Informal codes of conduct learned in the exclusive, fee-paying, public schools informed behaviour which was subtly policed through social networks such as gentlemen's clubs and leisure activities like polo matches, fox hunting and grouse shooting.

The Conservative Party promoted establishment interests and ruled in its interest. Because the Conservatives represented not only tradition but business and the idea of prospering from individual enterprise, it was able to reach across the class divide to a limited extent. The Conservative Party was traditionally the party of the British Empire. Members of the establishment were on the whole unlikely to be sympathetic to the Labour Party.

By the start of the twenty-first century both main political parties had jettisoned their core values. To give two examples: the Labour Party distanced itself from the working class in its formerly industrial heartlands, and; the Conservative Party was actively dismantling an important pillar of the British establishment, the civil service. At the core of government, roles and duties that had been fulfilled by experienced civil servants were increasingly likely to be devolved to management consultants.

Political parties' understanding of their purpose was now not about representing a set of social class interests and shaping a vision of the country but about competing for the honour of managing the economy. Ideology was history; their attitude to the country at large reflected the problems of their own cultural crises. This attitude, and the narrow version of economics that informed it, is most succinctly expressed by the programme of privatisation followed by governments of all hues.

Here is an anecdote that serves as both example and allegory to illustrate this crisis in national culture: the imposing stone edifice of the Halifax central Post Office is now a pawn shop.

—

Historically, for politicians, high office has usually been achieved later in life, at the end of a political career. It is a moment that would have been prepared for by lengthy apprenticeships within government, long service to a political party and notable careers in business or industry. In recent decades this has changed. In 2020, Tom Sasse and others at the Institute of Government reported that in the previous quarter of a century cabinet ministers could on average expect to spend two years in post. This compares poorly with a generation earlier (pre – 1980) when, according to a 2005 report by Samuel Berlinski and others for the London School of Economics, ministers were more likely to serve for the term of their parliament. Some ministers, including Harold Wilson, even kept shadow positions for periods in opposition before returning to continue when their party returned to power. It is worthy of note that Boris Johnson had only served two years as a minister before becoming Prime Minister; his Chancellor, Rishi Sunak, had only been an MP for five years before ascending to that post. Boris Johnson had a background in journalism and his near predecessor, David Cameron, in the media and Conservative Party back office. Cameron had been an MP for only five years before becoming party leader, the youngest and most inexperienced Prime Minister in almost two hundred years.

If there is good reason to be concerned about the nation's leadership, it should be noted that this is not an entirely new problem. In his essay, *The Lion and the Unicorn,* George Orwell described England as "a family with the wrong members in control." Nor, is this an issue that is exclusive to the Conservative Party. On the opposition benches, Jeremy Corbyn was a long serving MP but had spent his political career in relative obscurity, campaigning on issues of interest only to the party's left wing. A disdain for TV presenters was easily interpreted by viewers at home as contempt for voters.

Corbyn's successor, despite being named after the most important figure in the early history of his party, hovered with the electrodes ready to revive the cadaver of New Labour. For the Liberal Democrats, hapless Nick Clegg styled himself as British politics' answer to Stan Laurel, meekly suffering as Cameron and Osbourne poured custard into his trousers; his successor, Jo Swinson, became the invisible woman.

That this failure of institutional capacity now extended beyond the political parties, to the heart of the civil service, became painfully evident in the Covid crisis. Instead of seeking to manage the spread of the virus using public health bodies, the government delegated this work to accountants and management consultants. Whether this was because, after the cuts of the government's austerity programme, the capacity no longer existed or that a remote, insular, Westminster clique could not trust locally based services isn't entirely clear. The fees for this project amounted to more than £10 billion and the consultant's work was considered to have delivered the same results as if the government had done nothing. This is not a problem restricted to government.

The benchmark of national cultural failure is surely the Grenfell fire. It seemed that there was a significant failing in every single body implicated in the disaster whether manufacturer, landlord or regulator, public or private sector. Five years after the fire there had not been a single prosecution despite the deaths of 72 people. These problems reflect broader trends in the higher echelons of British society.

In *Reckless Opportunists,* Aeron Davis argues that the establishment is being replaced by elites. The new elites may occupy the same strata of society as the old establishment but this is a landscape that is more fragmented and less homogenous. The elites are characterised by their independent self-interest. They are mobile, internationally mobile, not tied exclusively to a country or continent, and less attached to institutions, traditions and social obligations (Rishi Sunak fits this elite profile). Ironically, the new elites have not just diluted the establishment with graduates of Harvard or the Sorbonne; closer examination also reveals alumni of the bog-standard comprehensive and University of Anywhere (such as Sajid Javid). Some sectors of the elites are divided and even in open conflict, as seen in the different attitudes to Brexit within the financial sector.

Davis writes that the new leaders may "display a strong ethical outlook which conflict(ed) with their business roles," they say the right things even when their corporations don't do the right things. In negotiating the course between morality and profitability the new elite leaders employ a high degree of mental flexibility and self-deception. Davis considers the example of the former Tesco CEO Terry Leahy as a character study of the new elite personality.

In an interview with Davis, Leahy struck the high moral tone found in his management book, talking of benefits to society and the importance of value systems. However, when Leahy moved on from his post, it became clear Tesco had been massaging the figures for several years and using questionable cash-flow strategies, such as holding back payments to suppliers until legal action was threatened. The scale of Tesco's problems only became evident shortly after Leahy left. "In 2017, after a three-year investigation, it had to pay out £235 million in fines, compensation and legal costs."

Davis identified a short-term outlook in Leahy's thinking. As a modern mobile leader, he always knew that he could dodge decisions and pass them down the line to his successor. Elite leaders,

"can sacrifice all sorts of things for a result, then exit before the bankruptcy hits the fan...Mobility also means future opportunity, enabling leaders to move quickly on to the next post..."

Those looking for an example of how this attitude has infiltrated public life need look no further than David Cameron.

It always seemed to be David Cameron's intention to follow the example of his near predecessor, Tony Blair, and parlay the cachet of high office into a future consultancy career. The morality of his ambitions quickly caught up with him and his reputation subsequently sank faster than the Titanic.

The behaviour of politicians and political parties may seem a far remove from brass bands, however they play two important roles: they are exemplars of the values and mores that underpin society, of how we organise ourselves and relate to each other; they also continue to play a crucial role in shaping the forms, perceptions and promotion of culture in its artistic senses.

Politicians who are increasingly distanced from traditions of culture in its most general sense may also be prone to lack cultivation. An indication of this might be found in the fact that there is now a Department for Culture, Media and Sport (DCMS). Amongst other things, the DCMS is the department with ultimate oversight of the BBC.

Jonathon Rose notes that one of the crucial roles of the early BBC was to broadcast high culture, both literature and music. Broadcasts of great works from the classical canon would be eagerly anticipated by a stratum of working class listener with no other opportunity to hear these either on record or in concert.

In *English Culture and the Decline of the Industrial Spirit,* Martin Weiner observes that under Stanley Baldwin the Conservative Party took a paternalistic attitude to broadcasting. The consensus was that the radio should be used to promote high culture and to eschew a commercial ethos as this would lead to trivial and frivolous programming. Whilst there was always a populist strand to BBC output (for example, the self-explanatory Light Programme) it had a monopoly on legal radio broadcasting until the early 1970s. Paternalistic support for the BBC provided the opportunity for a broader musical cultivation.

The ethos of the Baldwin era finds itself implacably rejected by the current Conservative Party. It seems to have a visceral loathing for the BBC

224

and is keen to see a purely commercial broadcasting environment. This may not be an impartial and disinterested position.

In *The Cultural Industries,* David Hesmondhalgh poses the question:

"Does ownership of the cultural industries by the wealthy and powerful ultimately... lead to the circulation of texts that serve the interests of these wealthy and powerful owners and their governmental and business allies?"

In mitigation, it should be noted that unfettered market forces and the evolution of digital on-demand media have created a radically different world to that of the 1930s, current forms of media access are rapidly rendering the term broadcasting archaic and obsolete. However, in the era of paywalls and subscriptions, culture will be accessed not only by those who are aware of it but those who can afford it.

Current government opinion can be seen as at best a-cultural (i.e. unconcerned or indifferent to culture) and at worst anti-cultural. A perhaps unintended consequence of their actions is to close some of the doors to high culture.

Cultural Industries

Commercial values dominate society and now culture cannot be seen as separate from the cultural industries. To be clear about terminology: I mean a cultural industry to be any area of artistic (cultural) activity that produces goods or services (cultural products) for sale. For example, theatre companies, film studios, record companies and publishing houses, etc. are cultural industries: they are cultural producers. They make, or help others to make, cultural products for sale (for example, films, CDs and books). As far as government is concerned, cultural production is to be most cherished for its economic benefits.

It would be disingenuous to suggest that culture and economics have never embraced in so-called advanced societies. For example, it is hard to imagine Greek artists and sculptors working outside an economic wage or patronage system, similarly, John Ruskin made a healthy living from his beautiful watercolours. Indeed, there is still a range of economic activity that supports the brass band movement: from the services of teachers and conductors to the manufacturers of uniforms and instruments. However, traditional economies have allowed artists to produce artefacts and experiences for the entertainment, edification and appreciation of their peers. In the twenty-first century this balance has been upended: activities identified as cultural have become servants of the economy.

This last point was succinctly demonstrated by Manchester's Whitworth Gallery with an exhibition in 2023 titled *Economics the Blockbuster – it's not Business as Usual.* The publicity helpfully asked, "how can Artists re-imagine the economy?" The promotional material proclaimed:

"Economics the Blockbuster *is a group exhibition about art, economy and community action... that demonstrate(s) art as real-world economic systems. Together they propose new ways of 'doing business'....*

Economy is an everyday activity. It includes many things, from the exchange of gifts, money and finance, to caring for others, building trust and sustaining the environment. It happens not only in factories, shops, or offices but in parks, on the streets, and in museums.

From a community-led drinks company to an art collective reclaiming plantation land, the exhibition includes.... merchandise with a purpose, business collaborations..."

The implication of this exhibition is that art, or at least publicly funded art, must justify itself by referring to its economic value.

More broadly, the value of culture is assessed in terms of its economic contribution to the national bottom line, exports and the GDP. This has had its most pernicious effects in the visual arts where the uniqueness of paintings and sculptures has turned them into an asset class, a form of money.

Any cultural production now faces a major problem in that the most important criterion by which it is judged is saleability. This undermines other values of, for example, the art world whereby paintings might have been judged according to criteria such as subject matter, composition and technical skill. As Grayson Perry noted in his book *Playing to the Gallery,* this is hardly a novel state of affairs. Culture's primary value has become financial.

Culture is not just valued for its direct economic benefits but its indirect ones. Cultural processes have become instrumental: they have become tools to further other agendas. A good place to start in examining the economic co-option of culture is in the field of urban regeneration.

There are three important and interlinked strands in the thinking around culture and regeneration. The first is around reframing the profile of cities and attracting inward investment by commissioning extended festivals: the European City of Culture programme pioneered this approach.

A secondary strand of metropolitan regeneration has been the development of headline grabbing architecture to rebrand a city or region on the global stage. It could be argued that the Sydney Opera House blazed the trail in the 1970s but the trend was consolidated with the construction of the Bilbao Guggenheim Museum.

The third strand is about demographic manipulation. In particular this involves encouraging "cool" people to populate run down urban areas in order to lure the rich to follow - in much the same way as NASA considers using bacteria to create a breathable atmosphere on Mars. This process is the brainchild of Richard Florida and his groundbreaking 2002 book, *The Rise of the Creative Class.*

Taking the last point first, Florida argued that attracting young creatives (artists, designers and tech workers) to a thriving hipster scene was the fast-track to kick-start urban regeneration. He observed syllogistically that: creative people tended to live in bohemian quarters; all prosperous cities had bohemian quarters; and therefore, if a city attracted "creatives" it would become prosperous. Florida developed a more than healthy consultancy income on the back of this proposition, whether this benefit was reflected in the fortunes of the cities who sought his advice is a moot point.

Due to the effects these initiatives had on demographics and property prices, Florida's philosophy became a form of gentrification. In an excellent assessment of his home city, *The Last Days of Detroit,* Mark Binelli pithily observes that this process merely sloshes property boom cash into creating middle class, whitish ghettoes in the midst of cities that remain otherwise unimproved.

There is another issue at play here which affects our understanding of culture. We live in an age of lexical looseness; our attention is not always focussed on the details of language and the specific uses and meanings of words. As Raymond Williams observed, culture has for a long time been a highly adaptable word with very flexible meanings. In contemporary society it is easily drawn into webs of synonym and association and becomes vulnerable to the abuses of branding and marketing.

Branding and marketing (like their evil twin, propaganda) thrive on creating associations between words, memory and experience. They require that we merely accept but don't consider their propositions and inferences. As Daniel Kahneman reminds us in *Thinking Fast and Slow*, the trick of marketing is to place meaning and understanding outside our conscious processes of reflection and consideration.

Marketers never want customers to think critically about the message, they want us to respond to it emotionally, spontaneously. Bearing this in mind, it should be noted that cities drawn to the ideas of Richard Florida often label urban districts as creative or cultural quarters interchangeably, but the two are very different words. Whilst such strategies may promote special and exciting feelings, this cavalier use of key terms contributes to a broader confusion in the understanding of culture in society. In the long view Florida's philosophy was a relatively late arrival on the regeneration scene, the plans for the Bilbao Guggenheim preceded it by over a decade.

In 1991 the City of Bilbao commissioned a new art gallery to promote the city as a tourist destination. This was an attempt to compensate for the blow to the local economy of its failing port; the strategy was generally considered to have been a great success. Following Bilbao's example, under Tony Blair's New Labour, the UK Millennium Lottery funded cultural centres (libraries, art galleries, etc.) in struggling towns in order to stimulate their revival.

The Lottery commissions didn't always bring the anticipated benefits and a number of prominent buildings soon closed. Notable failures included: the Centre for Popular Music in Sheffield - shaped like an aluminium drum kit; and The Public, a large art gallery in West Bromwich with windows like the empty speech bubbles from a superhero cartoon. The successes included the Tate Modern in London (perhaps not a failing town) and the celebrated Walsall Art Gallery.

The success or failures of these buildings seemed to rest on a variety of factors: the quality and utility of the building designs – the Tate Modern was well designed, The Public, not; the case for a particular building or project - the Centre for Popular Music failed in Sheffield because there was no demand for it, and finally; location - the Earth Centre.

There are many reasons city centres decline or become abandoned and the construction of an arbitrarily commissioned, flashy new building is unlikely to address these. As this book is being finished Huddersfield is about to repeat this costly mistake.

Finally, to consider the first point in this chain: the European City of Culture programme. The City of Culture initiative began (in 1985) with twin aims, one of which could be seen to be generally cultural; it sought to encourage a neighbourly understanding across the international community.

Whatever the initial intentions, the current thinking behind the City of Culture initiatives has very little to do with artistic or cultural values as Ruskin or Arnold would have recognised them. This is especially true of the UK City of Culture programme. They are focussed on the calculus of economic multipliers, the way in which upfront funding may draw in substantially more cash through a range of related and secondary economic activity.

City of Culture initiatives are planned with spreadsheets demonstrating that if the culture grant is awarded a range of objectives will be met in the following manner: there will be five art exhibitions with a total attendance of 250,000 people; during the period of the event 1,000 people will stay in local hotels; there will be a major event attracting a crowd of 10,000 people. Each of these tourists will be expected to spend, to contribute to the local economy; this is where the City of Culture justifies itself and earns its keep.

A City of Culture initiative is likely to have some social objectives too. A headline event may, for example feature: 300 local performers who will attend six workshop sessions to prepare for their participation; support 250 young people aged between 14 and 19 to attend theatre workshops, they will be from specific postcodes within the bottom 25% of the economic deprivation index; and so it will go on. The workshops may surreptitiously include employability skills if their ultimate purpose is to get people into work or education.

The headline outcomes of this type of Culture programme will include some vague uplifting statement about how the spirit and the profile of the city will change. For example, the website *visithull.org* offered,

"...a transformational year of cultural events, showcasing the exceptional talent and creativity in Hull. (and)...inspire and empower residents and communities to celebrate and participate in all this vibrant city has to offer and create a lifelong legacy."

The actual output figures for Hull: City of Culture 2017 are available on the Visit Hull website. By the way, have you ever been to Hull?

Beyond a boost to hospitality revenues, the tangible objectives from these initiatives are likely to be around: the improvement of the employability of marginalised groups; encouraging a spurt in start–up businesses; and an overall boost to a town's economic profile which encourages businesses to relocate to the area.

The key issue here is economic regeneration, culture (whatever that happens to be in these situations) is just the means to an end. We could just as well have the European Capital of Fish if this achieved the same goals. Whilst we're on the subject, what finer venue could there be for such a project than... Hull?

It is worth asking the question, is it wrong for a city to be a City of Culture? With a slight change of terminology, it is evident there is a long tradition of major cities hosting festivals with cultural activities such as music and theatre. These have been for the benefit and edification of their citizens but also provided visitor income for the local economy, all fine.

On a smaller scale, a good example of this is Marsden Jazz Festival. Marsden: is driven by a community charity with a board of local volunteers; involves local people in planning and organising the event (promoting community spirit); creates opportunities for local performers, allows some fine musicians to earn an honest crust; and brings in tourist income for local businesses. As the festival is hosted in the heart of the pennine sheep farming belt, this is also accomplished with a minimum of bullshit.

To properly assess the economic benefits of the City of Culture initiative it may be worth considering the history of attempts to rebalance the economy within the UK. From as early as the 1920s governments recognised that the prosperity of the south was beginning to outstrip that of the regions and also that patterns of pay and employment were better there too. Up until the end of the 1970s there was a regional economic policy to address this, as explained by Paul N Balchin.

From the 1980s onwards regional development was largely abandoned, although there were targeted initiatives for particular sub-regions or cities. Governments also became inclined to introduce a competitive element into the allocation of funds, areas that wrote better bids were likely to get better funding. City of Culture programmes are merely an extremely brief and specifically focussed version of these. Given the history of economic regeneration programmes it is unrealistic for a one year project to have any lasting economic benefit but they will provide a temporary glut of jobs.

What is also questionable is the type of guff and gush that appears on the *visithull* website. Rather than paint a glowing picture of a place and its cultural traditions, demonstrating how a City of Culture event is built on strong foundations, it is likely to be an indicator of an absence or erosion of these traditions. This will usually be exemplified by the glib commission of an artist to produce a work using the techniques of some long dead local craft to point up how the initiative is strongly rooted in a sense of place. The Coventry City of Culture programme offers a succinct example of this.

Coventry's City of Culture programme was built on the legacy of Two-Tone, a pop music movement of the late 1970s and early 80's. Two-tone was significant because it offered an optimistic, multicultural model of youth culture that was a welcome alternative to the dour, racist belligerence of the National Front. Before they split, The Specials (the most prominent of the Two-Tone groups) observed, "this town is getting like a ghost town."

One of the stated goals of the regeneration programmes will often be about "linking communities to culture." Implicit in statements of this sort is the assumption that communities are now places without culture and that culture (whatever that is) is something that can be doled out to a grateful populace.

In practice the frameworks for delivering cultural programmes are devised by central agencies, the Arts Council being a well-known example. The money may be awarded directly to recipient bodies and there has been a trend in public funding of developing partnership arrangements.

For money to be released to a regional or sub-regional level the relevant "stakeholders" must usually form boards and consortia to draw it down (Music Hubs are a recent example). These are composed of local arts organisations, city council officers, voluntary sector umbrella bodies and the like who devise their own grant programmes to be "responsive to local need". An administrative structure may be drawn up locally but this is usually a veil to mask centrally determined criteria.

One thing this type of process does very effectively is to produce convoluted (and expensive) bureaucratic and administrative structures. As a consequence, or perhaps as a raison d'etre, the production of the statistics and reports may become more important than the actual "project delivery" itself.

A number of conclusions can be drawn from this: the first is that any commitment to decentralise and devolve cultural control to communities is an illusion. The second is that the veiled centralisation conceals a deep distrust by funding bodies, and especially the core of government, of those below them; finally, and more insidiously is that the intensive accumulation of statistics and data are required to build a picture that represents an acceptable version of the objectives.

These programmes are creating an officially sanctioned, statistical simulation of reality. This is not the reality inhabited by the project beneficiaries. In his book *Capitalist Realism,* Mark Fisher argues this world of illusions bears an uncanny resemblance to the five year plans of Stalin's Soviet Union.

To develop a better understanding of these themes it is necessary to consider other ways in which culture is the indirect means of delivering social policy. It can be demonstrated that such projects are also indirectly economic in that their primary goal is to produce cost savings in areas of public service provision. Before this can be addressed it is worth reminding ourselves of some of the ways in which culture has manifested itself at community level.

Cultural Services

Activities that can be termed cultural have often served more than one social purpose. There are well established traditions of using culture, or for that matter sport, to address social problems stretching back to at least Victorian times. This has typically been presented as: diversion - the hoary old cliché that kids who are training down the gym are not robbing old ladies; safety - providing safe spaces for children and young people to gather under the care of sympathetic adults, or; inspiration - people only engage in socially destructive behaviour until they realise there are better things they could be doing. At its best this tradition has introduced young tearaways to fulfilling careers, Louis Armstrong is a prime example. These activities may have been delivered under the auspices of religion, formal authorities such as the legal system, charities or community organisations.

Adult recreation has a similar history, with church and chapel groups typically offering wholesome activities to parishioners. At times employers have provided opportunities for purposeful recreation and there are other traditions of community activity, one example of this being the Mechanics' Institutes. The Mechanics' Institutes were standard bearers for community education; this tradition was expanded at the turn of the twentieth century with university extension programmes and the Workers' Educational Association. One of the problems with these examples is inconsistency, some areas would have rich interlocking traditions whilst others very little.

In the post-war era there was a growth of state and local authority involvement, reaching a peak in the 1970s. I suspect this was driven from two ends: the first to address a change in patterns of community activity (for example, church attendance was falling); and at the other an effort to fill in the considerable gaps in community-led provision. In particular, FE colleges were encouraged to provide a range of activities under the heading of adult education; a network of community centres offered more local opportunities.

Community workers based in neighbourhood centres aimed to promote self-managed activity groups. These were typically for social purposes, however, the nearest community centre to my childhood home had a stage. It was often used as a venue for Gilbert and Sullivan and other amateur dramatic or musical productions. These were performed by self-directed, community-based organisations paying their own way through ticket sales.

When the estate was built the council clearly expected its new tenants would engage in a lively cultural life. Socialistically inclined local authorities can be considered to have been bringing Ruskin's Victorian ideal of vital beauty into the lives of their twentieth century constituents.

From the early 1980s onwards support for adult education and community activity began to be withdrawn due to budget cuts. Community centres closed and grant support to community organisations was removed. In this parched environment, a strand of entrepreneurial arts organisations developed to hoover up the remaining small grant funds. The concept of the time limited arts project is something that has arisen from this.

There are two ways community-focussed arts organisations tend to operate. The first is to identify funding regimes and then create community groups to be the front for grant applications. In this way the arts organisations secure income and the funders can claim they are supporting and empowering the grass roots. An alternative is for the input to be brokered by voluntary sector advisors who administer the grant fund. The nature of the funding restricts the scope of the projects, they are time limited and may only be open to specific demographics.

In their study *Culture is Bad For You*, Brook, O'Brien and Taylor suggest the problems are not restricted to the environment these organisations work in. The organisations themselves can be problematic for the workers.

It is not unusual for the only salaried staff employed by community arts organisations to be those who work in the administrative core. The face-to-face work is often delivered by sessional staff whose pay rates may not reflect the additional costs involved in preparation, travel and group support. Moreover, the sessional hours available may not add up to what most people might consider a working week or indeed a working wage. The position of freelance staff is also affected by the availability of graduates willing to work without pay to begin a career in the creative industries.

Community arts work can be a precarious occupation. If it was not for the cachet of being associated with artistic endeavour, it might well be discussed in the same terms as casualised warehouse work or the food delivery of the gig economy.

Community arts projects can give people very positive experiences. And the reason arts workers tolerate the bureaucracy is because of their love of what they do. However, this is a ministration. It is something people receive rather than something they develop and direct for themselves. It is a top-down version of affordable culture and it is a thin gruel. From the perspective of high culture there will not be the time and resources to develop artistic skills of any meaningful quality, although afterwards there may be some residue of inspiration. The most likely positive outcomes are that a talented arts worker enables a group to produce something that they are proud of.

As the open-ended grant and direct funding regimes dried up due to cuts, another change in direction was simultaneously being pushed by government policy. There was a drive to contract out services. This was the case across all major areas of public service, such as health and social care, and has led to some interesting developments in the uses and understanding of culture.

—

Economic regeneration isn't the only public agenda that has become "cultured". A body of research is steadily building about the health benefits, both physical and psychological, of participation in the arts (including music). There is already a well-established tradition of this in relation to exercise. This is leading to forms of advocacy based on cost–benefit analyses of health spending; that in certain cases the health service spends less if it encourages exercise than by prescribing drugs. The coming years should see an increase in arts projects funded by the NHS and related bodies through social subscribing schemes: this is culture as social policy.

The change in government attitude to culture has not escaped the notice of academics with an interest in brass music. Victoria Williamson and Michael Bonshor from the University of Sheffield have conducted research into the effects on well-being of playing in a brass band. What is significant here is that, as with urban regeneration, society is losing the capacity to recognise that art or cultural activities have intrinsic value: that is to say they are worth pursuing *for their own sake.*

For cultural initiatives to gain public funding they must now be linked to an issue that has an underlying economic objective. Culture is now the water in your cup rather than the sea that you swim in.

If insights about the community arts, health, welfare and economic regeneration agendas are combined, we can begin to understand how centralised funding and monitoring regimes are shaping notions of acceptable public culture. They define culture in exclusively quantifiable economic terms, by what can be weighed and measured, bought and sold. This new overarching agenda thereby deftly walls off whole worlds of experience, opportunity and possibility.

Current, officially sanctioned attitudes to culture are in stark contrast to those of the early 1950s. The post-war era saw a huge expansion in the provision of music education, by any measure a joyous and generous project. This musical wave was (probably unconsciously) rooted in the principles of Arnold's pursuit of sweetness and light and Ruskin's view that the virtues of the individual were manifested in the virtue of society. What is little noted is that on a most profound level Arnold had managed to transfer religious principles into secular life: these principles were belief and faith.

After Arnold the country was left with the thoroughly modern belief that a humanistic enlightenment could be achieved through engagement with the best that has been thought and said. As for faith, this can be taken as trust in a person, thing or a course of action. In the sense that the gardener trusts that the seeds that are planted will grow with careful nurture, the provision of post war music education was an act of faith. There was the trust that providing these opportunities would produce cultured individuals who would contribute to a more rounded, whole and - in the light of the Second World War - healed society. This project was conceived as permanent and open ended: it was the future.

In contrast, the economic and social policy version of culture is very narrow, very specific and lacking in any transcendental impulse. To the extent that, say, young people are offered the chance to develop their own skills they are restricted to several weeks or possibly months of activity. The benchmark for this is the six week Wednesday night DJ workshop for the kids on the former council estate - the same young people who no longer have a youth service.

From the health angle it is easy to envisage an arts project tackling loneliness in older people. The same people who not too long ago would have been able to meet in the community centre or library shut by the governments' austerity cuts. In these cases, "cultural" activities are a meagre attempt to try and mitigate the effects of deeper economic catastrophes.

The developments around community arts obscure the case that at grass roots level the evidence based, economic regeneration and health agendas are at best doing no more than reinstate the type of activity supported in community and adult education centres in the four post war decades. It is also worth noting these activities originally existed for no other reason than the satisfaction of the participants: with no other justification than that *people enjoyed them*. Moreover, this is being done on a far smaller and more limited scale than before. But now, it has been given a marketing edge to present itself as something "innovative" - a word that should always come with a health warning.

This new agenda is the service work of the cultural industries: this is culture as community care, culture as social care. Where higher forms of culture are involved, funds are likely to be devolved to already trained performers (e.g. a string quartet visiting an old peoples' home). To the extent that culture is funded in this sphere it is purchased like a bag of potatoes in a Grantham grocer's shop. The watch words here are value for money, it is very clear how much is being bought and what it costs. What was it Oscar Wilde said?

The spread sheets of economic regeneration and social welfare reveal deeper contours as aerial photos reveal the skeleton outlines of archaeological remains. That hidden truth is the government's contempt for and distrust of the recipients of this largesse. The money has so many strings attached it is hard to use with any freedom. Rather than "curating" a "passionate", "vibrant", "accessible"," empowered", "forward-looking", "inclusive" and "innovative" society it has created an empty culture of cynicism, distrust and resentment.

If Brexit is viewed as a rebellion by those who felt unrepresented by the existing political order, this crisis of values was surely a driver for the strength of feelings in the Leave vote.

Understanding British Culture

At this point there needs to be some sort of statement about what might be meant by British culture. This book has tried to find its way to identifying some underlying principles, to create a more nuanced picture of the current state of play requires a project in the style of Jeremy Paxman's *The English.* And therein lies a problem that has been avoided by this very English writer: where to draw the distinctions between Britishness and Englishness. The lack of clarity around these terms was also an issue in Brexit. Scotland and Wales have their own devolved parliaments within the UK but England doesn't; Scotland wanted to stay and Wales voted to leave.

Overall, Brexit was essentially an English affair. The main political protagonists, such as Boris Johnson and Nigel Farage are creatures of London and the English public school system, the so-called Metropolitan Elite. There wasn't a prominent politician based in Edinburgh or Cardiff joining in the charge. This wasn't the case in the most anxiously yet ambiguously British part of the UK. As might be expected, Ulster's Democratic Unionists strode purposefully in the opposite direction to their Celtic siblings, living up to their reputation as the party that walks into lamp posts and untended manholes. This picture is further complicated by the fact that, prior to the Brexit referendum, Scotland had its own independence vote and was closer to leaving the union than at any time in the previous 300 years. One of the unintended ironies of Brexit is that the first province to depart the union may be the six counties of Northern Ireland.

If Brexit was an ideological attempt to re-assert an essential British identity it was doomed to fail because the biggest piece was missing. It might be that only when there is a statement of English identity as clear as those of Scotland and Wales can a clear conception of Britishness be understood. This also leaves the possibility that when Englishness is understood Britishness becomes an impossibility. We might also find there is no unifying, essential English identity; regional sentiments may be more powerful than a national ideal (eg. Cornwall). Another irony is that membership of the EU might have provided a forum to accommodate more fragmented and distributed English and British identities.

My enquiry about the nature of Britishness stemmed from a failure to identify with the postures of the main Brexit protagonists. After considering issues around the North/South divide, I feel that my English identity rests firmly in the North. This is compounded by the feeling of being governed by people who appear to be living in a different country. It seems that the biases of a Westminster government no longer have the North's interests at heart; consider the cynical travesties of "Northern Powerhouse" and "Levelling Up". With tongue only half-way in cheek it is tempting to suggest that the next independence referendum might allow the North to escape from the Norman yoke. But that doesn't settle the principles of Britishness.

Obviously, Britishness has taken a wrong turn, it's not what it used to be and we need to go back to where the rot set in. Personally, I think everything was great until Doggerland was submerged. Or, maybe it was the Latin legions; coming over here with their fancy straight roads, sneering down their snooty Roman noses at those beautiful, English, winding country lanes. Even then, we could have still put things right if it wasn't for the Vikings... The point being that we always try to establish some fixed point of reference but we are always part of a larger fluid process.

It is my suspicion that for us common or garden nostalgics any Eden we can return to is always populated by the cultural furniture of childhood. Or perhaps the most compelling ideal is the one our parents described to us from their childhoods. In the formative years they are always greater authorities than ourselves. When I look at the values and activities of my own childhood it sometimes feels like I grew up in an earlier era. I am reminded of a cover from Private Eye during the Brexit campaign: Nigel Farage hails a black cab, the driver asks "Where to guv?" Farage replies, "take me to the

1950s." Nostalgia is a legitimate leisure pursuit when conducted in solitary moments or between consenting adults, but we should be wary of what we say in front of the children.

To get to the point: the essential elements of British culture that can be distilled from the brass band experience. Since the brass band is a product of industrial society, we can set aside for the time being: the extended, intertwined households; the commons and small rural farms; the cottage industries and small craft workshops; and the other features that Peter Laslett describes as characteristic of the previous agrarian age. Taking Nigel Farage's view, a good place to start might be back in the post-war years. This makes it clear that at the end of the discussion some work will still need to be done to make sure that it is fit for the twenty-first century. It also introduces the nostalgic's conundrum of whether or not we can settle on fixed, eternal principles of culture.

The post-war years are a good datum, a good point of reference, because: brass bands were still a major cultural force; it marked a decisive break with the Downton Abbey incarnation of the British class system and the rise of a more egalitarian current in the national psyche. In his study of the village of Ringmer, *The Quiet Revolution,* Peter Ambrose suggests: patterns of localised village life were still extant; the consumer society of the post-war boom was still waiting to be born; and the industrial society still waiting to die. The process of immigration from the contracting empire would begin with the arrival of the Windrush in 1948.

—

The quintessential brass band is the village band, the factory band or the colliery band. These are ensembles founded in very tight localities, whatever shenanigans may have been employed in recruitment. In their names bands refer to a variety of communities beyond location and work, such as: health (temperance); religion (Sally Army); the military; gender; other interests (even the caravan club has a band); age (Vintage Brass, youth bands); education (uni brass, school bands) and more that don't immediately spring to mind. This speaks to Edmund Burke's ideal of the little platoons but the little platoons don't stand alone.

Bands exist for the pleasure of their members and the service of their community. The strength of bands has traditionally correlated with the opportunities for performance, the opportunity to earn income. This in turn has related to the number of venues, organisations and events requiring their services. Brokering opportunities for performance has required unseen social skills: negotiating fees; and maintaining the relationships that will ensure subsequent commissions. In his classic account of Dobcross Band, Henry Livings demonstrates that the fallout from even the slight mishandling of community relations might last generations. Culture and community happen over time as well as in place.

This interwoven fabric of contact and relationship was developed through workplaces, schools, religion, community leisure activity, neighbourliness, childcare, shopping, politics, drinking in pubs and clubs. In *Working Class Community*, his landmark study of Huddersfield in the 1960s, Brian Jackson demonstrates the strength of networks established in that particular stratum of society. Peter Ambrose shows the Sussex village of Ringmer to be rigorously socially segregated, however, there were opportunities for mixing across social class provided by the cricket club and mutual benefit societies. There was also greater gender segregation.

Brian Jackson also depicts a quite marked divide between the worlds of men and women. Much of the social world outside the home is either exclusively male or dominated by men.

Richard Hoggart notes that, in a world before domestic appliances, homebound working class women were worn out in the service of their household and extended family.

Bill Morrison's archive documentary, *The Miners' Hymns*, illustrates women's condition with the female faces at the Durham gala. For brass bands it is worth remembering the role of the Ladies Committees and the relatively late arrival of women musicians in significant numbers.

Peter Ambrose records that, for most of the Victorian era and beyond, the women "cottagers" of Ringmer would have invariably ended their lives in the workhouse.

Up to the Second World War, communities of place were reinforced by limited opportunities for mobility. In the immediate post-war years car ownership was not yet widespread, and according to William Plowden in *The Motor Car and Politics in Britain*, particularly concentrated in the south east. This meant that distant travel for most people was by train or bus: shopping trips to a nearby town; or short commutes to work (incidentally, Huddersfield began its town public transport system in the 1880s).

Brian Jackson's chapter on Crowther's Mill in Milnsbridge shows that the workforce, to their best advantage, rotated around a number of major textile employer's. He observes a bus queue at the end of the shift; these workers would most likely live on the edge of Huddersfield or in Thornton Lodge one way, Linthwaite, even Slaithwaite or Marsden the other. The rest of the workforce might walk home to Paddock, Golcar or Cowlersley (the one-time home of Harold Wilson).

Peter Ambrose observed that by the mid 1960s up to a third of the workers in his village commuted over ten miles daily, another third at least three. A rapid expansion in housing was transforming Ringmer from an agricultural community to a dormitory suburb for Lewes and Brighton.

The late 1940s saw a continuation of pre-war trends for the consumption of domestic media. Newspaper circulation continued to boom into the nineteen fifties as did radio use. The immediate post-war years saw little electronic media in most homes beyond the radio, much entertainment would still be largely self-made.

As late as the 1970s, I remember church social evenings with performances from members of the congregation, perhaps supplemented by a local folk group. The pop music of the 1960s and 70s was sometimes inflected with memories of this type of popular culture. Ian Dury and The Kinks produced music with the ghost of the East End singalong, Chas and Dave reinvented it as TV entertainment.

Television finally arrived in 1953, just in time for the coronation and the so-called Stanley Matthews FA Cup final, consequently the most famous in football history. Television seemed to offer the opportunity to develop a new form of national consciousness. The following year saw the end of wartime rationing. Together these events marked the dawn of a new age.

Peter Ambrose analyses this moment using the systems theory that became popular in the social sciences at the end of the 1960s and early 1970s. He considers the traditional village to be a "closed cell". Nostalgics are fond of the idea of this intimate world where everyone knew each other and rallied round in times of crisis, but there is also another side. In many respects this was a surveillance society, as one of Ambrose's respondents notes, most people walked everywhere and so were always observed by other villagers. Tenants dependent on the goodwill of landlords for their home needed to regulate their behaviour, likewise those reliant on work from a small pool of farmers. This was still very much the world of the Tolpuddle Martyrs. Only the independently affluent could afford to flout convention or indulge in eccentricity. Opportunities were limited for many, as was education. In contrast the "open system" that emerged after the 1950s introduced a world of instant information through the mass media and greater freedoms and opportunities through travel and education.

Alan Macfarlane noted that mobility was a feature of English life from at least the sixteenth century. Surveys of the parish records he cites often show that less than half the people born in a particular district would die there too (this also includes infant mortality). The ideal of the stable community disturbed by unwelcome comers-in was always a sentimental myth.

It is no surprise that Ambrose notes that over the twentieth century there was remarkable fluidity in the composition of his village. At the start of the century over half the population would be born and die there, by 1970 this had shrunk to less than ten per cent. This was caused by two factors: a greater turnover of population; and an expansion of housing within the village. (These issues are often neglected in discussions of the international immigration that took place during this period; it was part of a larger change that was affecting the stability of populations in urban areas.)

When demographic change is alloyed with the development of commuting, it can be seen that people were now freed from the tyranny of place. Lives were diffused across often unconnected worlds of work, home and leisure. As Doctor Who might say, there was a fracture in the space/time continuum: everyone had their own TARDIS. Released from traditions and obligations that would have bound them in the past, people could: express parts of themselves that would have historically been repressed; and pursue their desires however they saw them. It was now more possible than ever to follow individual agendas and this was to have radical consequences.

Ambrose's open system world was the world of the generation gap, the permissive society, feminism, gay liberation, sex equality, race equality and social mobility. It was also the world of central heating, television, car ownership, foreign holidays, consumerism and supermarkets. Economically and politically this eventually became the age of globalisation.

As the open system unleashed the forces that redefined the village of Ringmer and fractured the working class of Huddersfield, it also reconfigured the establishment. Reverberations are also still being felt from the later technological waves of the internet revolution. The social revolution continues in the trans-gender moment and the hashtag campaigns of #metoo and #blacklivesmatter. A rearguard defence against the currents of the times has found expression in the so-called "culture wars".

—

As the name suggests, the culture warriors are in conflict, they are fighting a battle of ideas and more importantly ideals. Their nostalgia is for a world of clear indisputable values. They struggle to accept a world where negotiations are constantly occurring amongst competing value systems and are frustrated by having to contend with relative morality. Culture warriors yearn for a clearly defined social order. In his book *The Way We Live Now,* Richard Hoggart suggests this is a Britain that existed before the second world war. However, this is also the Britain that was definitively tried and condemned in J.B Priestley's classic play *An Inspector Calls.*

In inter-war Britain it was expected: the humble would defer to and respect their so–called betters; the respectable might still have domestic servants; the subjects of empire would serve their colonial masters; women would be generally based in the home; and consensual sex between men was illegal. Since the culture warriors are often found opposing wind farms it is relevant to observe that this was also a time when Britain was powered by coal. The culture warriors' aversion to so-called green technologies might be viewed as not just a nostalgia for historical energy sources but a form of anxiety about the future. A distrust of changes to the sources of physical power generation might also be construed as a metaphor for concern about changes to the sources of political, social and moral power within society.

The culture warriors do not exist in isolation, they often find vindication for their views in the activities of their opponents (whom they describe as "the wokerati") such as the dumping of the Colston statue in Bristol dock. Perhaps the most notable battle the culture warriors have undertaken is to attempt to take over the board of the National Trust. They sought to do this because the trust was drawing attention to the ways in which wealth from the slave trade and slave plantations was used to fund the construction of English stately homes. The culture warriors felt that this undermined the proud legacy of the British Empire. Their campaign up to the publication of this book has been unsuccessful.

The problem for the culture warriors is they are trying to promote ideas of culture and identity that are built on deference, assumption and received wisdom. These presently fare badly in the face of choice, reason, and historical fact. Theirs appears a vainglorious charge in a battle that was lost some time ago.

On the one hand the culture warriors can be seen as part of a thoroughly modern patriotic tradition improvising on a theme by Winston Churchill (himself in thrall to a late-Victorian fantasy) performed variously by Enoch Powell (the Tiber variation), Margaret Thatcher (the Falklands variation) and more recently Boris Johnson (the Brexit variation). In this sense the culture warriors can be seen as the keepers of the romantic flame of Imperial Britain. However, there are other ways to consider their nostalgic philosophy. In particular, the twentieth century provides several examples of successful political projects based on national mythology, most notably in Germany and Italy during the nineteen thirties. Their admirers will note these movements briefly dominated their respective societies but both examples ended in apocalyptic destruction. History tends to view them in a less than favourable light.

The focus on patriotism also makes it difficult to see the culture warriors as providing a credible cultural message. Patriotism is fundamentally the symbolic expression of abstract ideas and ideals within political boundaries. Patriotism may colour and enliven culture but is too insubstantial to constitute an encompassing form of culture in its own right.

No matter how easy it is to dismiss the culture warriors, beneath the bluster they are making a point that is essential to our times. They are seeking a form of British identity that confers pride, dignity and self-respect. However, they feel unable to do this in a process of negotiation with other communities and interest groups. Instead, they turn their backs on the public square and retreat into nostalgic fantasy. The key problem the culture warriors need to acknowledge is that the traditions they seek to draw from were achieved at the expense of others. These can be characterised and even caricatured as amongst other things: male dominance; a racial hierarchy; and hereditary class or wealth based social position.

More subtly, beneath the British veneer of the culture war lurks the understanding that the Empire was essentially English and not only that but a project centred on the establishment, the City of London and its comforting belt of home counties: it was not at heart a "national" project. The ideals that the culture warriors celebrate were only ever beneficial for a narrow stratum of English society. Theirs is a project of *nostos*, to recreate a now moribund version of the English class system. This would give them the dignity of a guaranteed, respected social status, and the administration of an unchallenged value system. For the majority of the population this archaic version of Britain was one without a public education system, universal health care and welfare systems. Historically, the poverty of this situation meant that the majority of the population were engaged in a constant struggle to achieve dignity, self-respect and basic rights; this was not an equitable state of affairs. Ultimately, the prospectus of the culture warriors is unable to offer a persuasive vision of British culture.

The current challenge is to develop a model of national dignity and self-respect based on mutual recognition, shared values and senses of equality. A larger sense of a unifying cultural identity also needs to be rooted in individual, local and national (even international) stories: in history; in tradition; and in shared values. Multiculturalism has been one attempt to address this.

Multiculturalism has been partially successful, especially in some cities and mixed urban areas; for example, the racially inflected civil unrest of the 1980s and early 2000s has been largely dampened. Multiculturalism has had its most enduring influence in public attempts to acknowledge the diversity of ethnic and cultural origins of the present UK population. One example is the high profile given to celebrations of the Windrush anniversary. It can be argued that as a result, there is a public recognition of the unacceptability of racial discrimination. Notably, the booing that greeted Black and Minority Ethnic (BME) footballers at the 2020 Euros (and supported by prominent politicians including the then Prime Minister) was drowned out by a far weightier public disapproval. The multicultural ideal of tolerance prevailed.

—

We can't go back in time and live in a theme park world of 1950's Britain, now the province of archaeology and nostalgia. We can't dismantle a century of technological development or reverse the unprecedented social change it unleashed. We can't put the genie back in the bottle but we can decide how we live with it.

What we can do is make some decisions about how we embrace technology and construct social and cultural traditions. These must be informed by history and the needs and opportunities of the present. We have the power of choice in the development of culture in ways that were previously impossible, similarly, we have the means to avoid culture as never before. A cultural revival has to be a matter of conscious decision and collective will.

Redefining Culture

Having explored some issues that affect and underpin British culture, the next task is to try and develop a viable model and definition for modern times. If we are to construct a culture for the twenty-first century we need to agree on some fundamental principles, some essential and unifying elements. The components of culture are probably best viewed as trends or tendencies of varying quality and strength. A cultural organisation or movement may be strong in all its aspects or have a few weak spots. Assessing culture in this way allows many different experiences to fit within the category. The following cultural elements can be identified from our understanding of brass bands.

Place is a primary condition of culture, it needs to be rooted somewhere in however loose a fashion. Culture also needs to represent continuity, a sense of history and tradition, an ongoing project that is handed on. There needs to be a sense of commitment, obligation or service; cultural activities require some dedication - all culture needs to feel essential, not optional. This also implies the exercise, maintenance or development of some form of skill or quality. Skills need to be practised (ideally, on Monday and Thursday evenings) and qualities expressed interacting with other people (helping to pack up at the end of a concert); there has to be a physical meeting involved. Skills and qualities are determined and assessed by values. Values are expressed as moral codes (for example, the ways we do or don't behave) or aesthetic standards (for example, understanding what constitutes good and bad art). Culture also needs to be owned and directed by its participants, this does not preclude paid, professional involvement. Finally, a cultural group needs to be linked into something greater than itself, a network of community institutions, a national organisation, or both.

Next, we need to identify some models to inspire or guide us, to test out the soundness of these principles and also make sure nothing has been omitted. I propose democracy as the ultimate exemplar of British culture, something that clearly encompasses the full spectrum of opinion; indeed, both Michael Gove and Gordon Brown included it in their British Values.

The reason for choosing democracy is because at times it has involved mass participation of the majority of specific communities in a common cause. Taking one of the key moments in democratic history, Peterloo, figures for the attendance range up to 80,000 – the population of Manchester at that time was 120,000. Here was something that could be said to have brought the whole city onto the streets. Even if the attendance was 10% of that figure it would still qualify as a hugely significant event. The Chartist movement that followed attracted similarly vast crowds to meetings and protests. The proposition that democracy is a cultural phenomenon now needs to be tested against the criteria above, first of all its connection to place.

The democracy campaigns were national but rooted in specific places with small meetings, gatherings and branches. Some of the most celebrated events were regional, for example Calderdale (the plug riots) and of course Manchester. Mike Leigh's film of *Peterloo* gives a flavour of the range of local activity that supported the campaign with meetings in fields, on factory floors and in smoky pubs.

Continuity was essential in the campaign for popular democracy. The initial stirrings were in 1647 at the height of the first English Revolution. The Levellers, a faction of Cromwell's New Model Army (for its time an exceptionally egalitarian organisation) demanded a meeting with their leaders. This became known as the Putney Debates. They argued for free and fair elections open to all (men) regardless of their property holdings.

The Putney Debates conceal another principle that should be considered an essential element of British culture: literacy. In *The World we Have Lost*, Peter Laslett proposes that in 1640 only a small part of the population could be said to be part of England. He argues that most people did not live as free and independent individuals but in families and as servants of families.

"England was an association between heads of such families... largely confined to those who were literate," all members of what he calls the "ruling minority". For the Levellers to demand their debate they had to be literate, they had to be able to take ideas and principles and discuss them in abstract terms; these are the higher skills of literacy.

Commitment to democracy was evident from the start. Some of the Leveller's were shot for their beliefs and Peterloo retains its place in the history books because of the massacre. Everyone involved in the three centuries of campaigning considered it an essential undertaking. In the final decades of the historic struggle, suffragettes were being imprisoned and some went on hunger strike. People literally lay down their lives for the democratic cause.

As for the development of skills and qualities, the campaign for democracy required its participants to develop all manner of talents from public speaking, to organising, to fundraising. National and local campaigns allowed relatively humble people to develop capacities beyond their station. This social phenomenon is described by American academic Theda Skopcol in her analysis of American civil society.

Values are the foundation for the campaign for democracy; it was underpinned by a desire for a society that treats everyone equally regardless of their property and wealth. This ultimately extended to men and women but the popular media celebrations of democracy seem to begin and end with the suffragettes. I suspect they have become democratic standard bearers for a number of reasons: there is a visual record of them on photographs and film; they were masters of PR and used high profile stunts to secure media coverage; they were publicly led by articulate and sometimes well-connected middle class figures, and; the issue of women's suffrage cuts across all social classes. An exclusive focus on the suffragettes also allows the construction of a deceptive narrative that the vote was always a universal demand.

Without denying the significant achievements of the suffragettes, the door they levered open had been forced ajar by the democracy campaigns of the nineteenth century. These are not widely celebrated and have now become obscure in the public consciousness. The reasons for this may lie in the conditions of the media at the time but I suspect there are two greater factors. Firstly, popular democracy was a sectarian project actively resisted by the upper classes; they believed that the franchise should be backed by property. Second, history has not presented us with popular figureheads such as the Pankhursts or, say, William Wilberforce.

There is a further point to be made by considering the nineteenth century experience. The campaigns of this period provide examples of a rich network of interlinked organisations. Movements such as the Chartists were also intertwined with the birth of the Co-operative movement, the precursors of trade unionism and therefore the birth of the Labour Party. We should also note that this is the world that brass bands emerged from. This was a world rich in cultural networks, association and regular meetings. In the twenty-first century many argue that face to face meetings are no longer necessary, that we can achieve the same results in the virtual, online world of social media.

Social media has played a useful role in helping to organise friendship networks and more formal associations. During the Covid lockdown, platforms such as *Zoom* provided a means of mitigating the absence of in-person contact. Even in these circumstances its champions neglect to recognise any shortcomings. There is a quantum difference between the experience of talking to an image on a screen and being in the same room as other people. Ironically, the most significant demonstration of the organising potential of social media has also become the most incisive exposure of its weakness.

In 2011, a wave of demonstrations in Egypt toppled the military dictatorship and established free and fair elections. Using social media platforms, such as *facebook*, young people were able to organise and sustain public protests against the regime. This campaign emerged swiftly and spontaneously and harnessed a reservoir of popular resentment. However, during its period of rule, the dictatorship had successfully squashed an effective civil society within Egypt. That is to say, there were no strong political parties or campaigning organisations in a position to take over, with one exception: the Muslim Brotherhood. This religious organisation had a strong structure with local participation through mosques and related activities. In the absence of any effective opposition, the Brotherhood swept to power, but their uncompromising take on Islam was at odds with a secularised society. Within a few years, the detested military dictatorship was welcomed back into power as the lesser of two evils; Egyptian society did not have the cultural capacity to sustain democracy.

The final point in the definition of culture is that it is ultimately owned and directed by its participants. Contemporary writers such as Michael Lind, in *The New Class War,* and Paul Embery, in *Despised,* argue that this is no longer the case for western democracy and that across the political spectrum government now represents a set of affluent, educated, liberal interests. Both authors argue that one reading of Brexit is as a protest vote against this new liberal status quo that would force politicians to deliver on a specific illiberal promise. Lind and Embery suggest that Britain's representative democracy is no longer providing a voice for the descendants of its creators, the industrial working class.

If democracy is the jewel in Britain's cultural crown the observations at the start of this section suggest it is in poor health, this is a view shared across the political spectrum. In his book *The Strange Death of Tory England,* the former literary editor of The Spectator, Geoffrey Wheatcroft, blamed Tony Blair. He complained that in 1997 less than a third of voters supported New Labour and in 2001 less than a fifth.

"For the first time in British history those voting for the largest party were outnumbered by those who didn't vote at all."

Wheatcroft sardonically categorises this as Blair's greatest success,

"he was both cause and effect of the steady depoliticizing of society; had come to dominate the land by voiding politics of its content, or by taking the politics out of politics."

Wheatcroft's analysis might be further refined. In D*reams of Leaving and Remaining,* David Meek describes politics as the arena where culture and economics meet. It can be argued that prior to Blair one of the triumphs of the Thatcher years was to reduce political debate to being largely a matter of economic calculation, summed up by Bill Clinton in 1992 with the phrase "it's the economy, stupid." In the wake of Brexit, Meek and Michael Lind argue, the spectre of culture returned to the feast in the guise of the populism of Nigel Farage. Farage's particular talent was to articulate the barroom grumbles of those who felt they were no longer represented by mainstream politics.

On the left of the political spectrum, Colin Crouch offered a less personalised and more systemic view of the problems facing democracy in *the Strange non-death of Neoliberalism.* He argued that politicians had become too remote from the electorate and too close to corporate influence;

political parties and the mass media were no longer able to fulfil their roles. As politicians have lost contact with grassroots opinion they are increasingly resorting to the techniques of marketing, such as focus groups, to create a simulation of this relationship: hence Blair's rebranding of New Labour. This expensive process gives an idea of the views of the electorate but is not an adequate replacement for effective political engagement. More worryingly, "the only major sources of large funds are corporations and extremely wealthy individuals."

An aura of what the British press are too polite or circumspect to term corruption has dogged all the governments of the twenty-first century from Tony Blair to Boris Johnson and will no doubt continue to do so. Indeed, one of the pillars of Blair's first election campaign was as the clean alternative to the corruption that tainted John Major's government of the 1990s.

The pool of wealthy individuals who are bankrolling politics also contains the owners of the media outlets that aim to form public opinion. This situation achieved its most egregious expression in Italy where Silvio Berlusconi, possibly the wealthiest Italian of his era and owner of the majority of media outlets, became president. Money is determining the course of democracy, not culture. This begs the question: if Britain lacks a strong civic culture, is an electoral cycle on its own sufficient to qualify it as a democracy?

This digression allows us to see a final, essential component of British culture: conflict. Cultural conflict: has been the process that has allowed society to grow and change; creates a healthy diversity of opinion to exist simultaneously; and offers templates of how differences may be successfully resolved. For cultural conflict to occur there has to be cultural activity and in politics, as in the arts, culture is in poor health. This begs the question as to what might be done to revive it.

Promoting Culture

In *Mind the Gap,* Ferdinand Mount expresses his nostalgia for the Victorian age of working class self-determination; he argues against the involvement of government agencies in promoting culture. This position is in accord with one of the characteristics that has been identified above: culture must be owned and directed by its participants. In this sense Mount is in opposition to the views of writers such as Brook, O'Brien and Taylor who see culture as the occupation of a priestly caste.

The cultural priesthood interpret holy texts and reveal sacred icons to supplicant congregations in theatres and art galleries (for the record, theatres and art galleries are wonderful things). Contrary to expectations, they protest that this elite is exclusive and unrepresentative - ostensibly the defining characteristics of an elite. Their nuanced mission has a social purpose: to create a diverse and representative cultural class.

Mount is rightly wary of these professional ministrations; he recognises the virtues of participation and agency in culture. Whilst these principles are laudable, they do not address the problem of how to reinvigorate culture in British society and what new forms it might take. It is not entirely realistic to reinstitute Britain as a form of Victorian theme park and so new ground will have to be broken, new cultural traditions created. One approach might be to reinvent community workers to foster autonomous, self-directed groups. However, if this includes political groups there is a conflict of interest around (local) government sponsored workers creating activities that will compete to direct their employer. This problem doesn't arise for arts focussed projects although as we have seen there is the issue of who decides the scope of such activities.

An activist, but hands off, approach is to create cultural habits not cultural institutions, to develop the skills, instincts and reflexes in citizens to think and act in cultivated ways. This could be achieved by establishing an organisation of national cultural renewal, an idea first proposed by Coleridge two hundred years ago. The question is: what would this organisation of national cultivation look like and what would it be called? This can be answered by considering the synonyms of cultivation, one of which is education.

Concerns about the performance of the education system come around more regularly than buses. However, it seems quite a while since there was a politician who understood that education and schooling are not necessarily the same thing. In Britain, schooling is the process of teaching the skills and aptitudes that lead toward tests and examinations. On the other hand, education is the means by which young people are enabled to develop their talents and capacities to become active participants in a society. Education is ultimately the means by which a culture renews itself. For a long time governments have focussed on strategies for improving the techniques of teaching, on the how of school rather than the why. It is therefore no surprise the crisis in culture is accompanied by a corresponding crisis in education; this is most succinctly articulated by the rising levels of existential angst of British youth.

The rise in anxiety is most often framed in terms relating to "mental health", but this is misleading. The problem is not medical; it is a crisis of meaning and belonging. At the heart of the education system and at the heart of society there is a void where there should be reason, purpose and transcendent ideals. Matters came to a head for many young people during the Covid lockdown when they were isolated at home. Not only did this experience weaken a sense of their place in the world, the contemporary source of reassurance from beyond the family became the fractured hall of mirrors that is the online environment. The answers they were offered to the anxieties of their developing identities were unrealistic, fantastical and allowed them little sense of a coherent place in the world. Young people need guiding lights that are visible beyond their front doors and the school gates.

Neil Postman addressed these concerns in *The End of Education,* he argued that both a society and a place of education need a god or gods to serve. By god he didn't necessarily mean an actual deity but a transcendent narrative, the measure of which are its consequences. "Does it provide people with a sense of personal identity, a sense of community life, a basis for moral conduct, explanations of that which cannot be known?" The gods also require a unifying power.

This crisis has been caused by replacing the ideals of culture (including religion) and society with the model of the independent economic agent, the individual in the free market. Our highest ideal is the pursuit of personal desire; celebrity, fame and material wealth are its ultimate expressions. Our mythology is built around the notion of the individual determining their own destiny. Aeron Davis noted that this provides a working model at the elite level of society, observing that when things are about to hit the fan the elite are usually able to walk away. This is not always the case at the other end of the playing field. If you are solely responsible for your own circumstances, what does this say about you if your circumstances are dire? How do you make sense of this if you are a child? The contemporary high priests of the free market assert that the accumulation of choices made through enlightened self-interest will allow society to achieve its optimum condition. The exemplary lessons of Victorian culture are of communities seeking solutions to individual problems through the habits of co-operative endeavour and mutual aid, through a social approach.

Britain's current school system serves as a temple of the new religion, its deity is the exam board. Students learn the catechism: work hard and good grades will be secured; economic opportunity will be offered in due proportion. For some this creed holds true, for others it is irrelevant as their economic security is already assured, for others it is merely a deception. The destinies of young people are largely determined beyond the classroom.

If school is a service mechanism for producing exam grades, then it is entirely appropriate that it is delivered by private businesses offering value for money. If a school is run as a business, then, following Milton Friedman, its primary purpose is to deliver value to shareholders, a financial surplus for distribution. Although the academy system is restrained from doing this directly it is able to do it indirectly through executive pay and consultancy fees. The profit motive rather than becoming a spur to an expansive excellence will thus drive many schools to achieving success in the most narrowly defined way possible to avoid excess expenditure: it will tend to steer them away from culture.

The most cynical reading of this situation would place young people as production line workers in a statistics factory, their teachers the shop floor supervisors. No-one (teacher or pupil) could survive school on such a bleak assessment and experience suggests that this is not the spirit with which people enter the classroom. Nevertheless, it is still a spectre in the corridor. Schools run on the business model will struggle to be places of education, that is places of cultivation: sites of cultural renewal. Unfortunately, this may be the intended purpose of recent education policy.

If schools are to be the new cultivators they need to be embedded in the most fertile soil of British culture, they need to be democratically governed and rooted in their local communities; they must be run for public benefit not private profit. Schools will continue to prepare students for exams but to play a part in cultural renewal they need some gods to serve.

Neil Postman proposes four myths for the education system to live by, these occasionally include significant endeavours that take place beyond the classroom's four walls. Since this is a book that primarily focuses on brass bands and British culture, I propose that one of the gods of a British education system could be Britain as a cultivated nation.

—

Since culture has been on the sidelines of national consciousness for too long it is appropriate to throw a couple of ideas into the ring to get a discussion started. A cultural curriculum would need to provide students with an aptitude for harmonious collaboration: an awareness of their own presence and the presence of others. In the infant years it might place a fundamental emphasis on the skills of painting, song, dance and discussion (the roots of philosophy). Juniors might be introduced to instrumental music, dramatic productions, poetry reading and more formally philosophical discussion. These skills would be supported in high schools which would develop reputations for the quality of their artistic productions. Efforts would also be made to establish and support community cultural activity such as music and theatre.

Culture does not have to mean monoculture and broad horizons are to be encouraged. Within the Western classical music tradition for example, its last great period of innovation, Minimalism, was driven by composers such as Terry Riley and Steve Reich who had studied musical forms in Asia and Africa respectively. Similarly, British curricula might reflect and respond to local tradition and circumstances including the diversity of cultural origins. For example; a community with links to Caribbean carnivals could develop skills in textile design and costume manufacture. Economically, this might have the knock-on effect of developing a distinctive local fashion industry that would add to the overall character of place.

Considering the basic principles, the commitment would be to achieve high standards of cultural value. Criticisms of this approach might be anticipated, suggesting that it is elitist. However, offering a grounding of this type does not prevent young people inspired by classic poetry from using their knowledge in rap. Those who would protest that the tales of Ovid have no relevance for the twenty-first century are clearly unaware of that most contemporary of characters, the sex-shifting Tiresius. Nor does a grounding in Shakespeare prevent the development of new forms of theatre productions that reflect contemporary circumstances or experience. Knowledge of the skills and theory of the western musical tradition might be one of the pillars of a music curriculum but it would help to raise the standards of pop music. Greater skill and knowledge offers greater possibilities. Also bear in mind, students don't tend to suffer from high expectations; those from whom little is expected often fail.

The overt aptitudes developed within this scenario relate to creative expression, however, skills of social organisation and influence are also required to produce and reproduce the arts. The two sets of skills should be inseparable. Soft skills are also directly transferable, indeed are essential to a meaningful community life. They may translate into the ability to campaign for improved bus services or develop forms of local economic activity. The school curriculum subjects that politicians seem to regard as peripheral or luxuries are in fact the essential elements of British culture.

Before moving on we should not forget the other role education has to play in British culture: the transmission of literacy.

Brass bands and British culture in uncertain times

As the book enters its final pages it is time to return to the opening statement and consider whether or not it has fulfilled its purpose. The months spent in the company of Upperthong Band have hopefully allowed the reader to get inside the village band experience. That sense of commitment, of what it is like to belong to a band, should serve as an intuitive guide as to how to measure cultural experience, cultural strength. If that has been communicated, then I hope the arguments about the principles of British culture ring true.

If the definitions of culture have been accepted, then it is only a small step to recognise that British culture is in poor shape. But all is not doom and gloom, finding a way to address these problems can set up a very optimistic path for the future. It is my hope that brass bands will continue to be part of that future and with that in mind the last words will be left to the brass bands on their own.

—

Brass bands are truly popular music; they are an art form from and of the people, but they have only a marginal presence in the modern world. They do not feature in the listings of the mainstream media and even specialist websites will only list a few concerts or recordings. Brass bands are not immersed in consumer culture and the market society, the musical form has largely dropped out of popular consciousness.

Bands are absent from commercial culture for a number of reasons. The first is that they still have a resolutely amateur and community focussed tradition. The second is that they were unable to ride the waves of changing styles, tastes and uses of music at the start of the twentieth century. Roy Newsome notes, at that time orchestral music and popular music were experimenting with different textures and timbres which bands struggled to emulate. The rising demand for social dances also bypassed brass bands; whilst they had at times played music for people to dance to, they were nudged out of this role by the new dance band formats from across the Atlantic. This situation was not helped by the advent of recorded music. The final element is that just as brass bands were more likely to play in concert halls rather than the open air, a class divide in listening habits was reinforced.

The start of the twentieth century saw the introduction of the terms highbrow and lowbrow in America. Roy Newsome suggests this reflected the social status of the occasion as much as the quality and style of music. Even though the best bands and repertoire deserved comparison with the classical orchestral canon they were a lower-class concern and not fully accepted in the concert hall. Whilst they had a loyal community-based following, brass bands became an afterthought to the general categories of mainstream entertainment.

The problem for bands at the end of the twentieth century was that they became a fish out of water. They had arisen as the pre-eminent cultural expression of the industrial working class but that formation of society began to erode and fragment in the post-war era. Initially this was due to the rise of consumerism, changes in patterns of employment and the reshaping of the urban landscape. This was exacerbated by the de-industrialisation of Britain. The coup de grace was the government's programme to disrupt self-conscious forms of working class organisation. If there was one faction of society who believed in class war rhetoric more than Militant and the Socialist Workers Party it would appear to have been Margaret Thatcher's cabinet committee. Gradually many of the community institutions that bands both served and drew support from ceased to exist. The world so keenly described by Brian Jackson slipped beyond memory.

Remarkably, brass bands have survived this radical transformation of society. Their very survival suggests that, even though it may be difficult to discern the pattern, they are slowly finding ways to reinvent themselves as a twenty-first century form of community music. The future may still not be certain but there are grounds for optimism.

—

When the public policy aspects of culture are considered, it is easy to see why spreadsheet culture, output culture, cannot accommodate brass bands. It costs a small fortune to train and equip competent musicians and the timescales this requires are immense. The official version of community focussed culture operates to tight timescales on a shoestring budget. Spreadsheet culture is not necessarily averse to the idea of brass bands, it is more that it would be happy to pick the apple but be reluctant to help grow the tree. The same can be said of any therapeutic uses of brass bands with respect to a health and well-being agenda, ukuleles may be a different matter.

If brass bands are not an attractive proposition for commissioned culture the feeling is probably mutual. From the band's point of view the sums on offer would have to be considerable for it to entertain becoming involved in any complex administration. Bands are autonomous, fiercely independent and on that basis not easily ministered to or directed by external agents. They do not readily become the grateful recipients of expert involvement or conform to someone else's agenda. There is also a conflict with one of the pillars of the band tradition; the day to day running costs have traditionally been met by the sweat of the band's brow, by undertaking paying jobs (although generous sponsorship has always been greatly appreciated). That is not to say that a brass band would be unwilling to take part in the type of City of Culture programme set out above and in fact would probably be keen to participate to reach new audiences. Brass bands are problematic for contemporary cultural policy because of their autonomy.

Band culture is self-directed and self-determined. The musical traditions of the banding world also mean that they retain very fixed notions of artistic value both in terms of acceptable repertoire and technical standards of performance. That is not to say they are resistant to change, more that they adapt and assimilate over relatively long timescales.

Bands may also struggle to fit into the niches of the officially sanctioned culture of the twenty-first century because they have something more precious to offer. Brass bands have the answer to the thorny question of where to find the essence of British culture.

—

Culture is found in the real world, in real places, real communities, in the lives of the people who live and breathe a tradition. When a cultural process becomes a dynamic, vital entity within a group of people and then becomes an important element in the life of their community then that culture has profound presence and authority.

It may be tempting to paint a picture of bands as an island unto themselves but they have proved the ability to engage with changes in society at large. They are a great example of durable and adaptable institutions. They have: accommodated women into a formerly male environment (there are also women only bands); adapted to changing values around sexuality (there is an LGBT brass band); and continued to support young people (in youth and training bands): but yet have retained an internal sense of moral authority and moral responsibility, band values.

One key area where bands have not adapted to the twenty-first century is in the ethnic diversity of their membership. There is no doubt that *en masse* bands do not reflect changes in the ethnic constitution of the country. There are a variety of factors that have affected this. I am in no position to judge whether attitudes within the band room are one of these.

Speaking from my own experience, from the world of Upperthong band, the traditional Pennine village bands are based in the outlying metropolitan areas. This must have a very strong effect on recruitment, training and retention of band members. Membership is likely to reflect the surrounding demographic. For example, urban Huddersfield has an extremely diverse population; the former mill towns of the Holme and Colne Valleys, where the bands are, have an overwhelmingly white population. The same is true when considering Oldham and Saddleworth. It should also be remembered that family tradition plays an important part in brass bands, this will also reinforce the profile of bands.

One reason that bands have survived in the Pennine villages may be because they are managing to adapt to the changes in the local population. Many of the villages in the areas mentioned above have slowly transformed. They are no longer the industrial and textile centres of the 1960s but the white-collar commuter hubs and working from homes of the twenty-first.

Government's hostility to music education in schools has had an effect on the opportunities for all young people to learn instruments and participate in ensembles. Where schools have a positive approach to music, they may also have strong views on what is appropriate for their school community; brass bands may not always be viewed with sympathy by key staff. Again, this may be a factor in reducing the opportunity for bands to adapt their profile.

I suspect the definitive study on bands and ethnic diversity is still to be written. In the meantime, bands should not apologise for being white, but embrace opportunities to become more closely aligned with the wider world as they arise.

—

Finally, it is worth restating the importance of brass bands as a culture. In the best sense it could be said that bands have brought Victorian values into the twenty first century. Bands are defined by:

- an artistic and cultural purpose.
- strong artistic and aesthetic values.
- strong moral, mutual and social values.
- a strong sense of autonomy and self-organisation.
- a connection and sense of service to wider forms of community and community institutions. A sense of place.
- a sense of cultural and historical continuity.

When this is compared to the prevailing cultural conditions bands take on a new meaning. They are no longer those funny people in bizarre uniforms playing old-fashioned music: they are a vital resource; they are like the seed banks stored in the arctic in case of natural disasters.

Brass bands are store houses of value lying in wait for the seasons to change so that Culture can bloom once more.

Bibliography

Ambrose, Peter (1974) *The Quiet Revolution: Social Change in a Sussex Village 1871 - 1971.* Sussex University Press

Arban, Jean Baptiste (1907) *The Complete Method for Cornet.* Boosey & Hawkes

Arnold, Matthew ( ) *Culture and Anarchy.* Cambridge University Press

Ayers, John (1973) *Architecture in Bradford.* Watmoughs / Bradford Civic Society

Balchin, Paul N. (1990) *Regional Policy in Britain: The North South Divide.* Paul Chapman

Banfield, Edward C. (1958) *The Moral Basis of a Backward Society.* Free Press

Bergreen, Laurence (1998) *Louis Armstrong: An Extravagant Life.* Crown

Berlin, Isaiah (1976) *Vico and Herder: Two Studies in the History of Ideas* Hogarth Press

Berliner, David ed. (2014) *Nostalgia and Anthropology* Berghahn Books

Berlinski, Samuel; Dewan, Torun; Dowding, Keith (2005) *The Length of Ministerial Tenure in the UK 1945 - 1997.* The Suntory Centre (LSE) (https://eprints.lse.ac.uk/19293/1/The_Length_of_Ministerial_Tenure_ in_the_UK_1945-1997.pdf)

Binelli, Mark (2013) *The Last Days of Detroit: Motor Cars, Motown and the Collapse of an Industrial Giant.* Bodley Head

Bishop, Jeff and Hoggett, Paul (1986) *Organising Around Enthusiasms*: *Patterns of Mutual Aid in Leisure.* Comedia

Boym, Svetlana (2002) *The Future of Nostalgia*, Basic Books

Brook, O'Brien and Taylor (2020) *Culture is Bad For You: Inequality in the Cultural and Creative Industries.* Manchester University Press

Brown, Clifford (1991) *Brass Band Contests: Art or Sport?* In Herbert, Trevor (ed.)

Byrne, David (2013) *How Music Works.* Canongate

Crouch, Colin (2011) *The Strange non-death of Neoliberalism.* Polity Press

Davis, Aeron (2018) *Reckless Opportunists: Elites at the End of the Establishment.* Manchester University Press

Dorling, Danny, et al (2007) *Poverty, Wealth and Place in Britain 1968 - 2005.* Policy Press

Eagleton, Terry (2016) *Culture.* Yale University Press

Edgerton, David (2018) *The Rise and Fall of the British Nation: A Twentieth Century History.* Penguin

Eldredge, Niles (2002) *A Brief history of Piston-valved Cornets.* Historic Brass Society Journal 14 (www.historicbrass.org/edocman/hbj-2002/HBSJ_2002_JL01_013_Eldredge_Divided1.pdf)

Elliot, Larry (2012) *Going South: Why Britain will have a third world economy by 2014* Palgrave Macmillan

Embery, Paul (2020) *Despised: Why the Modern Left Loathes the Working Class.* Polity

Fisher, Mark (2009) *Capitalist Realism: Is There no Alternative?* Zero Books

Friedman, Milton (1970) *A Friedman Doctrine - The Social Responsibility of Business is to Increase its Profits* New York Times (13/09/70) (https://www.nytimes.com/1970/09/13/archives/a-friedman-doctrine-the-social-responsibility-of-business-is-to.html)

Gammond, Peter & Horricks, Raymond (eds.) (1980*) Music on Record 1: Brass Bands.* Patrick Stephens Ltd.

Greenhalgh, Alec (1988) *Hail, Smiling Morn: Whit Friday Brass Band Contests 1884 - 1991* Oldham Education and Leisure Services

Herbert, Trevor (ed.) (1991) *Bands: The Brass Band Movement in the 19th and 20th Centuries.* Open University

Hazeldine, Tom (2020) *The Northern Question: A History of a Divided Country.* Verso

Hazen, Margaret H. & Robert M. (1987) *The Music Men: Illustrated History of Brass Bands in America 1800-1920.* Smithsonian Books

Hesmondhalgh, David (2012) *The Cultural Industries, 3rd Ed.* Sage

Hilton, Matthew (2010) *'Is civic society really in decline'*
(www.birmingham.ac.uk/news/thebirminghambrief/items/civicsociet
ydecline.aspx;)

Hoggart, Richard (1957) *The Uses of LIteracy: Aspects of Working Class Life.*
Penguin

Hoggart, Richard (1995) *The Way We Live Now.* Pimlico

Holman, Gavin (2018) *How Many Brass Bands? An Analysis of the
Distribution of bands in Britain and Ireland Over the Past 200 years.*
(https://www.ibew.org.uk/GH018-howmanybands.pdf)

Holman, Gavin (2018) *Brass Bands of the British Isles.*
(www.ibew.org.uk/GH019-brassbandsofbritisles.pdf)

Hutton, Will (1995) *The State We're in: Why Britain is in Crisis and How to
Overcome it.* Penguin/Random House

Jackson, Brian (1968) *Working Class Community: Some General Notions
Raised by a Series of Studies in Northern England.* Routledge

Jewel, Helen M. (1994) *The North-South Divide: The Origins of Northern
Consciousness in England.* Manchester University Press

Kahneman, Daniel (2012) *Thinking, Fast and Slow.* Penguin

Keay, Douglas (1987) *Aids, Education and the year 2000!* Woman's Own
31/10/1987 (https://www.margaretthatcher.org/document/106689)

Kelly, Thomas (1970) *A History of Adult Education in Britain.* Liverpool
University Press

Knight, John (1980) *Brass, Youth and Education* in Gammond & Horricks
(eds)

Laslett, Peter (1979) *The World we Have Lost,* Methuen

Lind, Michael (2021) *The New Class War.* Atlantic Books

Livings, Henry (1975) *That the Medals and the Baton be Put On View: the
Story of a Village Band 1875 - 1975* David & Charles

Meek, David (2019) *Dreams of Leaving and Remaining: fragments of a
Nation.* Verso

McLuhan, Marshall (1964) *Understanding Media.* Routledge

Macfarlane, Alan (1979) *The Origins of English Individualism: Family,
Property and Social Transition.* Basil Blackwell

Massey, Ron (Undated) *Marsden Senior School Boys' Band.*
(marsdenhistory.co.uk/downloads/marsden_boys_band.pdf)

Mount, Ferdinand (2010) *Mind the Gap: The New Class Divide in Britain.*
Short Books

Mumford, Lewis (1955) *Technics and Civilization.* Routledge and Kegan Paul

Newsome, Roy (1999) *The Nineteenth Century Brass Band in Northern England: Musical and Social Factors in the Development of a Major Amateur Musical Medium* (PhD Thesis, Salford University)

Newsome, Roy (2006) *The Modern Brass Band: From the 1930s to the New Millennium.* Ashgate

Newsome, Roy (2020) *Brass Roots: A Hundred Years of Brass Bands and Their Music* Routledge re-issue

Norman, Jesse (2010) *The Big Society: The Anatomy of the New Politics.* University of Buckingham Press

Norman, Jesse (2014) *Edmund Burke: The Visionary who Invented Modern Politics.* Harper Collins

Ong, Walter (1982) *Orality and Literacy: The Technologizing of the Word.* Routledge

Orwell, George (1941) *The Lion and the Unicorn: Socialism and the English Genius.* Penguin

Pawley, Martin (1972) *The Private Future: Causes and Consequences of Community Collapse in the West.* Pan

Perry, Grayson (2014) *Playing to the Gallery: Helping Contemporary Art in its Struggle to be Understood.* Penguin

Plowden, William (1973) *The Motor Car and Politics in Britain 1896 - 1970.* Penguin

Postman, Neil (1995) *The End of Education: Redefining the Value of School.* Alfred Knopf

Putnam, Robert (1994) *Making Democracy Work: Civic Traditions in Modern Italy.* Princeton University Press

Putnam, Robert (2000) *Bowling Alone: the Collapse and Revival of American Community.* Simon & Schuster

Rose, Jonathon (2003) *The Intellectual Life of the British Working Classes.* Yale University Press

Russell, Dave (1997) *Popular Music in England 1840 - 1914: A Social History.* Manchester University Press

Russell, Dave (2004) *Looking North: Northern England and the National Imagination.* Manchester University Press

Sasse, Tom; Durrant, Tim; Norris, Emma; Zodgekar, Ketaki (2020) *Government Reshuffles: The Case for Keeping Ministers in Post Longer.* Institute for Government

(https://www.instituteforgovernment.org.uk/publication/report/gove
rnment-reshuffles-case-keeping-ministers-post-longer)

Schafer, William (1977) *Brass Bands and New Orleans Jazz.* Louisiana State
University Press

Scruton, Roger (2017) *Where we are: the State of Britain Now.* Bloomsbury

Seabrook, Jeremy and Blackwell, Trevor (1985) *A World Still to Win: The
Reconstruction of the Post-War Working Class.* Faber and Faber

Sennett, Richard (1998) *The Corrosion of Character: the Personal
Consequences of Work in the New Capitalism.* W.W. Norton

Sennett, Richard (2003) *Respect: The Formation of character in a World of
Inequality.* Allen Lane

Skocpol, Theda (2003) *Diminished Democracy: From Membership to
Management in American Life* University of Oklahoma Press

Smith, Adrian ed. (2000) *Music Making in the West Riding of Yorkshire.* R.H.
Wood

Steenstrup, Kristian (2017) *Blow Your Mind.* Royal Academy of Music,
Aarhus

Storr, Anthony (1997) *Music and the Mind.* Harper Perennial

Swales, Kirby & Tipping, Sarah (2018) *Fragmented Communities? The role
of cohesion, community involvement and social mixing.* National Centre
for Social Research (retrieved from British Library)

Sykes, John (1926) *Slawit in the Sixties.* Schofield and Sims

Taylor, Arthur (1979) *Brass Bands.* Granada

Taylor, Arthur (1983) *Labour and Love: An Oral History of the Brass Band
Movement.* Elm Tree

Thompson, Dorothy (1986) *The Chartists: Popular Politics in the Industrial
Revolution.* Ashgate

Thompson, E.P. (1968) *The Making of the English Working Class.* Penguin

Tipper, David & Haynes, Hannah (1994) *De Balderston II.* self-published

Tylecote, Mabel (1957) *The Mechanics Institutes of Lancashire and Yorkshire
before 1851.* Manchester University Press

Visit Hull Website (2018) https://www.hull.ac.uk/work-with-
us/more/media-centre/news/2018/city-of-culture-evaluation.aspx.

Vygotsky, Lev (1986) *Thought and Language.* MIT Press

Weiner, Martin (1981) *English Culture and the Decline of the Industrial
Spirit 1850 -1980.* Cambridge University Press

Wheatcroft, Geoffrey (2005) *The Strange Death of Tory England.* Allen Lane

Whitworth Art Gallery *website* (2023)
  https://www.whitworth.manchester.ac.uk/whats-
  on/exhibitions/currentexhibitions/economicstheblockbuster/
Williams, Raymond ( ) *Culture and Society (1780-1950)* Penguin
Williams, Raymond(1983) *Keywords.* Flamingo
Williamson, Victoria J. and Bonshor, Michael (2019) *Wellbeing in Brass*
  Bands: The Benefits and Challenges of Group Music Making. Frontiers in
  Psychology vol. 10
  (www.frontiersin.org/articles/10.3389/fpsyg.2019.01176/full)